S
TRANSFORMATION
AND HEALING

SPIRITUAL TRANSFORMATION AND HEALING

Anthropological, Theological, Neuroscientific, and Clinical Perspectives

Joan D. Koss-Chioino
and Philip Hefner

ALTAMIRA
PRESS

A Division of
Rowman & Littlefield Publishers, Inc.
Lanham • New York • Toronto • Oxford

ALTAMIRA PRESS
A Division of Rowman & Littlefield Publishers, Inc.
A wholly owned subsidary of The Rowman & Littlefield Publishing Group, Inc.
4501 Forbes Boulevard, Suite 200
Lanham, MD 20706
www.altamirapress.com

PO Box 317, Oxford, OX2 9RU, UK

British Library Cataloguing in Publication Information Available

Library of Congress Cataloguing-in-Publication Data

Spiritual transformation and healing : anthropological, theological, neuro-
    scientific, and clinical perspectives / edited by Joan D. Koss-Chioino
    and Philip Hefner.
      p. cm.
    Includes bibliographical references and index.
    ISBN-13: 978-0-7591-0866-0 (cloth : alk. paper)
    ISBN-10: 0-7591-0866-8 (cloth : alk. paper)
    ISBN-13: 978-0-7591-0867-7 (pbk. : alk. paper)
    ISBN-10: 0-7591-0867-6 (pbk. : alk. paper)
    1. Conversion. 2. Healing—Religious aspects.   I. Koss-Chioino,
Joan. II. Hefner, Philip J.
    BL639.S65 2006
    204'.2—dc22

                                            2005037632

Printed in the United States of America

$\otimes^{TM}$ The paper used in this publication meets the minimum requirements of
American National Standard for Information Sciences—Permanence of Paper for
Printed Library Materials, ANSI/NISO Z39.48-1992.

Contents

Foreword

Solomon H. Katz

Although there has long been wide acknowledgment that spiritual transformations occur and that they can have a profound effect on the life of a person, group, or society, such as the classic biblical example of Saul on the road to Damascus, we are witnessing today renewed and more intensive efforts to chart these transformations and understand them more fully. One example of this renewed attention is the Spiritual Transformation Scientific Research Program (STP), a multidisciplinary, multimillion-dollar research program. This project was launched in the spring of 2002 to provide integrated scientific studies that can account for the nature of the various biological, psychosocial, and cultural conditions and factors that underlie spiritual transformations.

This book that Joan Koss-Chioino and Philip Hefner have assembled is closely related to the STP: the deliberations of this project provide the background for the design of the book, and seven of the book's authors are associated with the STP. The STP had a pyramidal effect for this book—providing impetus for new work and refocusing existing work and studies.

With this in mind, it may be useful to elaborate certain key elements that mark the thinking that guides the STP—both as a framework in which to place the essays of this book and also as a way of charting what they contribute and what challenges still lie ahead in this field of study.

When we began our studies of spiritual transformation we developed a series of scientific questions that create an agenda for scientific investigation that may lead to the formation of a new field of study. We began with an initial operational definition of *spiritual transformation* (Kenneth Pargament includes a full discussion of this definition in chapter 2). We expected that as the field developed, our understanding would quickly grow and other more comprehensive definitions and questions would emerge as various empirical results of the research yielded more subtle distinctions and catalyzed further studies.

The questions that shaped the agenda were the following:

(1) What is spiritual transformation and is there more than one kind?

(2) Are the processes of spiritual transformation the same as those, for example, of political transformation, but simply involving different content? Are there spiritually transforming events and processes that are distinctly religious?

(3) Are there universal elements in the processes of spiritual transformation?

(4) Are the contemporary psychosocial and biosocial models, theories, and methods of study sufficient for these studies and how can they be enlarged to account for the various aspects of spiritual transformation?

(5) Are there biological characteristics that predispose individuals to different pathways of spiritual transformation? What factors underlie spontaneous experiences of spiritual transformation? What factors influence the stability of various spiritual transformation outcomes? What is the role of significant personal experiences and life events in the processes of spiritual transformation?

(6) What are the pathways (processes, antecedents, and outcomes) of various forms of spiritual transformation (both incremental and rapid)?

(7) Do individual and group characteristics facilitate or inhibit spiritual transformations? Are specific techniques or practices, such as fasting, use of pharmacological substances, solitude, singing and music, confession, and celebrations in religious and nonreligious practices, pathways to spiritual

transformation? What roles do prayer and meditation, worship, pilgrimage, readings of scriptures or other sacred texts and stories, "telling one's story," artistic endeavor, relationship toward nature, acts of service, and various other religious and nonreligious rituals play in the process of spiritual transformation?

(8) What are the outcomes for individuals who undergo a spiritual transformation experience and for the groups with whom these individuals interact? What are the benefits or costs of these spiritual transformation experiences for these individuals and groups?

We also knew that in formulating these questions we would not be able to address all of them in our initial series of projects. This book, however, represents one of the most important of these initial projects, and a very distinctive one: spiritual transformation as a medium of healing.

As readers work through the chapters that lie before them in this volume, they will recognize that they are encountering a domain that is in fact marked by a partnership of research and reflection, a cross-disciplinary network of researchers—ranging from neuroscientists to philosophers of religion—that is, as we write, exploring a vast terrain with methods that are both tried and true and also novel. This book is an early signal of what awaits us as we seek fuller understanding of spiritual transformation and healing.

Preface

Ralph W. Hood Jr.

Joan Koss-Chioino and Philip Hefner have produced a marvelous work that is more than a simple compilation of authors and chapters centered on a common theme, and it would be unwise not to read this book in its entirety, regardless of what one's personal interest is. The book itself is logically divided into an introduction and four interrelated parts.

Definitional and ontological issues are the focus of part I, "Finding Our Way through New Terrain," and resurface throughout the text. In the introduction, chapter 1, the editors provide a prospective commentary on what they call the "new terrain" that is being opened up by research into spiritual transformation and healing. In addition to surveying issues raised by the varying contributors to this volume, they give their own take on further developments necessary to advance the field. Kenneth Pargament in chapter 2 then reminds us that spiritual transformation necessarily centers on one's relation to the sacred, and, despite varieties of transformation, that only when there is a qualitative change with respect to the sacred is it fair to speak of *spiritual* transformation. In chapter 3, David Hufford and Mary Ann Bucklin craft a careful discussion that reminds us that *spiritual transformation* references the word *spirit*. They remind us that there are social-scientific limitations to be overcome when academic and scholarly efforts consider belief in spirit or spirits to be problematic (especially in the West).

However, people in the West remain as committed to the existence of spirits as do people in non-Western cultures. At a minimum, Hufford and Bucklin suggest that academic arrogance and limited methodological relevance often too quickly seek reductive explanations of spiritual phenomena that require a more sensitive and appreciative effort to be understood properly.

If I might jump ahead for a moment, the text of this book ends with two chapters dealing with clinical perspectives, each based partly on empirical data. In the first of these chapters, chapter 15, Gail Ironson, Heidemarie Kremer, and Dale Ironson present preliminary results from an empirical study of persons living with HIV, and we learn that the crisis of being diagnosed with HIV can lead to spiritual transformation and a deeper and richer life. It can even perhaps, as in Buddhism, lead to a more meaningful moment of death. In the second and concluding chapter, Jean Kristeller and Leonard Hummel present empirical evidence that physicians who take a moment (no more than five or six minutes) to merely inquire about a cancer patient's spiritual resources can provide a form of more meaningful care to those patients. The symmetry between the opening chapters of this volume, which confront conceptual issues, and the reality of the importance of the spiritual issues identified in the two empirical studies of the closing chapters should be noted.

The text becomes richer in parts II–IV. In part II, which addresses spiritual transformation and indigenous healing systems, the methodological focus comes largely from anthropology informed by psychological and feminist thought. Several chapters extend Joan Koss-Chioino's theory of radical empathy (explored fully by Koss-Chioino in chapter 4), which is not simply an empathic and spiritually transformative understanding of another's plight, but rather a sense of experiencing this plight, *as if it were one's own*. Koss-Chioino implies a possible neurophysiological basis for this, as do others throughout the book. Using examples from shamans in Peru, for instance, Bonnie Glass-Coffin in chapter 5 notes that females seem most adept at expressing radical empathy. It may be that females rather than males have cultivated the capacity to share suffering with the afflicted, but the explanation for the range and possible basis for gender differences in radical empathy remains to be more fully explored. In chapter 7 Edith Turner focuses on the process by which shamans are made. She refuses to accept a psychological rhetoric of healing that levels the process as if it were merely rational. She appropriately parallels Aristotle's view that the soul is the form of the body. She finds similar processes operating in African, Nepalese, and Inuit (Christian) healers. She also demands that we recognize the reality of the soul and our own spiritual interconnectedness. Earlier in chapter 6, however, Marjorie Balzer has reminded us of a central theme of this text, that spiritual transformation is a universal potential of human life. Her study of the nostalgia of inhabitants of the former Soviet Union for a lost wisdom explores the pitfalls of too readily accepting any healer's claim of authenticity as a healer. Foreshadowing Turner's refusal to reduce the shaman's calling to a purely rational process, Balzer notes that the Marxist regimes of the former Soviet Union failed to eliminate what common folk knew to be valid means of healing. The challenge to modern inhabitants of these regions is to carefully navigate between identifying authentic and would-be healers and to seek a way to revitalize the ability of a culture to discern legitimate healers from charlatans, within a spiritual tradition whose obituary has proven to be premature.

Part III explores spiritual transformation from a religious perspective, and the shift is from anthropology to psychology and theology. Philip Hefner elaborates on Kenneth Pargament's discussion of the sacred in spiritual transformation and healing, and calls for new methodologies in this field of research. Karl Peters next reflects, in the light of evolutionary theology, on the untimely death of his first wife. Rather than death by disease, Peters and his wife overcome *dis-ease* as the cancer demands withdrawal from merely material attachments and the foregoing of the present for future goals. Here the disease that overcomes *dis-ease* functions much as meditation and mindfulness, allowing Peters and his wife to focus fully on experiencing the present. Even disease that ends in death, we find, can be both healing and spiritually transforming. Peters's reflections also illuminate the empirical findings reported by Ironson and her coauthors on spiritual transformation in HIV patients, as noted above. Fraser Watts in chapter 10 reminds us that spiritual transformation has long been a concern of both psychology and theology, and that the interface of these disciplines, if explored with humility, may allow psychology to illuminate processes of concern to theology, and theology in turn to broaden and extend the range of psychology. The following chapter, written by Carol Rausch Albright, then explores Fowler's well-known stages of faith development in novel terms linked to complexity theory, and embedded in insights from contemporary neuroscience.

Part IV continues the discussion by exploring biological and neurological perspectives with a focus on neural plasticity and embeddedness. The theme of neural plasticity appears in the work of Andrew Newberg. His chapter in this volume presents a model of spiritual transformation largely informed by empirical research based upon new technologies, especially the variety of functional neuroimaging techniques now available. He notes that neuroplasticity, a change in connections of neurons over time, is not an instantaneous process. Thus he suggests that *sudden* spiritual transformation must make use of neural connections that are either not activated or are suppressed in primary modes of consciousness. One consequence of this view is support for the major theme of this text that spiritual transformation is a human potential we all harbor within us. Michael Spezio next presents cogent arguments in chapter 13 that elaborate on the theme of embeddedness. Using simulation theory, he argues that the radical empathy required for both spiritual transformation and healing requires the accurate reading of the emotions and intentions of others, either automatically or by means of imagination. This reciprocal awareness of a shared intersubjectivity is rooted in the very nature of our shared biology and allows for radical empathy. With this Spezio appropriately anticipates David Hogue's view that the Christian notion of a resurrected body applies to a modern, scientifically informed view of the soul. If religious discourse has neglected the body, this neglect is balanced by a social-science discourse that has neglected the soul. David Hogue reminds us that within the Christian tradition, the focus upon a resurrected body refuses the easy dualism of soul and body. Socrates, we remember, goes to his death calmly, noting that because he is a denizen of this world, only death can release his soul from its bodily prison. Christian theology however insists on a resurrected *body*. The implications of this claim are not simply restricted to theology. They spill over into any concern with the soul as embedded or as embodied. Hogue notes how neuroplasticity, the ability of the brain to "rewire" itself, allows for a top-down determinism, in which spiritual experiences of transcendence are embedded in narratives linked to the very neural plasticity that is fundamentally involved in all our relatedness to others, including the divine. Neuroplasticity allows narratives both to nourish the soul and to allow its expression in terms of a soulful body.

This text will go a long way in helping scholars and researchers navigate the difficult path between the Scylla of a theology that ignores the body and the Charybdis of a science that ignores the soul. While I have given here only an inkling of the variety and rich depth of the various chapters of this edited work, it would be a shame for the reader to think these chapters ought to be read in isolation. The themes that cut across the chapters of this book are obvious: the power of narrative; the refusal of spiritual concepts to yield to reductionism; the emerging, sophisticated technologies of minimally invasive exploration of the neurological correlates of experience; and the need for consistent recognition of the role of radical empathy in healing and spiritual transformation, to mention only a few. However, perhaps Edith Turner gives us the proper way to read a text such as this one that applies to reading the "texts" of persons' lives as well. She reminds us that we are not isolated, disembodied souls. We are not unconnected bodies. We are interconnected, and in Turner's delightful term, *permeable*. And so are the chapters of this wonderful text.

PART I

FINDING OUR WAY THROUGH NEW TERRAIN

1

Exploring Spiritual Transformation and Healing: Fundamental Issues

Philip Hefner and Joan D. Koss-Chioino

This book explores the relationship between spiritual transformation and healing from various disciplinary perspectives. All of the authors are scholars in the social sciences, academic medicine, neuroscience, or theology who have conducted research or engaged in reflection on spiritual transformation and healing. The book focuses on generic, widespread aspects of the healing process within diverse cultural, religious, and biological contexts. It rests on the premise that spiritual transformation is a universal potential of human life and a central element in the actions and interactions of the healing process. In the present climate of Western culture and elsewhere, spiritual transformation appears to be a sought-after experience for considerable numbers of people.

Although "mind cures" and their investigation through magnetism and other techniques were common in Europe throughout the nineteenth century (Ellenberger 1970), William James, in *The Varieties of Religious Experience* (1902), can be thought of as the initiator of the study of spiritual transformation and healing in the twentieth century. In James's discussions of "healthy mindedness," "the sick soul," and "conversion" in chapters 4 through 10 of *The Varieties of Religious Experience*, and especially when he talks about cases in which individuals—either famous persons or friends—were cured through conversion, he clearly describes a connection between spirituality and healing. James referred to *religion* when he described transformation and transformative experiences, and this is repeated in most of the subsequent literature. However in more recent times, spirituality and religion are increasingly viewed as distinct phenomena. *Spirituality* is reserved to refer to individual experience (see chap. 2), whereas *religion* is attached to social institutions and corporate practices and includes spirituality and spiritual practices (see chap. 14). But personal spirituality versus organized religion is too strict a dichotomy; they are clearly intimately related for many people (Pargament 1997). Religious communities have perennially considered themselves communities of spirituality, and they continue to do so. The concept (and experience) of spirituality is under continuous scrutiny; the exploration is vigorous and still in its beginning stages.

In this introductory chapter we briefly explore perspectives and foundational issues, and their implications in the study of spiritual transformation associated with healing. Our aim in this book is to provide a snapshot of current thinking and newer perspectives on spiritual transformation that reach beyond the existing literature. Additionally, exploration of and evidence for universal elements of the healing process are found in the following fifteen chapters that describe and explore diverse anthropological, theological, neurobiological, and clinical perspectives on the relationship between spiritual transformation and healing.

Perspectives

Behavioral/Social Sciences

Spiritual transformation is a concept that labels a special type of personal transformation in which a deep sense of spirituality is incorporated into an individual's consciousness and cosmic perspective. Pargament (see chap. 2) defines it as a "fundamental change in the place of the sacred or the character of the sacred in the life of the individual." Under different terms, such as *personal transformation* or *conversion experience*, this fundamental change has been described in numerous theological, ethnographic, and popular accounts of healing. As will be evident, each of the chapters in this book departs on its own path of exploration of the notion of spiritual transformation and, as a result, changes or elaborates upon it.

There are a number of significant works on spiritual transformation (usually labeled "conversion") in the social-science literature of the twentieth century, such as Rambo (1993). It is unfortunate that from the 1970s to the 1990s the major focus of the literature was on religious-cult activities and on conversion as negative, as a form of "brain washing" (Singer and Lalich 1995). This emphasis obscured for a time the positive effects of conversion. However, as chapters 4 through 7 illustrate, there are abundant ethnographic descriptions of spiritual transformation in the anthropological literature that, with a significant increase of medical anthropological research, have provided experiential reports that clearly connect spiritual transformation to healers and healing.

There are now scholarly treatises and research linking spirituality and health in psychology and psychiatry, but few of these examine the healing process as related to that association. This book builds on the assumption that spiritual transformation is an essential aspect of most healing systems, with the exception of systems such as biomedicine, which is based mostly on biophysical concepts and on experimental rather than experiential validity. In an excellent review of studies of ritual healing, Csordas and Lewton (1998) note the complexity of answering the question "What is healing?" One goal of this book is to explore that perennial query by examining how and why spiritual transformation—in healers or clients, doctors or patients—is important in understanding healing processes and their reported effectiveness. This approach focuses in part on a revision of the constructs of therapeutic or healing relationships that have been constructed through scientific studies of psychotherapy and biomedicine, and it includes what is defined as sacred and transformational across diverse cultural and religious contexts. *Healing* is a complex concept to define; but such a definition is important in any examination of what healing does. A common explanation of the English term translates the word *healing* as "wholeness," with all of its many implications. We might in turn define *healing* as a return to or acquisition of an optimal level of well-being. In this book the meanings of the construct *healing* emerge from the particular emphasis of each author. Each author has a specific notion relative to the perspectives that he or she develops to examine the relationship between spiritual transformation and healing.

Religious Traditions and Practices

Spirituality, spiritual transformation, and healing have been at or near the center of most religious traditions and practices throughout recorded history, sometimes as discrete phenomena, but more frequently as interrelated elements that are considered essential to religious life. Iconic figures of religion from earliest times are known to have had spiritual transformations and to have practiced healing. The traditions of the world's religions, including those from human prehistory, encompass both in quality and quantity an inconceivably large array of reflections, practices and procedures, personal testimonies, descriptions, and interpretations of spiritual transformation and healing. The range of these traditions includes transformations and healing that occur suddenly in idiosyncratic forms as well as those that take place in meticulously disciplined, almost routine experiences. Religious communities over the millennia have expended enormous effort in training practitioners whose goal is to engender spiritual transformation and healing among their adherents.

Scientific perspectives are opening up new approaches to the understanding of what religious communities bring to spiritual transformation and healing. Albright (see chap. 11) makes use of newer research that relates spiritual transformation to well-known concepts and methods employed in the study of individual human development. Even more recent are insights that Albright and Hogue (see chap. 14) have brought to bear from the neurosciences to explain the processes of transformation and healing. And in chapter 10, Fraser Watts represents the kind of sophisticated psychological analysis of spiritual transformation that has become a hallmark of pastoral caregivers.

Neuroscience and Clinical Perspectives

Newberg (see chap. 12) and Spezio (chap. 13) exemplify approaches to understanding spiritual transformation through recent scientific methods. Newberg's imaging research points to how we can chart and measure the effects of transformative experiences on the brain, and encourages our understanding of the possibility that spiritual experiences are panhuman potentials. Spezio reviews social, neuroscientific evidence that shows that healing depends on the intersubjective interchange between practitioners and supplicants through embodied emotional processing. This is an independent confirmation, from a neuroscience perspective, of what the anthropological chapters of this book describe as spiritual transformation and healing across cultures. As we implied earlier, a multidisciplinary approach seems to have more than a simple confirmatory effect; it doubly augments the findings on the topic from another discipline—a kind of enriched mix. These chapters, and clinical research by Ironson et al. (see chap. 15) and Kristeller (chap. 16), are included to illustrate potential applications of this topic, which will be legion once we can more precisely specify the processes involved in spiritual transformation and healing. In addition, the work of Ironson and her colleagues points to an important area for significant further research, that of spiritual transformation and healing as a gradual process or set of processes within certain pathways. The antecedents and consequences of spiritual experiences have long received attention from psychologists, spiritual mentors, and pastoral caregivers; that attention will result in broader, even more significant insights when it takes newer methodologies into account and focuses on both the overarching processes of transformation and healing as well as on their constituent microprocesses. Among other researchers, Newberg explores the effect of meditation practices on the brain in advanced meditators, and Kristeller describes a clinical experiment with cancer patients limited to introducing spiritual experiences. All of these chapters experimentally address the question of how spiritual transformations might develop as a stage- or phase-wise process, using spiritual experience as a potential platform for undergoing spiritual transformation at a later time.

Issues

Critical Methodology

A major question that arises is whether and to what extent scientific methodologies can take the measure of spiritual transformation and healing. In chapter 2 of this book Pargament states,

"We have no tools to measure God, nor can we assess the authenticity of miraculous healings. However, we can study perceptions of sacredness and their implications for people's lives." Thus he describes the parameters of both the possibilities and limitations of scientific methodologies for engaging spiritual transformation and healing. All of the authors in this book work with the adequacies and inadequacies those parameters allow. We submit that one of the major contributions of this book is in its attempt to raise the question of whether spiritual transformation can be adequately described and understood using scientific methodology. As has been the case in the past, do we need to rely for this understanding upon experiential and phenomenological descriptions? Can the two approaches, experiential and phenomenological, be meaningfully combined, or can more innovative methods be developed for this area of study?

Hufford's discussion (see chap. 3), as well as Hefner's (chap. 8), articulates forcefully a particular facet of the methodological issue: The vast majority of those who experience spiritual transformation and healing (and also many of the agents of those experiences) entertain specific beliefs and hold to worldviews that modern science in general and many scientists in particular believe are not tenable. Under such conditions, is it possible for scientific studies to approach the subject of spiritual transformation and healing in ways that are both valid and reliable?

An additional consideration is that of adequacy; some scientific methods abstract from experience in a way that leaves the experience incomplete and lacking its essence. Can we develop a way to understand spiritual transformation and healing as a complex, multidimensional phenomenon that honors its extraordinary as well as its nonextraordinary aspects?

The Exploratory Nature of this Book

We underscore the exploratory nature of this collection of chapters for several reasons. First, as our comments on the interdisciplinary character of the discussion suggest, we have brought together representatives from several different fields of study, some of whom have seldom or never found themselves working together. Although the psychological and clinical disciplines have a long history of collaboration with both religious studies and the neurosciences (and peripheral collaboration more recently with anthropology), and a similar history of cooperation has marked relations between religious studies and anthropology, interaction between these latter disciplines and the neurosciences is still in its early phases.

In the years ahead, multidisciplinarity will fundamentally reshape the terrain in which research in spiritual transformation and healing is carried out. Consequently we can expect that new studies will be essentially exploratory rather than definitive in character, as new research partnerships are formed. Furthermore, these new evaluations will necessarily call for reevaluation and reinterpretation of much of the existing research—which is the way most science proceeds, with the exception that these new studies will be mostly provisional until multidisciplinary approaches and methods are clarified and accepted.

We offer the research and interpretations in this book as material for others as they explore this area of human experience and move toward refinements both of methodology and interpretive theorizing.

References

Csordas, T., and E. Lewton. 1998. Practice, performance and experience in ritual healing. *Transcultural Psychiatry* 35 (December): 435–512.

Ellenberger, H. E. 1970. *The Discovery of the Unconscious*. New York: Basic Books.

James, W. 1902. *The Varieties of Religious Experience: A Study in Human Nature*. New York: Modern Library, 2002.

Pargament, K. I. 1997. *The Psychology of Religion and Coping: Theory, Research, Practice*. New York: Guilford.

Rambo, L. 1993. *Understanding Religious Conversion*. New Haven, Conn.: Yale University Press.

Saliba, J. A. 2003. *Understanding New Religious Movements*. 2nd ed. Walnut Creek, Calif.: AltaMira.

Singer, Margaret Thaler, with Janja Lalich. 1995. *Cults in Our Midst*. San Francisco: Jossey-Bass.

2

The Meaning of
Spiritual Transformation

Kenneth I. Pargament

I was unusually troubled in my soul. Suddenly I heard a voice, just as clearly as I have ever heard anyone. . . . The voice said to me, "You must get rid of your self; you must renounce your self; you must reject your self." These were surprising words. I should have not been surprised if the voice had commanded me to stop drinking. But this was not the message at all. It was my self that I was commanded to give up. My self was my trouble—my love of myself, my fear of anything that might frustrate my wishes. My will had always been the central interest in my life. False pride had erected a barrier between my soul and God. (Candler 1951, 55–56)

Laura was raised as a Roman Catholic. Although she knew that [her father] cared about her, she felt that rules, order, and the Catholic church were more important to him than her mother or herself. She saw God very much like her father. . . . After an aborted suicide attempt, Laura asked her father for help, but none was received. "Dad told me, in a not-so-nice tone of voice, that he didn't want to hear anything like that again." . . . In the next few years Laura began to change. She grew attracted to her mother's Methodist church, which portrayed the deity in more personal, less fearful terms. Over time, God took on the characteristics of the father she wanted but never had, someone who would love her unconditionally. In fact, she now refers to God as her "Papa." (Pargament 1997, 214–15)

My motivations and my whole sense of direction have changed. My values changed. What I thought was important changed. I just completely shifted gears. It's given me a sense of purpose and direction I never had before, and I've been searching different avenues but never found exactly what I was supposed to be doing. I've tried a lot of different things, a lot of different jobs, traveled a lot, had lots of experiences in my life. Yet always there was that kind of restless searching, searching. Now I feel like I know exactly what I'm supposed to do. (Miller and C'de Baca 2001, 130)

How could you in all your greatness have abandoned me, a little girl, to the merciless hands of my father? How could you let this happen to me? I demand to know why this happened? Why didn't you protect me? I have been faithful, and for what, to be raped and abused by my own father? I hate and despise you. I regret the first time I ever laid eyes on you; your name is like salt on my tongue. I vomit it from my being. I wish death upon you. You are no more. You are dead. (Flaherty 1992, 101)

Introduction

Traditionally, spirituality has been viewed by social scientists as a source of stability in life, a way to conserve a sense of meaning, identity, connectedness with others, peace of mind, or transcendence. Spirituality has another side, though. It can also be a source of deep and profound change. Although the founding figures in psychology devoted considerable attention to the links between religion and radical change, the topic lay relatively dormant for many years. More recently, however, social scientists have become increasingly interested in the phenomenon of spiritual transformation. This topic is attracting the attention of scholars and scientists from diverse research communities, including psychology, sociology, anthropology, medicine, and theology. As yet, however, a clear and compelling definition of this construct has not emerged. Although definitional consensus at this early point would be premature, it is not too soon for researchers to begin grappling with the meaning of spiritual transformation. Without a general sense of where this phenomenon of interest begins and ends, this domain of study is unlikely to advance.

Consider the four vignettes above. Each illustrates some form of spiritual change. But do they represent spiritual transformations? In the first vignette, Asa Candler Jr. (son of the founder of Coca-Cola) describes his own religious conversion, his born-again experience, which led to radical changes in his life. Most social scientists would agree that conversions of this kind represent spiritual transformations. What is it about conversions, however, that represents transformations? In the second vignette, we hear the story of a college student who switches her religious affiliation and image of God in an effort to find the love and acceptance she was unable to experience with her father. Does this form of switching qualify as a spiritual transformation? The third vignette describes someone who experiences a "quantum change" (cf. Miller and C'de Baca 2001), a shift in core values in living. Yet there is no mention of God in this account. Is God or transcendence an essential component of spiritual transformation? In the fourth vignette, we hear a victim of incest tell God that He is no more, He is dead. Does the loss of spirituality also qualify as a spiritual transformation? These are simply a few of the thorny questions that arise in the effort to define the meaning of this term.

In this chapter I present one way to think about spiritual transformation. My goal here is not to present the last word on spiritual transformation, but rather some first words. Though my thoughts will not be convincing or satisfying to all, I hope they represent a starting point for further discussion and dialogue about the meaning of this rich and fascinating construct. I will begin by discussing the meaning of spirituality.

A Definition of Spirituality

Elsewhere I have defined spirituality as "a search for the sacred" (Pargament 1999, 12). There are two key terms in this definition: *search* and *sacred*. Before elaborating on these terms, I should emphasize that this definition rests on a particular assumption about human nature: that people are more than reactive beings, shaped by evolution, genetics, biology, early childhood, or the environment. People also strive (cf. Emmons 1999). Striving toward goals is a basic imperative of life, one that organizes and directs other dimensions of human functioning: cognitive, affective, and behavioral (Klinger 1998). Empirical studies have shown that goals and intentions can be the strongest predictors of human behavior (e.g., Fishbein and Ajzen 1975). Of course, people strive toward a variety of significant ends: psychological (e.g., meaning, self-esteem, peace of mind); social (e.g., marriage, family, status); physical (e.g., health, fitness, appearance); and material (e.g., money, possessions). Differences in configurations of goals help distinguish individuals and groups from each other, and have important implications for health and well-being (e.g., Ford and Nichols 1987; Kasser and Ryan 1996). One goal many people strive toward is the sacred.

The Sacred

Though scholars have defined the sacred in a variety of ways (Idinopulos and Yonan 1996), my view of the sacred is grounded most deeply in the works of Durkheim (1915) and Eliade (1958). In the Oxford English Dictionary, the word *sacred* is defined as the holy, those things set apart from the ordinary and worthy of veneration and respect. The sacred includes concepts of God and the divine (Oxford English Dictionary 1980). Other aspects of life though can become sacred or can take on transcendent character and significance by virtue of their association with, or representation of, divinity (Pargament and Mahoney 2002). As Durkheim wrote: "By sacred things one must not understand simply those personal beings which are called gods or spirits; a rock, a tree, a pebble, a piece of wood, a house, in a word anything can be sacred" (52). Sacred objects include time and space (the Sabbath, churches); events and transitions (birth, death); materials (wine, a crucifix); cultural products (music, literature); people (saints, cult leaders); psychological attributes (self, meaning); social attributes (compassion, community); and roles (spouse, parent, employer or employee). Regardless of its particular form, however, the sacred is, in the words of Eliade, "the one unique and irreducible element in [religious phenomena]" (xii).

The sacred can be understood from both traditional theistic and nontheistic perspectives. From a theistic vantage point, the sacred encompasses both concepts of the divine and embodiments, manifestations, or symbols of a higher power. Nontheists can also hold many aspects of their lives sacred by imbuing them with divine-like qualities, such as transcendence, ultimacy, and boundlessness. For example, Durkheim (1915) noted that "in default of gods, [Buddhism] admits the existence of sacred things, namely, the four noble truths and the practices derived from them" (52).

It is important to stress that the reality of the sacred cannot be determined from a social-scientific perspective. We have no tools to measure God, nor can we assess the authenticity of miraculous healings. However, we can study perceptions of sacredness and their implications for people's lives. In fact, there is growing evidence that people who see the world through a sacred lens experience life quite differently than do their more secular counterparts (Pargament and Mahoney 2005).

The Search

The sacred is the central focus of spirituality, the feature that gives spirituality its distinctive, even unique, character, for no other human phenomenon centers itself around the sacred. However, spirituality involves more than the sacred; it is a search for the sacred. The term *search* indicates that spirituality represents an active verb rather than a passive noun. Spirituality is not static. It does not refer to a stable, unvarying set of beliefs, practices, or experiences. It is, instead, a process in motion. There are three critical, interrelated elements of this process: discovery, conservation, and transformation.

The search for the sacred begins in childhood. Although questions have been raised about the child's capacity to grapple with spiritual abstractions (Goldman 1964), rich anecdotal accounts of children suggest otherwise. Consider the words of one nine-year-old Jewish boy:

> I'd like to find God! But He wouldn't just be there, waiting for some spaceship to land! He's not a person, you know! He's a spirit. He's like the fog and the mist. Maybe He's like something—something we've never seen here. So how can we know? You can't imagine Him, because He's so different—you've never seen anything like Him. . . . I should remember that God is God, and we're us. I guess I'm trying to get from me, from us, to Him with my ideas when I'm looking up at the sky! (Coles 1990, 141–42)

The discovery of the sacred may grow out of several forces. Some have suggested that there is an innate, genetic basis for spirituality (e.g., Bouchard et al. 1990). Others maintain that conceptions of God are rooted in the child's intrapsychic capacity to symbolize and fantasize superhuman beings (Rizzuto 1979). Some have asserted that spirituality is stimulated by critical life events and challenges that reveal human limitations (Johnson 1959; Pargament 1997). And others have emphasized the importance of the social context of family, institution, and culture in shaping the child's spirituality (Kaufman 1981).

Empirical research on the origins of spirituality is not plentiful. In one exception to this rule, Lee Kirkpatrick (2004) has elaborated on Bowlby's (1988) attachment theory, and posited that the child's mental models of God are likely to correspond to the models of self and others that emerge out of repeated interactions with primary attachment figures. In support of this notion, Kirkpatrick cites a number of studies among children, adolescents, and adults that demonstrate parallels between the quality of attachment to God (e.g., secure or insecure) and the quality of attachment to parents. Research such as that of Kirkpatrick suggests that the discovery of the sacred grows out of a variety of personal and social factors. Even so, this research cannot tell the full story, for the child's emerging spirituality is more than a reaction to his or her personal and social world. Interview studies of children underscore their capacity to reject, elaborate, or move well beyond the spiritual views of their parents, teachers, and religious leaders. Consider, for example, the words of one ten-year-old Brazilian girl whose mother was dying of tuberculosis:

> Mother used to tell us we'll go to heaven, because we're poor. I used to believe her. I don't think she really believes that herself. She just says that—it's a way of shutting us all up when we're hungry! Now, when I hear her say it, I look up at Him, and I ask Him: What do *You* say, Jesus? Do you believe her? (Coles 1990, 91)

It appears that children are far from passive when it comes to matters of faith. They might be described more accurately as spiritual pilgrims or seekers of something beyond themselves, motivated by a desire to discover the sacred itself.

The search for the sacred does not come to an end when people feel they have discovered something of spiritual value. People then try to hold on to it, to preserve it, to experience it, to consolidate it, and to integrate it more fully into their lives. There are a number of spiritual methods for conserving the individual's relationship with the sacred, including prayer, meditation, ritual participation, spiritual study, social action, and daily spiritual experiences (e.g., Poloma and Gallup 1991; Underwood 1999). In addition to these day-to-day forms of spiritual involvement, people can draw on a variety of spiritual coping methods to help them conserve the sacred in times of stress. For example, they may seek out spiritual support or reframe negative events from a benevolent spiritual perspective to sustain their connection to the sacred (Pargament 1997).

Much of the scientific study of spirituality has focused on the conservational functions of spirituality; that is, on how people sustain their relationship with the sacred over time. Important as these functions are, though, spirituality involves more than the discovery and conservation of the sacred. In spite of our best efforts, few of us are able to avoid threats to, challenges to, and losses of the sacred over the course of our lives. People may struggle to hold on to their relationship with the sacred, but faced with trauma and tragedy, normal developmental transitions, or simply personal growth and change, old sources of value and meaning may stop working. And when these sources lose their power, people enter a period of transformation when they have to fundamentally change their understanding and experience of the sacred. Transformation is the third process that is critical to the search for the sacred.

Spiritual Transformation

Although most social scientists have viewed spirituality as more of a force for conservation than transformation, not everyone has agreed. The connection between radical human change and the sacred was a core interest among many early psychologists, including William James, Edwin Starbuck, James Pratt, George Coe, and Elmer Clark. They focused much of their attention on religious conversion, a process that was understood to be a normal rather than a pathological human experience (Rambo 1993). Later, however, social scientists took on a more critical attitude to radical religious change, and the topic grew out of favor. Freud (1928), for instance, viewed religious conversion more critically as a regressive attempt to resolve hatred toward the father by total submission to a higher power. Other mental health professionals were alarmed that religious conversion represented a form of "brainwashing" or "thought reform" by new religious movements or cults (e.g., Sargant 1957). Only in the last twenty-five years has the study of spiritual transformation received new and more balanced attention.

What Transformation Is Not

As a prelude to defining spiritual transformation, it is important to consider the meaning of *transformation*. First, let me suggest a few things that transformation is not. Transformation is not doing more of the same thing. Watzlawick (1988) presents a striking illustration of this point. When NASA began building larger rockets in their race to the moon, they had to create larger hangars to protect the rockets from inclement weather. In designing the new hangars, they simply multiplied the dimensions of the hangars by a factor of ten. Unfortunately, they did not realize that hangars of this size create their own climate, including clouds, drizzle, and electricity. Paradoxically, this "more of the same" solution produced the very problem it was designed to eliminate. To solve the problem more effectively, NASA engineers had to go back to the drawing board and fundamentally rethink rocket hangars. Similarly, transformation refers to fundamental change, a change in the basic character of a system, rather than more of the same.

Transformation is not the same as statistical significance. As social scientists are well aware, even small changes in some dimension of human functioning can reach a high level of statistical significance when the changes are observed in a sufficiently large sample. Statistically significant changes in affect, cognition, or behavior that are associated with spirituality, then, do not necessarily indicate that a transformation has taken place. The more appropriate analogy for our purposes here is clinical significance rather than statistical significance. Clinical significance refers to changes that are large enough to hold practical and more profound implications for human functioning.

Transformation is not necessarily positive. If people are capable of extraordinarily powerful, life-affirming changes, they are equally capable of destructive changes that result in deep and long-lasting damage.

Finally, transformation is not necessarily spiritual. People can make profound changes in many aspects of their lives—career, residence, spouse, political affiliation, or values. Transformations of this kind may qualify as "quantum changes" in the words of Miller and C'de Baca (2001), but significant as they may be, none is necessarily a spiritual transformation unless it involves in some fashion the sacred.

The Meaning of Spiritual Transformation

What then is spiritual transformation? We can distinguish between two types of spiritual transformation: primary and secondary.

Primary Spiritual Transformation

At its heart, spiritual transformation refers to a fundamental change in the place of the sacred or the character of the sacred in the life of the individual. Spiritual transformation can be understood in terms of new configurations of strivings. In the classic conversion scenario, illustrated by Asa Candler Jr. (1951), the individual experiences a shift from self-centered strivings to God-centered strivings. Other forms of spiritual conversion are also possible. Mahoney and Pargament (2004) note that the classic form of conversion is particularly applicable to people "caught up in the trap of pride" who replace self-exaltation with self-sacrificial love (487). They contrast the traditional conversion model with the feminist model in which an abdication of personal dignity rather than excessive pride sets the stage for transformation: "Conversion from self-abnegation," they write, "involves learning self-affirmation in union with God and compassionate love" (487).

New configurations of strivings may center around sacred entities other than God or a higher power. The individual can reorient himself to a new religious group or to universal concerns. For religious group converts, the group, its leaders, and its mission become the new organizing force, lending coherence and direction to life. Universal converts attempt to re-create not only themselves but also the larger social matrix to more closely approximate an ideal transcendent vision. Thus, we find figures from Mahatma Gandhi to Martin Luther King Jr. promoting nonviolent resistance to social and political oppression and injustice throughout the world.

We can also speak of spiritual transformation in terms of a change in the character of the sacred. Changes in the nature of the sacred are not restricted to any particular period of life. In her classic text *The Birth of the Living God*, psychoanalyst Ana-Maria Rizzuto wrote: "The God representation changes along with us and our primary objects in the lifelong metamorphosis of becoming ourselves in a context of other relevant beings" (1979, 52). Consider one example. Following the death of his young son, Rabbi Harold Kushner found that he could no longer believe in a loving, all-powerful God. He could not reconcile the idea of a loving God with the notion of an all-powerful God who would allow the death of his son. After a great deal of struggle and soul-searching, Kushner ultimately transformed his understanding of God from a loving, all-powerful being to a loving, but limited God—a being unable to intervene directly in our lives but a being who could share in our pain and suffering. He concluded:

> I can worship a God who hates suffering but cannot eliminate it, more easily than I can worship a God who chooses to make children suffer and die, for whatever exalted reason. . . . Because the tragedy is not God's will we need not feel hurt or betrayed by God when tragedy strikes. We can turn to Him for help in overcoming it, precisely because we can tell ourselves that God is as outraged by it as we are. (1981, 231)

Kushner's is only one of many possible spiritual transformations people make in the character of the sacred. People can also shift from punitive to loving conceptions of God, from images of a distant to a personally involved being, from belief in a personal God to a sense of transcendence in all things, from "false Gods" (e.g., alcoholism, drug addiction) to "true Gods," and so on. It is also possible to envision negative spiritual transformations, such as changes from a sense of a larger presence in the universe to feelings of spiritual emptiness, or from belief in a loving God to belief in a harsh, malicious God. Thus, the loss of spirituality experienced by the victim of incest described in the introduction to this chapter would qualify as a spiritual transformation, albeit a negative one.

Secondary Spiritual Transformation

While primary spiritual transformations speak to fundamental changes in the place or character of the sacred as a goal or destination that guides the individual's life, secondary spiritual transformations have to do with changes not in goals or destinations, but in the pathways people take to the sacred. One type of secondary spiritual transformation is religious switching. For instance, Laura, in the second vignette of the introduction, switched denominations in an effort to find a God who would provide her with the unconditional love and acceptance she could not find from the denomination of her childhood and relationship with her father. This is not an unusual case. Empirical studies suggest that people are more likely to switch religious groups when they find alternatives that offer more compelling pathways to their personal, social, and spiritual goals. For instance, in a study of twenty-five people who became involved in the Divine Light Mission, Gartrell and Shannon (1985) found that 100 percent felt that their church of origin was hypocritical, 80 percent felt it could not help them with their most important needs, and 100 percent believed that the Divine Light Mission provided them with more viable solutions to their deepest problems.

Secondary spiritual transformations can also take the form of switches in other pathways people take to the sacred. In his book *A Generation of Seekers: The Spiritual Journeys of the Baby Boom Generation* (1993), Roof notes that many people in Western culture are now engaged in highly individualized spiritual experimentation in their quest for the sacred. Over several years, one person becomes a vegetarian, leaves his job in marketing, joins an eco-awareness group, and learns tai chi. Another jumps from interest in astrology and tarot card reading to music and meditation. Still another experiments with alcohol, drugs, and sexual liaisons. In spite of their differences, each of these individuals is involved in secondary spiritual transformations in the search for the sacred.

Secondary spiritual transformations also include efforts to overcome obstacles that block the individual's spiritual journey. These obstacles may be self-created, as in the case of spiritual transgressions that separate the individual from what he or she perceives as sacred. The religions of the world have developed a variety of purification rituals (e.g., repentance, sacrifice, exorcism, isolation, ablution, confession) to help people reorient themselves to the sacred following their transgressions (Pargament 1997). Other obstacles to the sacred may come upon the person, as in the case of a medical illness. Any illness can pose a threat not only to physical health and well-being, but also to the individual's sense of hope, meaning, and connection with the sacred (Csordas 1994). In response to this threat, many religious traditions encourage their adherents to redefine the meaning of healing from a "cure" to that of a final and ultimate union with God (see Poloma and Hoelter 1998). Spiritual direction and spiritually integrated psychotherapy are also called upon to help people overcome barriers to their search for the sacred.

Conclusion

Spiritual transformation refers primarily to a fundamental change in the place of the sacred or the character of the sacred as an object of significance in life, and secondarily to a fundamental change in the pathways the individual takes to the sacred. Defined in this manner, spiritual transformation is neither rare nor incomprehensible; it is, instead, part and parcel of spiritual life, one of the three processes critical to spirituality. In the search for the sacred, people engage in efforts to discover the sacred, conserve or sustain a relationship with the sacred once it has been discovered, and transform that relationship in response to internal or external trauma and transition. But the search for the sacred does not come to an end once the individual's relationship with the sacred has been transformed. Following this transformation, the individual's task shifts to the process of conserving this new understanding of the sacred. In this fashion, the search for the sacred evolves over the course of the individual's lifespan.

It is important to emphasize that people do not follow fixed and invariant stages in their search for the sacred; rather, each individual's search is likely to have a distinctive trajectory. Some people experience a relatively smooth process of spiritual development characterized by lengthy periods of conservation and gradual, unobtrusive transformations. For others, the spiritual journey is rockier, marked by sudden and unexpected twists and turns and only brief periods of spiritual continuity and calm. Still others, unable to transform their spirituality in response to internal or external change, may disengage from the spiritual search only to rediscover the sacred at a later point in life.

There are several advantages of this definition of spiritual transformation. First, it is inclusive, being broad enough to encompass the variety of subtypes of spiritual transformation that occur in cultures throughout the world. These subtypes include sudden and gradual spiritual transformation; spiritual transformation that occurs within a denomination, between denominations, or outside traditional religious institutions; and transformation in both theistic and nontheistic representations of the sacred. Second, though it is inclusive, the definition has a substantive core, the sacred, that sets it apart from other types of transformation, brings a potentially fuzzy construct into sharper focus, and lends a much needed boundary to this new area of inquiry. Finally, by defining spiritual transformation as a process rather than an outcome, the value of this construct is not prejudged or predetermined. Instead, social scientists can examine the implications of spiritual transformation empirically by studying how this construct relates, positively or negatively, to various physical, psychological, social, and spiritual outcomes.

For too many years, social scientists have neglected the study of spiritual transformation. Fortunately, the picture has begun to change. Knowledge about this phenomenon of interest is likely to expand in the years to come. Hopefully, these initial thoughts on the meaning of spiritual transformation will contribute to greater knowledge about a construct that is critical to an understanding of the meaning of spirituality and, more generally, of what it means to be human.

Note

Portions of this paper were adapted from Pargament and Mahoney (2002).

References

Bouchard, R. J. Jr., D. T. Lykken, M. McGue, N. L. Segal, and A. Tellegen. 1990. Sources of human psychological differences: The Minnesota study of twins reared apart. *Science* 250:223–50.

Bowlby, J. 1988. *A Secure Base: Parent-Child Attachment and Healthy Human Development*. New York: Basic Books.

Candler, A. G. Jr. 1951. Self-surrender. In *These Found the Way: Thirteen Converts to Protestant Christianity*, ed. D. W. Soper, 51–62. Philadelphia: Westminster.

Coles, R. 1990. *The Spiritual Life of Children*. Boston: Houghton Mifflin.

Csordas, T. J. 1994. *The Sacred Self: A Cultural Phenomenology of Charismatic Healing*. Berkeley: University of California Press.

Durkheim, E. 1915. *The Elementary Forms of the Religious Life*. New York: Free Press.

Eliade, M. 1958. *Patterns in Comparative Religion*. New York: Sheed and Ward.

Emmons, R. A. 1999. *The Psychology of Ultimate Concerns: Motivation and Spirituality in Personality*. New York: Guilford.

Fishbein, M., and J. Ajzen. 1975. *Belief, Attitude, Intention, and Behavior: An Introduction to Theory and Research*. Reading, Mass.: Addison-Wesley.

Flaherty, S. M. (1992). *Woman, Why Do You Weep?: Spirituality for Survivors of Childhood Sexual Abuse*. New York: Paulist.

Ford, M. E., and C. W. Nichols. 1987. A taxonomy of human goals and some possible applications. In *Humans as Self-Constructing Living Systems: Putting the Framework to Work*, ed. M. E. Ford and D. H. Ford, 289–311. Hillsdale, N.J.: Erlbaum.

Freud, S. 1928. A religious experience. In *The Standard Edition of the Complete Psychological Works of Sigmund Freud*, ed. and trans. J. Strachey, 21:169–72. London: Hogarth, 1961.

Gartrell, C. D., and Z. K. Shannon. 1985. Contacts, cognitions, and conversion: A rational choice approach. *Review of Religious Research* 27:31–48.

Goldman, R. 1964. *Religious Thinking from Childhood to Adolescence*. New York: Seabury.

Idinopulos, T. A., and E. A. Yonan, eds. 1996. *The Sacred and Its Scholars: Comparative Methodologies for the Study of Primary Religious Data*. Leiden: E. J. Brill.

Johnson, P. E. 1959. Psychology of Religion. Nashville, Tenn.: Abingdon.

Kasser, T., and R. M. Ryan. 1996. Further examining the American dream: The differential effects of intrinsic and extrinsic goal structures. *Personality and Social Psychology Bulletin* 22:280–87.

Kaufman, G. D. 1981. *The Theological Imagination: Constructing the Concept of God*. Philadelphia: Westminster.

Kirkpatrick, L. 2004. *Attachment, Evolution, and the Psychology of Religion*. New York: Guilford.

Klinger, E. 1998. The search for meaning in evolutionary perspective and its clinical implications. In *The Human Quest for Meaning*, ed. P. T. P. Wong and P. S. Fry, 27–50. Mahway, N.J.: Erlbaum.

Kushner, H. S. 1981. *When Bad Things Happen to Good People*. New York: Schocken Books.

Mahoney, A., and K. I. Pargament. 2004. Sacred changes: Spiritual conversion and transformation. *Journal of Clinical Psychology: In Session* 60:481–92.

Miller, W. R., and J. C'de Baca. 2001. *Quantum Change: When Epiphanies and Sudden Insights Transform Ordinary Lives.* New York: Guilford.

Oxford English Dictionary. 1980. 2nd ed., vol. 14. New York: Oxford University Press.

Pargament, K. I. 1997. *The Psychology of Religion and Coping: Theory, Research, Practice.* New York: Guilford.

———. 1999. The psychology of religion and spirituality? Yes and no. *International Journal for the Psychology of Religion* 9:3–16.

Pargament, K. I., and A. Mahoney. 2002. Spirituality: Discovering and conserving the sacred. In *Handbook of Positive Psychology,* ed. C. R. Snyder and S. J. Lopez, 646–59. Oxford: Oxford University Press.

———. 2005. Sacred matters: Sanctification as a vital topic for the psychology of religion. *International Journal for the Psychology of Religion* 15:179–98.

Poloma, M. M., and G. H. Gallup Jr. 1991. *Varieties of Prayer: A Survey Report.* Philadelphia: Trinity Press International.

Poloma, M. M, and L. Hoelter. 1998. The "Toronto blessing": A holistic model of healing. *Journal for the Scientific Study of Religion* 37:257–72.

Rambo, L. R. 1993. *Understanding Religious Conversion.* New Haven, Conn.: Yale University Press.

Rizzuto, A.-M. 1979. *The Birth of the Living God: A Psychoanalytic Study.* Chicago: University of Chicago Press.

Roof, W. C. 1993. *A Generation of Seekers: The Spiritual Journeys of the Baby Boom Generation.* San Francisco: Harper and Row.

Sargant, W. 1957. *Battle for the Mind.* Garden City, N.Y.: Doubleday.

Underwood, L. G. 1999. Daily spiritual experience. In *Multidimensional Measurement of Religiousness/Spirituality for Use in Health Research: A Report of the Fetzer Institute/National Institute on Aging Working Group,* 11–17. Kalamazoo, Mich.: Fetzer Institute.

Watzlawick, P. 1988. *Ultra-solutions, or, How to Fail Most Successfully.* New York: Norton.

3

The Spirit of Spiritual Healing in the United States

David J. Hufford and Mary Ann Bucklin

Mr. Jacobson (a pseudonym) had no experience with religious healing services, but he was seriously ill and facing surgery, which his physician gave a 50 percent likelihood of success. So when his wife read about a healing service at a local church, he attended.

> Friday morning before the evening service I became very sick and left work. . . . At the service I felt a little uneasy, but I became more at ease because the service was sedate, well done. . . . I got in the healing line . . . and one of the ministers laid his hands on my head and prayed for the Lord Jesus to heal me. I didn't feel anything.
>
> [Later, after the service ended,] on the way to my car I thought, "I wonder if I got healed? How are you supposed to feel when you get healed at one of these things?" And then I thought, "Well, it doesn't matter. Whether I get healed or not, I won't lose faith in God." Then suddenly, I felt like high voltage touched me on my head, and I had a feeling that I can only describe as like bubbling, boiling water rolling to my fingertips and back up. . . . And I felt the presence of God right there on the street. . . . I knew I had been healed. (Hufford 1993)

And medical tests the next week confirmed his return to health, contrary to all medical expectations. Mr. Jacobson's healing occurred not at the emotional height of an ecstatic service, not when a minister laid hands on him, and not when he "claimed his healing."

It occurred when he was met on the street outside the church by a spiritual presence and he was filled with boiling energy. This was a kind of spiritual healing, and it transformed Mr. Jacobson. From one with no prior experience with healing in a religious context, he became a deeply committed member of a religious healing group, a commitment he kept until his death fifteen years later.

Introduction

In popular language, the term *spiritual* refers to beliefs (we use the term in its cognitive sense; Hahn 1973, 208) that are contested in modern academic discourse. In this chapter we will address an aspect of the spiritual that is unconventional in academic work by calling attention to the implications of three points that in themselves are not controversial: (1) the adjective *spiritual* and the noun *spirituality* refer to the noun *spirit* (plural *spirits*); (2) belief in spirit(s) is problematic in modern discourse; and (3) contrary to the predictions of philosophers and social scientists since the nineteenth century, a wealth of data shows that belief in spirits is persistent and widespread among modern persons. These three facts are inherently related. But, although each has been much studied, their collective significance has received little attention.

Because the long-predicted "demise of the supernatural" (Berger 1990, 1–30) has not happened, modern theories of spiritual belief that have predicted that demise face serious challenges. One problem is the appropriation of terms such as *spiritual* from popular language and the redefinition of such terms for technical use in ways that differ substantially from their original meanings. Avoidance of the core reference to *spirit(s)* is common among such technical redefinitions. We will argue that it is the theoretical stigmatization of spirit belief that creates these lexical problems. We do not suggest that these problems have resulted in fatally flawed research on spirituality, transformation, and healing. But we do believe that our criticism of this scholarly convention can make an important contribution.

Spirit belief, the belief that spirits can and do exist, is a broad category ranging from beliefs conventionally considered religious (belief in God, belief in the human soul, belief in angels) to what are more often treated by scholars as folk beliefs (such as belief in ghosts). We are especially concerned with the way that modern intellectual attitudes toward spirit belief have stigmatized a broad range of spiritual experiences as pathological and the beliefs arising from those experiences as naive or irrational. Because these attitudes are pervasive, our analysis may seem polemic, and perhaps it is. But it is offered collegially, and we do not intend to dismiss or ignore the important contributions of those with whom we have some disagreement. Peter Berger provides an excellent example. We find Berger's analysis of the effects of modern secularization and pluralization of religion to be enormously helpful. But we disagree with his assumptions about spiritual experiences and the nonrational character of inferences based on them, and his emphasis on the need for institutional support for the plausibility of religious beliefs in general (Berger 1959; 1990; 1992). Our own approach is experience-centered (Hufford 1982; 1985a; 1995), and it yields a picture of dramatic spiritual experiences as remarkably common and providing a rational basis for a variety of basic religious beliefs independent of institutional religious sanction or elaboration. While this approach is novel, it is not opposed to other approaches. So we trust that the reader will take our critical analysis of the issues embedded in the meanings of *spirit(s)* as it is intended: with respect and an openness to dialogue.

Since research on spiritual matters involves surveys, ethnographic interviews, and other language-based methods, a mismatch between investigator and respondent on the meaning of key terms weakens the validity of the research. Because *religion* is defined in close relation to *spiritual(ity)*, an inappropriate definition of *spirituality* minus *spirit(s)* poses a large problem. Defining *spiritual* in terms of *spirit(s)* yields a simple and direct reference, congruent with popular usage, that allows for diverse findings: spiritual transformation may be either positive (toward something, e.g., conversion) or negative (away from something, e.g., loss of faith), healthy or unhealthy, incremental or sudden; it may involve transformation of spiritual beliefs (a cognitive spiritual transformation) or it may refer to one's spirit being changed (e.g., being "saved" or being spiritually corrupted); and it may refer to healing *by* a spirit, such as charismatic healing of a physical illness (healing by the Holy Spirit), or a healing *of* one's spirit.

Since our three basic points are not controversial, the following background is offered as an elucidation of their implications.

Spiritual Refers to Spirit(s)

Contemporary scholars have found *spiritual* and *spirituality* difficult to define, complaining that their meanings are "vague and contradictory" (Egbert, Mickley, and Coeling 2004, 8). The reason appears to be discomfort with the immaterial, supernatural meaning of *spirit*, the core reference of *spiritual* and *spirituality*. The meaning of *spiritual* has also become more contentious because of the 20–30 percent of Americans who describe themselves as "spiritual but not religious" (Gallup Organization 2001; Kurs 2001, 28). This group holds spiritual ideas not restrained by institutional doctrines. While often described as a recent phenomenon (e.g., New Age), this is actually characteristic of American religious life and was even more common at the time of the American Revolution (Butler 1990; Fuller 2001).

Space will not allow a survey of all the lexical data, so we will sketch the basic facts and give references to authoritative sources. In English, *spirit(s)* has consistently referred to the immaterial aspect of living beings (soul, animating principle) and in Western theology to the power of God. (Brown 1993; Jones 1986, xxiv; Skeat 1909). Its other usages are metaphorical extensions, as in *wine and spirits*, where *spirits* refers to alcohol, a consequence of seventeenth-century efforts to explain the "animating principle" in material terms using the volatility of alcohol as an analogy for subtle and highly refined "corpuscles" of matter coursing through the nerves (Frank 1990, 132–35).

Animating (i.e., life-giving) principle is not always taken in as personal a sense as *soul* is, despite its derivation from *anima*, the Latin word for "soul." It could be understood as more like the Chinese idea of *Qi*, often translated as "vital energy," which resonates with the élan vital of vitalism. Nonetheless, this animating principle, like soul and the power of God, is radically nonmaterial. This is why many Americans think of healing practices such as *qi gong* and therapeutic touch as spiritual. All such concepts break a basic rule of modernity, stated in a recent review of a book on the biological basis of consciousness, that there should be "no spooky forces that contravene thermodynamics" (Laureys 2005, 16). For the modern rejection of "mysterious, unpredictable forces" postulated in Weber's disenchantment thesis discussed below, all these ideas of "spooky," immaterial substances form a single category, the category to which the English word *spirit* points.

The following quote from National Public Radio's *All Things Considered* demonstrates that usage of *spirituality* as dependent on spirits is still current. Vina Drennan, widow of firefighter Captain John Drennan, killed in a fire in 1994, was being interviewed by Noah Adams in connection with the firefighters who died in the World Trade Center on September 11, 2001. She stated that the men in her late husband's company had prayed to him and that he had led them to find their fallen comrades.

> *Adams:* Mrs. Drennan, are you saying that those at the scene were, in a way, calling on the *spirit* of your husband to help them find those who had fallen?
>
> *Drennan:* Yes. You lose your religion somewhat after a large crisis, but you sure get a *spirituality* about it. (NPR 2002; italics added)

Spirituality refers to the domain of spirit(s): God or gods, souls, angels, jinni, demons—and only by metaphorical extension to other intangible and invisible things (e.g., ideas, such as "team spirit" or the "spirit of democracy"). However, using such metaphorical extensions to define spirituality is common today in academic circles, creating an unintentional equivocation.

Modernity and Spirit

The modern attitude tends to oppose the belief that there exist non-material spirit(s) that can influence and be influenced by events in the everyday world, treating that belief as primitive, naive, or psychopathological. Modern, well-educated people are not expected to hold such beliefs, and, therefore, it is thought that such ideas should disappear in the modern world. This tendency creates a strong bias that inclines modern discourse constantly away from acknowledging a widespread belief in interaction between humans and a complex world of spirits. This inclination is as common in modern theology as elsewhere among scholars, and it is embedded in modern language.

Typical modern definitions of *spiritual* avoid reference to *spirit(s)* and are therefore broad, "fuzzy" (Zinnbauer et al. 1998), or ambiguous. Such definitions are not well-aligned with popular usage. For example:

> I see spirituality as that which allows a person to experience transcendent meaning in life. This is often expressed as a relationship with God, but it can also be about nature, art, music, family, or community—whatever beliefs and values give a person a sense of meaning and purpose in life. (Puchalski and Romer 2000, 129)

Such definitions are common and show the influence of theologian Paul Tillich's definition of *religion* as "ultimate concern" (1959, 7–8). Like Tillich's, in the effort to be inclusive these definitions fail to distinguish religion and spirituality from other concepts. As Jonathan Z. Smith puts it, they make it "difficult if not impossible to distinguish religion from any other ideological category" (1998, 281).

Some scholars (e.g., Pargament 1997) have been careful to avoid highly ambiguous definitions and have noted the problems with divergent validity that are caused by the conflation of spiritual and psychological variables (Koenig, McCullough, and Larson 2001, 505–8). Their more specific definitions generally either refer to the divine or the sacred (relating to *deity*). The definition provided by Koenig, McCullough, and Larson in their *Handbook of Religion and Health* is an example:

> *Spirituality*: Spirituality is the personal quest for understanding answers to ultimate questions about life, about meaning and about relationship to the sacred or transcendent, which may (*or may not) lead to or arise from the development of religious rituals and the formation of community. (2001, 18)

The inclusion of *sacred* is helpful and works well for Protestant Christian religious doctrines. However, the avoidance of *spirit(s)* produces difficulty when applied to *spiritual healing* broadly, because many Americans have healing practices that they consider spiritual but that are not defined exclusively by reference to God. For example, Mexican *curanderos*, working on "the spiritual level,"

> are thought to be able to project their own souls or spirits out of their bodies, making the body a vessel for other spirits. . . . On the spiritual level, illness can be caused, diagnosed, and cured by spiritual forces called *corrientes espirituales* (spiritual currents) [Trotter and Chavira 1981, 63–64].

The same is true for such healing practices as Reiki, now quite popular throughout American society, that generally make no mention of God or the divine (e.g., "*rei* means 'universal' and refers to the energy of the spiritual dimension and soul. . . . *ki* refers to the vital life force that flows through all that is alive" [Fairbrass 2000, 436]). Also many traditional Catholic healing practices refer primarily to saints or the souls (spirits) in purgatory. It is not that these beliefs and practices are atheistic; they are not, and for most of those who use these practices, God is understood as the ultimate source of healing. Nonetheless, such beliefs and practices refer to a more complex social world of spirit than does the Protestant definition. The fact that these practices are generally omitted from the spirituality-religion-and-health literature reflects the fact that the Protestant definition is conventional.

Defining *spiritual* simply by reference to *spirit(s)* does not require the investigator to take a position on the existence of spirit(s). Calling a transformation or healing *spiritual* should not commit us to a theory about the ontological status of the human soul! It is with the meaning of *spiritual* in ordinary speech that research and interpretation must begin. This kind of definition is more common in the anthropological literature (e.g., Spiro 1966) perhaps because, while dealing with the cultural "other," anthropology has been less constrained by modern European theological formulations.

However we define modernity (since medieval times, or since the Enlightenment, et cetera), we find assumptions that are biased not only against the validity of belief in the existence of spirits but against the idea that such belief can be rationally warranted. These assumptions are found in theology as well as in philosophy and developing fields devoted to the study of humanity. This bias is not in itself the widely imagined rift between science and religion, because it does not arise from science per se but rather from scholarly reflections about science. But these assumptions are an important source of the idea that such a rift exists (Ferngren 2002).

Historical Developments

In sharp contrast to the medieval Catholic religious worldview, the theology of the Protestant Reformation, especially as reflected in Calvinism, sharply reduced the interactions between spirits and humans. As J. J. Cerullo puts it:

> The God described by Reformation thinkers (particularly, of course, by Calvin and those most directly influenced by him) simply will not irrupt into either the natural or social environment as directly or regularly as does that of Catholicism. The Catholic world was permeated by supernatural manifestations: miracles, saintly intercessions, even the sacraments themselves. Direct interventions by the heavenly realm were normal, expected (even invocable) features of reality in Catholic eyes. Protestantism denied most of them. The God it portrayed would not grant such "popish" boons to a mankind as utterly, frightfully fallen as Luther and Calvin believed. In the final analysis, only one undeniably supernatural event was allotted Protestant man: the devolution of God's sovereign grace. (1982, 3)

In secular philosophy a similar change was occurring. Although taking very diverse positions regarding religion, such philosophers as Hobbes, Hume, Kant, Hegel, Feuerbach, and Marx took positions that firmly rejected the possibility of a rational belief in spirit(s) on an empirical basis. The Enlightenment view of a division between science, in charge of rational knowledge, and religion, based on faith, feeling, and intuition, became conventional among intellectuals.

Even more striking is the fact that many theologians outside Calvinism responded to the growing materialism of modern philosophy with what Peter Berger calls "surrender" (1990; 1992). For example, in 1799 at the beginnings of liberal Protestant theology, Friedrich Schleiermacher in his first book, *On Religion: Speeches to Its Cultured Despisers*, rejected the very idea of supernatural causes of observable events and located the spiritual exclusively in the believer's feeling of religious significance about life in general. Theological existentialism further developed the subjectivity of religion. Søren Kierkegaard, for example, held that in religion, reasoned inference from observation undermines true faith by attempting to make "safe" that which should be accepted "by virtue of the absurd" (1941/1843, 47, 51).

The result of these parallel developments in very different intellectual traditions was the distinctively modern separation of the spiritual from the observable world. This was part of the construction of religion as affective rather than cognitive, in contrast to science, the domain of rationality and the observable. This shift clearly contradicts empirical ideas of spirit: that God (or others) could be directly encountered or would produce observable results in the world. Although resisted by experiential movements from Shakerism beginning in the eighteenth century to Christian Science and Pentecostalism in the nineteenth century and the charismatic movement in the twentieth century, this divorce of religion from observation and reason became conventional among American intellectuals. This is the aspect of modernity that Max Weber famously called "disenchantment."

> The growing process of intellectualization and rationalization . . . means that in principle, then, we are not ruled by mysterious, unpredictable forces, but that, on the contrary, we can in principle *control everything by means of calculation.* That in turn means the disenchantment of the world. Unlike the savage for whom such forces existed, we need no longer have recourse to magic in order to control the *spirits* [italics added] or pray to them. Instead, technology and calculation achieve our ends. This is the primary meaning of the process of intellectualization. (2004/1917, 12–13)

For Weber, the expulsion of spirits was necessitated by "intellectualization and rationalization"; only "savages" would hold such beliefs. This idea became a central characteristic of modernity, even among theologians and others positively disposed toward religion. For example Keith Thomas, in his landmark *Religion and the Decline of Magic*, says that the belief in ghosts is today "rightly disdained by intelligent persons" but was "taken seriously by equally intelligent persons in the past" (1971, ix). He places the change in the sixteenth and seventeenth centuries, saying that in the sixteenth century the belief in ghosts "distinguished Protestant from Catholic almost as effectively as belief in the Mass or the Papal Supremacy" (589). But, as Theo Brown's description of the post-Reformation period in West Country England states, "The church also had ceased officially to believe in ghosts. . . . This did not mean that ghosts ceased to appear, but merely that the church abdicated its authority over them" (1979, 190–91). However the shift Weber describes did not just concern ghosts. It extended to all sorts of spirit encounters and spiritual causes, religious visions, angels, and God. As Stanley Tambiah (1994, 31) points out, "Seventeenth century Protestant thought contributed to the demarcation of 'magic' from 'religion,' magic being . . . false manipulations of the supernatural and occult powers."

Although they are often conflated, *disenchantment* is different from *secularization*, which can mean primarily the shifting of political authority from religious institutions to the state. There is no doubt that secularization has been a characteristic of modernity. Enchantment can be found within religious institutions and (heretically) outside them. The secularization of society seems to have affected the enchanted view of religious institutions much more than of the popular spiritual practices not associated with them.

The modern theological move away from spirits is epitomized in the twentieth century by the existentialist Protestant theologian Rudolf Bultmann (1884–1976). Bultmann found religious beliefs based on observations of alleged spiritual cause in the world to be primitive, an offense to the modern mind. This led him to embark on the project of "demythologizing" Christian scripture. Bultmann (1953) claimed that

> the mythical view of the world is obsolete. . . . Now that the forces and the laws of nature have been discovered, we can no longer believe in *spirits*, whether good or evil. . . . It is impossible to use electric light and the wireless and to avail ourselves of modern medical and surgical discoveries, and at the same time to believe in . . . *spirits*. (3–5; italics added)

Contemporary Illustrations of the Modern Trend

Demythologizing continues, often under other names, as modern theologians struggle to maintain authentic religion without making any claims that might be either tested or subject to alternative explanation by skeptics. As Berger points out, the "death of God theology [was] short-lived . . . But many contemporary theologians using more moderate language are engaged in essentially the same act of surrender" (1992, 42). For example, theologian Nancy Murphy, in a 2001 interview, made the following statement:

> The interesting thing is that, over the past 100 years in biblical studies and church history, it [belief in an immaterial soul] has been gradually disappearing from mainline Christian thought, but that has not been widely shared with the folks in the pew. So, I suddenly realized some years back that I am a physicalist, I don't believe there is a soul. The soul is a hypothetical concept that seemed necessary way back when. We don't need it now for scientific purposes. (Giberson and Yerxa 2001, 33)

Murphy's reference to the "folks in the pew" suggests the elitism implicit in the development of the intellectual attitudes of modernity described above. Murphy's view has been echoed by a number of contemporary theologians and philosophers of religion (e.g., Barbour 2000; Brown, Murphy, and Malony 1998). This view is remarkably close to those of such well-known scientific skeptics as Francis Crick, who writes, "The idea of a soul, distinct from the body . . . is a myth" (1994, 4), or E. O. Wilson, who asserts in *Consilience* (1999) that neuroscience makes belief in the soul untenable and that this eliminates any grounds for belief in spirits. "The *spirits* our ancestors knew intimately fled the rocks and the trees, then the distant mountains. Now they are in the stars where their final extinction is possible" (289; italics added).

The equation of spirits with "our ancestors" reiterates the conventional view of such beliefs as antiquated and primitive—*not modern*. Centuries after Calvin and Hume, we find skeptical materialists and some prominent theologians moving in lockstep on the issue of spirit belief—despite the diverse spirit beliefs that have persisted in the American population (Gallup and Jones 2000; Gallup and Proctor 1982; Greeley 1975; 1987; Hufford 1985a).

In contrast, the modern discipline of anthropology was founded on efforts to avoid ethnocentric assumptions about the truth or falsity of the beliefs and values of others, and an interest in religion and spiritual belief has been a central aspect of the field since its inception. Nonetheless, anthropology has consistently located spirit belief in other cultures, assuming that in modern society the idea is made untenable by modern rationality. In 1952 Sir Edward Evans-Pritchard described the attitude of the discipline: "Religion is superstition to be explained by anthropologists, not something that any anthropologist, or indeed any rational person, could himself believe in" (Evans-Pritchard 1960, 10).

The most common anthropological mode of showing respect to spirit beliefs is to "take them seriously" as local views that are reasonable from the local perspective but not from that of the objective anthropologist. This is typically assumed rather than argued (e.g., Lambek 1981; 2002; Mageo and Howard 1996; Malinowski 1948/1925; Morris 1987).

Even some anthropologists who claim to have transcended the Western, rationalist worldview consider spirit beliefs untenable for the modern scholar. A clear example can be found in editors David Young and Jean-Guy Goulet's conclusion to *Being Changed by Cross-Cultural Encounters* (1994), in which they state a hermeneutic position remarkably similar in its outlook to Bultmann's demythologizing project.

> All the contributors to this book elaborate on their extraordinary experiences in terms that are foreign to the culture in which they lived these experiences. This is necessarily so . . . because the anthropological journey leads back home where they must communicate anew with friends and colleagues in a shared language of understanding. (322)

Even though at least two of the contributors to this collection, Edith Turner (1994) and Antonia Mills (1994), clearly take the beliefs of their informants as reasonable and probably valid, Young and Goulet seem unaware that many of the non-Western experiences and beliefs discussed in their book are actually prevalent in American society! Although some anthropologists courageously reject the dichotomy between spirit belief and modern knowledge, including Joan Koss-Chioino (see chap. 4) along with Edith Turner (1994; and chap. 7) and Antonia Mills (1994), the clarity with which the exceptions stand out emphasizes the prevalence of the standard view that belief in spirit(s) is indefensible for the modern person. Finding this view among theologians and anthropologists, we should scarcely be surprised that other fields have followed suit.

Spirit Belief among Modern Americans

Belief in and utilization of spiritual healing is very common in the United States. For example, a *Newsweek* poll utilizing a large national sample found that 87 percent of Americans believe "that God answers prayers," and 79 percent say God answers prayers for healing someone with an incurable disease (*Newsweek* 1997).

The best recent data on the utilization of prayer for healing is Barnes et al. (2004). Among the ten most common healing practices used, five were explicitly spiritual in nature: personal prayer for health (43 percent); prayer by others (24.4 percent); participation in a prayer group for one's own health (9.6 percent); meditation (7.6 percent); and yoga (5.1 percent); and the other five are often associated with religious and spiritual ideas and groups. According to Barnes et al., "About 45% of (English-speaking, American) adults used prayer specifically for health concerns during the past 12 months" (6; see also Eisenberg et al. 1993; 1998). Prayers for healing occur both within formal religious contexts and outside such settings among the "spiritual but not religious"; and spiritual healing is not limited to such prayers (e.g., Reiki, and yoga).

A great deal of additional data show that spiritual belief among Americans is often associated with experiential encounters, and that such experiences often are transformative and healing (Gallup and Jones 2000; Gallup and Proctor 1982; Greeley 1975; 1987; Hinton, Hufford, and Kirmayer 2005; Hufford 1982; 1985a; 2005; Moody 1975; Rees 1971; 2001; van Lommel, van Wees, Meyers, and Elfferich 2001). As discussed above, this seems to have been true throughout American history. For ordinary Americans, this is not the "second naiveté" envisioned by Paul Ricœur, an immediacy only available through hermeneutics: "we can only believe by interpreting" (1967, 352). It is a sustained tradition of belief rooted in experience that challenges the very use of the term *naive*. Disenchantment seems to have been a characteristic of intellectual discourse rather than of modern belief and experience—even among many intellectuals. Perhaps Bruno Latour is right when he claims that *We Have Never Been Modern* (1993).

Conclusion

The strength of public interest in spiritual aspects of health and healing is obvious in the popular literature and media. A search of Gale's *Onefile*, by five-year intervals from 1985 through 1999, showed a rise in *spirituality* citations from 323 to 929. "Across the board . . . surveys confirm a remarkable rise in spiritual concern" (Gallup and Jones 2000, 27). This public interest is driving growing research interest, especially in the health field. Between 1990 and 2000 the number of references for *spiritual* and *spirituality* in a one-year search of MEDLINE rose almost fivefold (from 50+ to 250+), and for *religion* and its cognates roughly doubled (from 300+ to 700+).

But a disconnect remains between the public and those investigators whose view of the topic remains heavily conditioned by the Weberian assumption that the modern world is disenchanted. Among religion and health investigators this produces a negative bias regarding American spiritual-healing approaches that are not religious, for example Reiki or therapeutic touch. But emphasis on religious healing ideas is further biased by the theological issues of modernity noted above. Even those specifically churchly healing approaches that appear nonmodern, the pilgrimages of Catholics to sacred sites such as Lourdes in France or Ste. Anne de Beaupré in Canada, for example, and prayers to the saints (Hufford 1985b), receive little attention in this literature.

The issue is not whether belief in spirit(s) is true. Neither do we dispute any particular theological position that restrains spirit belief on the basis of scripture or doctrine. Rather we are arguing that theological commitments, whether theist or atheist, ought not distort the facts of ordinary belief and experience. Belief in spirit(s) is widely held and is intimately and directly involved in *spiritual healing* and *spiritual transformation*, as most English-speakers use those words. The idea that such a belief cannot be held by the mainstream in the modern world is contradicted by a wealth of empirical data. Theories of modernity that assume a modern loss of spirit belief are wrong. (And even postmodern theories, generally no friendlier to spirit(s) than modern theories, are called into question by the persistence and widespread distribution of spirit belief.) Spirit belief is not one of the differences between modern Westerners and the rest of humanity. It is something that we and they have in common. And the prevalent tendency to avoid facing this startling and fascinating fact of modernity and postmodernity creates serious problems of validity in both data acquisition and interpretation.

References

Adams, N. 2002. Interview with Vina Drennan. *All Things Considered* (September 20). Washington, D.C.: National Public Radio.

Barbour, I. G. 2000. *When Science Meets Religion*. New York: HarperCollins.

Barnes, A. M., E. Powell-Griner, K. McFann, and R. L. Nahin. 2004. Complementary and alternative medicine use among adults: United States, 2002. *Advance Data from Vital and Health Statistics of the Centers for Disease Control*, no. 343 (May 27). Retrieved June 20, 2005 from http://nccam.nih.gov/news/report.pdf

Berger, P. L. 1959. *The Sacred Canopy*. Garden City, N.Y.: Doubleday.

———. 1990. *A Rumor of Angels: Modern Society and the Rediscovery of the Supernatural*. 2nd ed. Garden City, N.Y.: Doubleday.

———. 1992. *A Far Glory: The Quest for Faith in an Age of Credulity*. New York: Free Press.

Brown, L., ed. 1993. *The New Shorter Oxford English Dictionary on Historical Principles*. Vol. 2. Oxford: Clarendon.

Brown, T. 1979. *The Fate of the Dead: A Study in Folk Eschatology in the West Country after the Reformation*. London: D.S. Brewer.

Brown, W. S., N. Murphy, and H. N. Malony, eds. 1998. *Whatever Happened to the Soul: Scientific and Theological Portraits of Human Nature*. Minneapolis, Minn.: Fortress.

Bultmann, R. 1953. The New Testament and mythology. In *Kerygma and Myth*, ed. H. W. Bartsch, 1–44. London: SPCK.

Butler, J. 1990. *Awash in a Sea of Faith: Christianizing the American People*. Cambridge, Mass: Harvard University Press.

Cerullo, J. J. 1982. *The Secularization of the Soul: Psychical Research in Modern Britain*. Philadelphia: Institute for the Study of Human Issues.

Crick, F. 1994. *The Astonishing Hypothesis: The Scientific Search for the Soul*. New York: Macmillan Library Reference.

Egbert, N., J. Mickley, and H. Coeling. 2004. A review and application of social scientific measures of religiosity and spirituality: Assessing a missing component in health communication research. *Health Communication* 16 (1): 7–27.

Eisenberg, D. M., R. C. Kessler, C. Foster, F. E. Norlock, D. R. Calkins, and T. L. Delbanco. 1993. Unconventional medicine in the United States. *New England Journal of Medicine* 328 (4): 246–79.

Eisenberg, D. M., R. B. Davis, S. L. Ettner, S. Appel, S. Wilkey, and M. Van Rompay et al. 1998. Trends in alternative medicine use in the United States, 1990–1997: Results of a follow-up national survey. *Journal of the American Medical Association* 280 (18): 1569–75.

Evans-Pritchard, E. E. 1960. Religion and anthropologists. *Blackfriars* 41:104–18.

Fairbrass, J. 2000. Reiki. In *Clinician's Complete Reference to Complementary/Alternative Medicine*, ed. D. W. Novey, 435–43. St. Louis: Mosby.

Ferngren, G. B., ed. 2002. *Science and Religion: A Historical Introduction*. Baltimore, Md.: Johns Hopkins University Press.

Frank, R. G. Jr. 1990. Thomas Willis and his circle: Brain and mind in seventeenth-century medicine. In *The Languages of Psyche: Mind and Body in Enlightenment Thought*, ed. G. S. Rousseau, 107–46. Berkeley: University of California Press.

Fuller, R. C. 2001. *Spiritual But Not Religious: Understanding Unchurched America*. New York: Oxford University Press.

Gallup Organization. 2001. Religion. In *Gallup Poll Topics: A–Z*. Retrieved 2001 from www.gallup.com/poll/indicators/indreligion4.asp

Gallup, G. H. Jr., and T. Jones. 2000. *The Next American Spirituality: Finding God in the Twenty-first Century*. Colorado Springs, Colo.: Cook Communications.

Gallup, G. J., and W. W. Proctor. 1982. *Adventures in Immortality*. New York: McGraw-Hill.

Giberson, K., and D. Yerxa. 2001. Tiny holes for God: A conversation with Nancy Murphy. *Research News and Opportunities in Science and Theology* 1 (8): 21, 33.

Goulet, J.-G., and D. Young. 1994. Theoretical and methodological issues. In *Being Changed by Cross-Cultural Encounters: The Anthropology of Extraordinary Experience*, ed. D. Young and J.-G. Goulet, 298–35. Peterborough, Ontario: Broadview.

Greeley, A. M. 1975. *The Sociology of the Paranormal: A Reconnaissance*. Vol. 3, ser. 90-023. Beverly Hills, Calif.: Sage.

———. 1987. Hallucinations among the widowed. *Sociology of Social Research* 71 (4): 258–65.

Hahn, R. 1973. Understanding beliefs: An essay on the methodology of the statement and analysis of belief systems. *Current Anthropology* 14 (3): 207–29.

Hinton, D. E., D. J. Hufford, and L. J. Kirmayer. 2005. Sleep paralysis and culture. *Transcultural Psychiatry* 42 (1): 5–10.

Hufford, D. J. 1982. *The Terror That Comes in the Night: An Experience-Centered Study of Supernatural Assault Traditions*. Philadelphia: University of Pennsylvania Press.

———. 1985a. Commentary: Mystical experience in the modern world, a memoir by Genevieve Foster. In *The World Was Flooded with Light: A Mystical Experience Remembered*, ed. G. W. Foster, 87–183. Pittsburgh, Pa.: University of Pittsburgh Press.

———. 1985b. Ste. Anne de Beaupré: Roman Catholic pilgrimage and healing. *Western Folklore* 44:194–207.

———. 1993. Epistemologies of religious healing. *Journal of Philosophy and Medicine* 18 (2): 175–94.

———. 1995. Beings without bodies: An experience-centered theory of the belief in spirits. In *Out of the Ordinary: Folklore and the Supernatural*, ed. B. Walker, 11–45. Logan: University of Utah Press.

———. 2005. Sleep paralysis as spiritual experience. *Transcultural Psychiatry* 42 (1): 11–45.

Jones, C. P. M. 1986. Preface to *The Study of Spirituality*, ed. C. P. M. Jones, G. Wainwright, and E. Yarnold, xxi–xxvi. New York: Oxford University Press.

Kierkegaard, S. 1843. *Fear and Trembling*, trans. W. Lowrie. Princeton, N.J.: Princeton University Press, 1941.

Koenig, H. G., M. E. McCullough, and D. B. Larson. 2001. *Handbook of Religion and Health*. Oxford: Oxford University Press.

Kurs, K. 2001. Are you religious or are you spiritual? Voices of a new America. *Spirituality and Health* 4:28–31.

Lambek, M. 1981. *Human Spirits: A Cultural Account of Trance in Mayout*. Cambridge: Cambridge University Press.

———, ed. 2002. *A Reader in the Anthropology of Religion*. Malden, Mass.: Blackwell.

Larson, D. B., J. P. Swyers, and M. E. McCullough. 1998. *Scientific Research on Spirituality and Health: A Consensus Report*. Rockville, Md.: National Institute for Healthcare Research.

Latour, B. 1991. *We Have Never Been Modern*. Cambridge, Mass.: Harvard University Press.

Laureys, S. 2005. Review of *Wider than the Sky: The Phenomenal Gift of Consciousness*, by Gerald M. Edelman. *New England Journal of Medicine* 352:16.

Mageo, J. M., and A. Howard, eds. 1996. *Spirits in Culture, History, and Mind*. New York: Routledge.

Malinowski, B. 1925. *Magic, Science, and Religion, and Other Essays*. Garden City, N.Y.: Doubleday, 1948.

Mills, A. 1994. Making a scientific investigation of ethnographic cases suggestive of reincarnation. In *Being Changed by Cross-Cultural Encounters: The Anthropology of Extraordinary Experience*, ed. D. Young and J.-G. Goulet, 237–69. Peterborough, Ontario: Broadview.

Moody, R. 1975. *Life After Life*. Atlanta, Ga.: Mockingbird Books.

Morris, B. 1987. *Anthropological Studies of Religion: An Introductory Text*. Cambridge: Cambridge University Press.

New Oxford American Dictionary. 2005. Ed. E. McKean. 2nd ed. Oxford: Oxford University Press.

Newsweek. 1997. The mystery of prayer: Does God play favorites? March 31, 56–65.

Pargament, K. L. 1997. *The Psychology of Religion and Coping: Theory, Research, Practice*. New York: Guilford.

Puchalski, C. M., and A. L. Romer. 2000. Taking a spiritual history allows clinicians to understand patients more fully. *Journal of Palliative Medicine* 3 (1): 129–37.

Rees, D. 1971. The hallucinations of widowhood. *British Medical Journal* 4:37–41.

———. 2001. *Death and Bereavement: The Psychological, Religious and Cultural Interfaces*. 2nd ed. London: Whurr.

Ricœur, P. 1967. *The Symbolism of Evil*. New York: Harper and Row.

Schleiermacher, F. E. D. 1799. *On Religion: Speeches to Its Cultured Despisers*, trans. J. Oman. Louisville, Ky.: Westminster John Knox, 1958.

Skeat, W. W. 1909. *An Etymological Dictionary of the English Language*. Oxford: Oxford University Press.

Smith, J. Z. 1998. Religion, religions, religious. In *Critical Terms for Religious Studies*, ed. M. C. Taylor, 269–84. Chicago: University of Chicago Press.

Spiro, M. E. 1966. Religion: Problems of definition and explanation. In *Anthropological Approaches to the Study of Religion*, ed. M. Burton, 85–126. London: Tavistock.

Tambiah, S. J. 1994. *Magic, Science, Religion, and the Scope of Rationality*. Cambridge: Cambridge University Press.

Thomas, K. 1971. *Religion and the Decline of Magic*. New York: Charles Scribner's Sons.

Tillich, P. 1959. *Theology of Culture*. New York: Oxford University Press.

Trotter, R. T. II, and J. A. Chavira. 1981. *Curanderismo: Mexican American Folk Healing*. Athens: University of Georgia Press.

Turner, E. 1994. A visible spirit form in Zambiah. In *Being Changed by Cross-Cultural Encounters: The Anthropology of Extraordinary Experience*, ed. D. Young and J.-G. Goulet, 71–95. Peterborough, Ontario: Broadview.

van Lommel, P., R. van Wees, V. Meyers, and I. Elfferich. 2001. Near-death experience in survivors of cardiac arrest: A prospective study in the Netherlands, *Lancet* 358 (9298): 2039–45. Erratum. 2002. *Lancet* 359, no. 9313 (April 6): 1254.

Weber, M. 1917. Science as a vocation, trans. R. Livingstone. In *The Vocation Lectures*, ed. D. Owen and T. B. Strong. Indianapolis, Ind.: Hackett, 2004.

Wilson, E. O. 1999. *Consilience: The Unity of Knowledge*. New York: Vintage Books.

Young, D., and J.-G. Goulet, eds. 1994. *Being Changed by Cross-Cultural Encounters: The Anthropology of Extraordinary Experience*. Peterborough, Ontario: Broadview.

Zinnbauer, E. J., K. I. Pargament, B. Cole, M. S. Rye, E. M. Butter, and T. G. Belavich et al. 1998. Religion and spirituality: Unfuzzying the fuzzy. *Journal for the Scientific Study of Religion* 36:459–564.

PART II

TRADITIONAL AND INDIGENOUS HEALING SYSTEMS: ANTHROPOLOGICAL PERSPECTIVES

4

Spiritual Transformation and Radical Empathy in Ritual Healing and Therapeutic Relationships

Joan D. Koss-Chioino

> *Crees en los espiritus? No, pero que lo hay lo hay.*
> "Do you believe in spirits? No, but what exists, exists."
>
> —A spirit medium

In the early seventies, at the request of the Department of Health of Puerto Rico, I applied to the National Institute of Mental Health (NIMH) for a grant to develop an interface between Spiritist healers and the public health system. The health department proposed that encounters of traditional healers with mental health professionals might facilitate the health department's mandate to deliver community care to the mentally ill because popular healers saw more troubled persons than did mental health care professionals. At the San Juan airport I met a distinguished-looking older man, the site visitor from NIMH. He was somewhat distressed, claiming that my typical Puerto Rican hospitality was excessive, that I should not have met him or arranged accommodations. That evening I took him to a Spiritist healing session and was appalled when halfway through the three-hour session the spirits called him to the table to be treated. He went in good grace and afterwards demanded that I translate. In considerable discomfort I softened the spirits' words: He would suffer from a fatal cancer in the next several years. Despite his avowed disbelief in their prediction and my fears, he recommended that the project be funded. Three years into the project I received word from the NIMH that he was no longer there, having succumbed to cancer.

This sort of revelation occurred many times in the course of my research into Spiritism, or Spiritualism, a popular healing cult in Latin American countries. How could the spirit healers divine so accurately in the case of such visitors who had never before attended a spirit-healing session? It was this kind of experience, observed many times when involving Puerto Rican supplicants as well, that led to my three-decade-long exploration of the ritual-healing process.[1] Explanations in the anthropological literature simply did not fully account for the healers' work, the spirits' diagnoses and predictions, or the effects on healers and supplicants.

Core Elements of the Ritual-Healing Process

There are many rich, parallel descriptions of healing rituals that employ spirits, God(s), or other extraordinary beings across cultures, and these descriptions can serve as a basis for exploring core elements of healing process. My exploration in this chapter is based on an assumption that cultural elaborations—such as very different mythic worlds, diverse symbol systems, different schemas to identify illness and disorder, various types of ritual paraphernalia, and so on—are elaborations of content rather than process. The presence of core elements in the healing process appears to be particularly the case for spirit healing, which has very similar ritual forms, enhanced by local content, across diverse regions of the world. What I suggest here as foundational aspects of the ritual-healing process can also be identified in some psychotherapeutic modalities, although they appear of lesser importance to the healing process in these psychotherapeutic modalities.

My formulation of core components of the ritual-healing process uses spirit healing in Puerto Rico as a prototype.[2] It focuses on the nascent healer's experience of spiritual transformation, associated with a severe illness or period of intense distress, and an emergent ability visited upon them (see chap. 7) to commune with the sacred (however conceived in diverse cultures). Some sufferers undergo a spiritual transformation that, in about one-third of the cases seen by spirit healers, may lead to their "development" as a healer-medium. From this type of spiritual transformation emerges a capacity for *radical empathy* in the developing healer, which threads the healer's work for the rest of his or her life. A model of ritual healing, based on these foundational components, is described in the following sections.

Spiritual Transformation

Spiritual transformation, defined very generally as "fundamental change in the place of the sacred or the character of the sacred in the life of the individual" (see chap. 2), is foundational to the ritual-healing process. It might be defined more specifically as "dramatic changes in world and self views, purposes, religious beliefs, attitudes or behavior. These changes are often linked to discrete experiences that can occur gradually or over relatively short periods of time" (Katz 2004, 1). Spiritual transformation also has been described as a "transition from a lower to higher consciousness, transformation in the essence (soul) of the individual, or the experiencing of a fresh acquaintance with rare, dramatic . . . spiritual states" (McLean 1994, 76). Spiritual transformation, as the hallmark of spirit-healer initiation, is reported by many healers and sometimes also by their clients (see for example Csordas and Lewton 1998; Katz 1993; Peters 1981). It appears to be a central component of the healing process in many healing systems, with the exception of Western biomedicine and cosmopolitan healing systems, such as classical Chinese medicine, that are grounded in biophysical concepts. Furthermore, bodily and psychic incorporation of spirits or God(s) or other extraordinary beings, as outcomes of a spiritual transformation, are directly associated with being healed, whether or not all of the sufferer's symptoms remain (Csordas 1994; Kleinman and Sung 1979). The role and effect of spiritual transformation on healers and the healing process have been described in numerous reports of ritual healing in a number of societies and groups (e.g., Csordas 1994; Katz 1993; Koss-Chioino 1992).

The Wounded Healer

The anthropological literature contains numerous examples of how indigenous healers and shamans are initiated into their healing roles via a serious, often life-threatening, illness that is resolved when an extraordinary being(s) is introduced into their consciousness and life world. Behavioral and attitudinal changes ensue, once the spirit becomes an integral part of the novitiate's life and being. Initiation into the healer role is both preceded and accompanied by changes in self- and worldviews. These descriptions of healer initiation via life-threatening illness have led to the formulation of the *wounded healer*, whose source of power and authority as a healer is a continuous relationship to her own *woundedness*, and is exemplified by the healer's willingness to maintain an awareness of those parts of herself that are perpetually wounded (see Kirmayer 2003 for a history of the formulation). Whether the healer's wounds are physical, emotional, or existential, the healer often must confront them during encounters with ill and distressed clients.

The idea of the wounded healer continually repeating his own process of being healed is not new. Apart from the anthropological literature on shamanism, Jung viewed the wounded healer as a central archetype represented by Asklepios, the God-healer and founder of Greco-Roman healing cults. Jung and some post-Jungians view this archetype as a key aspect of the analyst-patient relationship, one that activates the endogenous healer in the patient and the remembered patient in the healer (Groesbeck 1975; Guggenbuhl-Craig 1978; and see Kirmayer [2003] for a discussion of the wounded physician or healer; also, Miller and Baldwin 2000). In the Jungian formulation, as explained by Groesbeck (1975), the patient projects his inner healer onto the analyst because the distress of the wound blocks the inner healer. If the analyst does not recognize the healer-wound polarity in himself, he may project his woundedness onto the patient, which prevents healing. The patient's wound can be successfully treated only when interaction with the analyst (who recognizes his woundedness) facilitates the patient's withdrawing of his projection of "healer" from the analyst so that the patient's inner healer is activated.

In his cogent discussion of the wounded healer Kirmayer (2003) cites Van Franz (1975), who relates Jung's work to that of "shamans and medicine men" who mediate between the spirit world and the suffering client. As noted above, the shamanic healer gains power and credibility through her own inner experience of severe illness and recovery. During this event, most often with the intervention of other spirit healers, the novitiate develops the capacity (Spiritists use the word *faculty*) to communicate with and control spirits or other extraordinary influences that can cause illness or distress. She also acquires one or more spirit guide-protectors to facilitate her new healing vocation.

In spirit healing in Puerto Rico, which I use as a prototype for this discussion, a willingness to confront one's own woundedness (related to partial recovery from a life-threatening illness) is commonly associated with new, life-shaking experiences of spirit beings who occupy a world parallel to that of living beings (see chap. 8 for a description of the qualities of and encounters with the sacred). Although over time the novitiate healer becomes familiar with the characteristics of the spirit personae who cohabit in his consciousness from that time forward, the spirits are also ineffable and inexplicable.

Communion with the sacred may take three main forms: (1) visions of the spirit world, (2) journeys to that spirit world, and (3) voluntary (involuntary for persons who are not "developed") intimacy (i.e., in embodiment or in possession trances) with spirit beings. In Spiritism for example, both spirit guide-protectors and intrusive, often harmful spirits may possess people (the latter type of possession resulting in displacement of the possessed individual's own spirit). Novitiate healers learn through tutelage and by observation of other healers how to control communication with spirits. They experience spirits in ways that are both personally and cosmically meaningful.

The experience of spirit beings during a life-threatening illness can make a significant impression upon the sufferer (who is in a state of high emotional arousal—confused, fearful, desperate, socially withdrawn, etc.). As Frankl (1959) observed (and many writers since), many reports of transcendence in the context of suffering are facilitated by both psychological and physical factors. If a healer is present and the healer establishes a significant association between a spiritual entity and the sufferer's hope of, or actual relief from, danger or suffering, that spiritual entity can take on significant personal meaning for the sufferer. This then appears to reinforce or establish belief in the power of extraordinary beings, as has been noted throughout years of anthropological writing on illness and healing. One might say, following Csordas (1994), for those who hold a worldview centered on the self, that the *spirit-other* becomes embodied within the self of those who become healers. The personal spirit guide-protector (or several) makes healing work not only possible but also safe from contagion; that is, the guide-protector protects the healer-medium from the effects of distress-causing spirit beings brought to the healing session by suffering clients.

Following such experiences, spiritual communion becomes the foundation for the healer's capacity for empathy. As I will describe in more detail later, the healer is not only empathic in her healing work but also comes to employ radical empathy in healing relationships constituted by visionary experiences, trance, and possession by spirits. Spirit work is based on the emergence of an intersubjective space where individual differences are melded into one field of feeling and experience shared by healer and sufferer. In Spiritism for example, intersubjectivity is essential to making a diagnosis that describes the spirits and the reasons they have for causing distress in the sufferer. It might be noted that strangers who seek help at a healing center are recognized by the healer as being made up of the same spiritual components as are persons in the local group, a universalistic orientation and approach to healing that levels out social-class and cultural difference.

Clients in many healing traditions undergo spiritual transformation as a result of their contact with a healing tradition that recognizes this phenomenon, though not all of them become healers. In my studies of spirit healing in Puerto Rico, approximately one-third of the sufferers were diagnosed as being "in development" to be a healer when they showed signs that indicated a spiritual transformation was taking place. The recognition that a person is in development as a healer requires not only reading the signs that a spiritual transformation has occurred or is in process, but also entering into the feelings and spirit experiences of that person.

Empathy in Psychotherapies and Ritual Healing

In this section I explore definitions and roles of empathy in therapeutic relationships—that is, in client-centered therapies (Rogers 1957; 1959), in the self psychology of Kohut (1984), and in some relational therapies (Bohart and Greenberg 1997)—and then compare these with how empathy works in ritual healing. I then describe my concept of radical empathy, as a kind of empathy that appears in spirit healing, which I propose goes beyond empathy as discussed in the literature on psychotherapy. Finally, I briefly explore some conceptual parallels in analytical (Jungian) psychology (Samuels 1985) and other analytic traditions in order to amplify this difference.

Mead (1932) proposed that *adequate empathy* is an ability to take the attitude of another person. There is now a plethora of meanings and explications of *empathy* in psychology and other literatures. In the social-psychological literature, for example, the concept may be referred to as "social insight," "interpersonal sensitivity," or "interpersonal judgment." In psychological research, empathy is the subject's ability to predict how another person will respond to items displaying certain psychological properties. Although empathy has for decades been a focus of client-centered therapy (Rogers 1957; 1959) and of object-relations work by Kohut (1984), interest in its clinical role as a component of clinical process has expanded only recently, going beyond the idea that empathy is useful only as a "kindly and supportive posture" when establishing a therapeutic relationship (Bohart and Greenberg 1997, 5). Bohart and Greenberg note:

> First, empathy includes the making of deep and sustained psychological contact with another [with awareness that] . . . the other is a unique other. . . . Second, empathic exploration includes deep sustained empathic exploration or immersing of oneself in the experience of the other. . . . Third, empathic exploration includes a resonant grasping of the "edges" or implicit aspects of a client's experience to help create new meanings. (5)

Rogers and Kohut, however, placed more emphasis on empathy in their therapies than most other schools in psychology.

Empathy in Psychotherapy: C. R. Rogers and H. Kohut

For Rogers (1959) the "state of being empathic" meant to "perceive the internal frame of reference of another with accuracy . . . as if one were the other person, but without ever losing the 'as if' condition" (210). Losing the "as if" meant a state of complete identification—which was to be avoided. Since the goal of client-centered therapy is to facilitate an authentic sense of self in the client, transiting personal boundaries is considered counter-therapeutic. In contrast, Kohut (1984) regarded empathy both as "vicarious introspection"—advocating that having a similar experience allows us to gauge what another person is feeling—and as a clinical tool. As a clinical tool, empathy is the "capacity to think and feel oneself into the inner life of another person" (82). Some of Kohut's followers have described "empathic attunement," or the "attempt to experience as closely as possible what the patient is experiencing" (Rowe and MacIsaac 1989). Throughout these discussions however, there is discomfort with the therapist's need to move in and out of an empathic state in order to preserve a sense of neutrality. Preston and Shumsky (2002) describe an "empathic dance" in which "empathy is understood as a co-created web of meanings that are negotiated moment-to-moment, weaving the fabric of a new relational experience" (48). The focus of the "dance" shifts from the analyst, to the patient and then to both (the *dyad*) as the therapy proceeds, but the main focus is on the therapist's commitment to create a bridge to the patient.

Since both of these schools, client-centered and self psychology among many others, subscribe to the ideal of the autonomous, integrated individual as normal (and preferable), any displacement or elimination of the boundaries between persons is considered counter-therapeutic (O'Hara 1997). O'Hara refers to Shweder and Bourne's (1982) description of the Western modernist self as based on an egocentric worldview in which the "person" (the inner self) is treated as if it lacks a social and cultural context, in contrast to individuals who possess a sociocentric worldview in nonmodernist societies. She asserts that modernist Western psychology limits and shapes the use and meaning of empathy in therapeutic interactions. This perspective is directly relevant to the discussion of radical empathy to be developed below. Much ritual healing is embedded in a pervasive, sociocentric worldview that focuses on individuals integrated into groups, societies, and the universe.

Empathy in Spirit Healing

Although the spirit healers I studied did not use the term or concept (I cannot find an equivalent or near equivalent Spanish word for *empathy* other than the word for "compassion," *compasión*), we might ask what would be labeled *empathic* behavior in the spirit-healing process. In order to answer this question I would like to briefly outline a generic Spiritist healing session, based on my observations of over 200 sessions in Puerto Rico over eight years.

A typical healing session is conducted in a spirit-healing center by a small group of mediums seated around a table at the head of a room or small hall most often added onto the home of the presiding medium, who has organized the center. The audience may include twenty to sixty persons who are seated facing the table on which sits a bowl of holy water, the fluid that encapsulates the spirits brought to the session. Very briefly, the ritual occurs in five stages. First, the president, or presiding medium, opens the session with a long prayer and readings from one of Allan Kardec's books, such as *The Spirits' Book* (1886; i.e., a Spanish translation of part of the text). This is aimed at focusing the attendees' attention on the spirit world and on God, the Holy Spirit. The president then requests silence, and at this point everyone ideally enters into a meditative state in which the mediums and sometimes the attendees receive communications from the spirits. During this second stage the spirit guide-protectors of the mediums come to the table and may announce themselves through the mediums. The spirits then leave the bodies of the mediums to stand behind them. At the third stage, the mediums concentrate on the spirit world for messages (*videncias*) about the attendees. If a spirit indicates a person in the audience to the medium, that person is called to the table to enter into a dialogue with the medium, who now has "seen" and "felt" the spirit-cause of the attendee's distress. A kind of probing by the medium ensues in which the indicated sufferer is queried as to his feelings—including physical complaints—and the circumstances in his life that may be causing him distress. The medium at this point has "captured" (*captar*) or "formed" (*plasmar*) within herself the inner experience of the sufferer, and she asks for verification from the sufferer (who replies affirmatively, in my experience, approximately 97 percent of the time).

At the fourth stage of the ritual, the spirit causing the attendee's distress comes to the session by possessing another medium, an adept at "bringing," or inviting possession by, these spirit-causes of distress. The sufferer then talks with the spirit-cause of his distress, and the other mediums admonish the spirit to leave the sufferer alone. When the spirit-cause (speaking through the possessed medium) consents, and repents of harming the sufferer, the sufferer is enjoined by the mediums to forgive the molesting spirit, and the spirit is "taken off" (*despohar*) him by one of the mediums. (This fourth stage is repeated until a number of the session's attendees have been called to the table to be treated.) A final, fifth stage closes the session with prayers (often Christian or Catholic in origin, such as the Our Father), and everyone is enjoined to "take off" any distress-causing spirits who may have clung to them.

This process includes a radical empathic exploration, in which the healer-medium first sees and feels the sufferer's distress through the agency of the spirits. The medium who enters into direct contact with the distress-causing spirit becomes deeply, often unconsciously immersed in the inner experience of the sufferer. Spirit-mediums report that they feel a great deal of tension during spirit contacts, typically described as an "electric charge" that starts in the fingertips and goes through the body, as well as an accelerated heart rate that can be very loud or violent. Those mediums who have developed the faculty of taking distress-causing spirits into their own bodies and becoming possessed by them may experience the spirit's feelings of anger and aggression toward the sufferer. Most often the mediums report the experience of possession by a distress-causing spirit as extremely unpleasant, even though they say that they are not conscious of actual events that occur when they are possessed by a spirit. They do report intense sensations of heat, sweaty hands, pain in their extremities, trembling, headaches, buzzing in their ears, hot and cold sensations deep within their bodies, high blood pressure, and a feeling like an electric current. In direct contrast, when their spirit guide-protectors enter them, mediums report mostly pleasant sensations. It might be noted that mediums are enjoined not to work at the table if they are ill or fatigued because they will be more vulnerable to the influence of illness- or distress-causing spirits. Moreover, they are instructed to prepare for the session by eating little or no food, meditating, and relaxing to prepare their bodies for difficult takeovers by spirits.

The spirit-healing process completely sidesteps the concerns of many psychotherapists and analysts about the negative effect of mutuality in the therapeutic dyad, when empathy in treatment means attunement to, sharing, or even resonating with the inner experiences of the client. The medium is only an intermediary for spirits; the drama of the sufferer's inner life does not touch her personally except as a call to use his faculties (with all the difficulties associated with that use). However, distress and suffering are calls to which the medium must respond even outside of the ritual session, if asked to do so by his guide-protectors, on whom her own well-being depends. Moreover, healer-mediums often express and act upon a collective sentiment central to their version of Spiritism (and a traditional sentiment in Puerto Rican culture, though it may be changing) that a person is continually affected by what other persons are feeling, particularly within families (Koss 1990). It must be further noted that the mediums at all ritual sessions refer to individuals as small units of the universe ("grains of sand"). Their spirit guide-protectors preach about the need for all persons to contribute to universal progress of the spirit (i.e., peace, harmony, and balance) in exercising *agape*.

Radical Empathy: A Step beyond Empathy

Radical empathy takes empathic behavior to a further degree, in that the wounded healer actually enters into the feelings of suffering and distress of those persons who attend the sessions and who a spirit indicates need help. (At rare times these persons may be those the wounded healer meets in the course of her life.) The wounded healer experiences the feelings as felt by the sufferer (*plasmaciones*) as communicated through spirit visions (*videncias*) or through possession by a spirit. Importantly, the wounded healer has the guidance and authority of her spirit guide-protectors who prevent her from being overwhelmed or seriously affected by a client's suffering. When a healer's own well-being and continued healing avocation depend upon a spiritual connection, the interpersonal space in which healing takes place becomes sacred space, and radical empathy acts as a path to transcendence.

We can explore the concept of empathy in other contexts that parallel radical empathy. Spezio (see chap. 13) notes a widespread variation in the definition of *empathy* and suggests that for some, such as Scheler (1954), *sympathy* is the more accurate term. Spezio's use of *sympathic* is similar to the concept of radical empathy that I develop here because it includes the idea not only of experiencing what another person feels but also of participating in that experience. Further, in some psychoanalytic schools the concept of therapeutic relationship closely parallels that of the radical empathy I describe. Winnicott (1971) suggests that patient and analyst coincide psychologically in an "area of illusion," which is the area in which the analyst meets the psychic reality of the patient via his own psychic reality. Samuels (1985) describes a process found in Jungian analysis as an "embodied transference," which he defines as a "physical, actual, material, sensual expression in the analyst of something in the patient's inner world, a drawing together and solidification of this, an incarnation by the analyst of a part of the patient's psyche" (52). To compare these articulations to Spiritist healing, in Spiritist healing the sufferer's inner state is mirrored by the medium-healer, who reports that he feels the same pains, distress, or confusion as the sufferer with whom he is working. These feelings often come on unbidden, especially in novitiate mediums. A vivid example is that of a research assistant working in one of my projects, who had been told by several Spiritist healers that she was in development as a medium.

> Sarah accompanied Doña Maria on a visit to a bed-ridden client who had been paralyzed for four years. Sarah reported that at first she felt "deeply sorry for this woman." Shortly afterwards she "felt a creeping heaviness in her arm which traveled down her spine to the middle." Then she got the same feeling in her legs—especially one leg. Suddenly she was unable to move her legs. The client reported that the paralysis came upon her in exactly the same way over four days. She had never told anyone exactly how it happened. Doña Maria told Sarah that the feelings would leave if she described them verbally to the client, and they did. Sarah then felt "a calmness inside."

To amplify the parallels, I note that Samuels (1985, 58–59) talks about embodied transference in analytic work as the sharing of a mythic world, a *mundus imaginalis*, which "refers to a precise order or level of reality," "an intermediate dimension . . . in-between patient and analyst," in-between body and mind, and in-between the analyst's conscious and unconscious. It is a world constellated by the analyst-patient relationship, "imaginally but not subjectively real." While these concepts and terms are mainly meaningful to analytical psychologists, who work with the model of a therapeutic dyad in which the separateness of the individual actors may be transcended by an "embodied transference," as described by Samuels, the parallels to Spiritist concepts and the spirit-healing process are striking. For those who subscribe to the idea that spirits exist in a parallel world, there is the shared imagery of spirit phenomena (Koss 1979). In contrast to the dyadic-analytic situation described by Samuels, however, the imaginal world in spirit healing is constellated by a three-party relationship between the sufferer, the medium-healer (or mediums, all of whom are the sufferer's conduit to the spirit world), and the particular spirit or spirits brought to the healing table. This imaginal world is also shared, but to a lesser extent, by all who attend the sessions. Moreover, spirits are not perceived as imaginal in the sense of existing only in the minds of persons. As noted in the epigraph, for those who are involved and experience them, spirits exist.

I must point out that the operation of radical empathy is facilitated by the very different structural relationship of the principal figures in the spirit-healing process, which offers some advantage to the spirit healer. The spirit healer does not have responsibility for the effect of spirits on a sufferer, either positive or negative, or for a cure; healer-mediums do not themselves "heal." Despite a strict code of ethics in Spiritism, there is no need for healer-mediums to fear that they have transgressed personal boundaries (as therapists may fear) since it is the spirits who invade the sufferer's personal space and the healers who endeavor to "take off" (despohar) these invaders using the faculties given them by their spirit guide-protectors.

Speculation about how radical empathy is learned is perhaps worthwhile. Its origin in novitiate healers may begin with a first, impressive experience of spirits during an index illness. When the novitiate healer is introduced into the ritual session and enjoined to have visions—to open her body to her spirit guide-protector or to "take a spirit into her body"—some new healers report that earlier memories of alterations of consciousness are immediately replayed. (I had this experience on two occasions when at healing sessions I reexperienced the feelings of dizziness, sinking, and loss of control associated with entry into a state of trance. At the time, I was pulled back by friends who shook me as we sat together at the session. Later I was able to recognize these feelings and to pull myself back to reality before they could engulf me.)

Conclusion

Radical empathy, as I have defined it, takes the healer across a wide and deep emotional spectrum that relatively few psychotherapists or medical doctors—apart perhaps from some psychoanalysts—are willing to enter (Groesbeck 1975). It appears that certain persons, especially those who have the emotional flexibility and courage needed to deal with alterations in consciousness and with experiences in the fascinating but often fearsome sacred realms of spirits and gods, are able to become healers (see chap. 8). However, the belief systems of spirit healers also provide ways for the healer to deal with the impact of the emotional intensity and intense feelings of distress coming from his or her client, through both depersonalization (i.e., it is the spirits, the gods, or God that heals, not healers themselves) and through the healer's belief in the mythic structures that explain these experiences. Rules governing how to deal with vulnerability and to avoid contagion from sufferers are transmitted during the informal tutelage that follows the healer's initiatory spiritual transformation, so that a sense of security is provided. In addition, spirit healers most often work in teams, using their spirit guide-protectors to support each other when distress-causing spirits descend upon the healer-medium or the session.

My perspective on spiritual transformation parallels Hufford's (2005) idea of "core spiritual experiences" that "show complex and consistent subjective patterns independent of cultural context" (33). Hufford proposes that core spiritual experiences form a "distinct class of experience with a stable perceptual pattern." I propose that spiritual transformation might be considered a type of core spiritual experience. Spiritual transformation appears to be especially, but not exclusively, associated with rituals that heal with spirits (or in other cultural contexts, gods or God), which have very similar forms across diverse cultures and regions of the world. The model presented in this chapter is an attempt to explain some extremely widespread parallels in ritual healing by describing these core elements as foundational to the ritual-healing process. These occur within diverse cultural contexts that thereby supply the content (symbols, liturgy, narratives, etc.) and structure of the ritual forms.

Notes

1. Four studies were funded by the National Institute of Mental Health (NIMH) and sponsored by the Department of Health of Puerto Rico, to whom I am indebted: (1) *1968–1969 Social and Psychological Aspects of Spiritism in Puerto Rico*, NIMH (MH-14246-01), Health Department of Puerto Rico, Rio Piedras, Puerto Rico; (2) *1969–1970 Social and Psychological Aspects of Spiritism in Puerto Rico*, NIMH (MH-17997-01), Health Department of Puerto Rico, Rio Piedras, Puerto Rico; (3) *1976–1979 Therapist-Spiritist Training Project in Puerto Rico*, NIMH (MH-14310-03), Health Department of Puerto Rico, Rio Piedras, Puerto Rico; and (4) *1979–1980 Therapist-Spiritist Training Project in Puerto Rico*, NIMH (MH-15992-01), Health Department of Puerto Rico, Rio Piedras, Puerto Rico. See Koss-Chioino (1992; 1996) for details on the projects and the subject. I acknowledge my appreciation to the Department of Health of Puerto Rico, who sponsored the projects, and to the National Institute of Mental Health who funded them. They are in no way responsible for what I report, however.

2. *Espiritismo* (Spiritism) in Puerto Rico parallels very widespread healing cults throughout Latin America, Mediterranean countries, and the Philippines. Based on folk Catholicism and innovative nineteenth-century ideas about spirits of the dead who exist in a parallel world, the cult was initiated by Leon Hippolyte Denizarth Rivail (1803–1869), a scholar in Paris, France, in the latter part of the nineteenth century. Under the pen name of *Allan Kardec*, he published seven books that reported his exploration of the spirit world through young, female mediums. The first of these books, *The Spirits' Book* (1886), may have been published as early as 1853. Rivail's books and ideas spread to Spain and thence to the Western hemisphere through Latin-American intellectuals. Wherever found, Spiritism has been syncretized with local cultural content, Afro-Caribbean, Native American, or popular folk belief. It is variously called Spiritualism, Umbanda, Kardecismo, Trincadismo, and in some cases, merely Curanderismo (Koss-Chioino 1992).

References

Bohart, A. C., and L. S. Greenberg. 1997. *Empathy Reconsidered: New Directions in Psychotherapy*. Washington, D.C.: American Psychological Association.

Csordas, T. 1994. *The Sacred Self: A Cultural Phenomenology of Charismatic Healing*. Berkeley: University of California Press.

Csordas, T., and E. Lewton. 1998. Practice, performance and experience in ritual healing. *Transcultural Psychiatry* 35 (December): 435–512.

Frankl, V. E. 1959. *Man's Search for Meaning*. Boston, Mass.: Beacon.

Groesbeck, C. J. 1975. The archetypal image of the wounded healer. *Journal of Analytical Psychology* 20 (2): 122–45.

Guggenbuhl-Craig, A. 1978. *Power in the Helping Professions*. Dallas, Tex.: Spring.

Hufford, D. J. 2005. Sleep paralysis as spiritual experience. *Transcultural Psychiatry* 42 (March): 11–45.

Kardec, A., received by. 1886. *The Spirits' Book*. 14th ed. Boston: Colby and Rich. Originally published as *Le livre des esprits*. Paris: Didier et Cie.

Katz, R. 1993. *The Straight Path: A Story of Healing and Transformation in Fiji*. Reading, Mass.: Addison-Wesley.

Katz, S. H. 2004. *The Spiritual Transformation Scientific Research Program*. Philadelphia: Metanexus Institute on Religion and Science.

Kirmayer, L. J. 2003. Asklepian dreams: The ethos of the wounded-healer in the clinical encounter. *Transcultural Psychiatry* 40 (June): 248–77.

Kleinman, A., and L. Sung. 1979. Why do indigenous practitioners successfully heal? *Social Science and Medicine* 13B, pp. 7–26.

Kohut, H. 1984. *How Does Analysis Cure?* Chicago: University of Chicago Press.

Koss, J. 1979. Artistic expression and creative process in Caribbean possession cult rituals. In *The Visual Arts: Graphic and Plastic*, ed. J. M. Cordwell, 373–410. The Hague: Mouton.

———. 1990. Somatization and somatic complaint syndromes among Hispanics: Overview and ethnopsychological perspectives. *Transcultural Psychiatric Research Review* 27 (1): 5–29.

Koss-Chioino, J. D. 1992. *Women as Healers, Women as Patients: Mental Health Care and Traditional Healing in Puerto Rico*. Boulder, Colo.: Westview.

———. 1996. The experience of spirits: Ritual healing as transactions of emotion (Puerto Rico). In *Yearbook of Cross-Cultural Medicine and Psychotherapy*, ed. W. Andritzky. Vol. 1993, *Ethnopsychotherapy*, 251–71. Berlin: Verlag für Wissenschaft und Bildung.

McLean, J. A. 1994. *Dimensions in Spirituality*. Oxford: George Ronald.

Mead, G. H. 1932. *The Philosophy of the Present*. Chicago: University of Chicago Press.

Miller, G. D., and D. C. Baldwin Jr. 2000. Implications of the wounded healer paradigm for the use of self in therapy. In *The Use of Self in Therapy*, ed. M. Baldwin. 2nd ed, 243–62. New York: Haworth.

O'Hara, M. 1997. Relational empathy: Beyond modernist egocentrism to postmodern holistic contextualism. In *Empathy Reconsidered*, ed. A. C. Bohart and L. S. Greenberg, 295–319. Washington, D.C.: American Psychological Association.

Peters, L. 1981. An experiential study of Nepalese shamanism. *Journal of Transpersonal Psychology* 13:1–26.

Preston, L., and E. Shumsky. 2002. From an empathic stance to an empathic dance: Negotiation. In *Progress in Self Psychology*, ed. A. Goldberg, 47–61. Hillsdale, N.J.: Analytic.

Rogers, C. R. 1957. The necessary and sufficient conditions of therapeutic personality change. *Journal of Consulting and Clinical Psychology* 21:95–103.

———. 1959. A theory of therapy, personality and interpersonal relationships, as developed in the client-centered framework. In *Psychology: A Study of a Science,* ed. S. Koch, 184–256. New York: McGraw Hill.

Rowe, C., and D. S. MacIsaac. 1989. *Empathic Attunement: The Technique of Psychoanalytic Self Psychology.* Northvale, N.J.: Jason Aronson.

Samuels, A. 1985. Countertransference: The mundus imaginalis and a research project. *Journal of Analytical Psychology* 30:47–71.

Scheler, M. 1954. *The Nature of Sympathy,* trans. P. Heath. London: Routledge and Kegan Paul.

Shweder, R., and E. J. Bourne. 1982. Does the concept of person vary cross-culturally? In *Cultural Conceptions of Mental Health and Therapy,* ed. A. J. Marsella and G. M. White, 997–1037. Boston: Kluver.

Van Franz, M. 1975. *C. G. Jung: His Myth in Our Time.* Toronto: Little, Brown.

Winnicott, D. W. 1971. *Playing and Reality.* London: Tavistock.

5

Radical Empathy, Gender, and Shamanic Healing: Examples from Peru

Bonnie Glass-Coffin

Between 1987 and 1989 I worked with eight female shamanic healers in northern Peru, studying the ways in which they conceptualized illness and structured therapeutic strategies for their patients—most of whom were believed to be victims of "sorcery." My research focused on the ways in which male and female shamans in that region of the world diverge in both their understanding of the causes of illness and the strategies they employ for restoring health (Glass-Coffin 1996; 1998; 1999). In this chapter, I present these findings in terms of the concept of *radical empathy* (see chap. 4). In the interest of space this chapter focuses the discussion on the therapeutic strategies of two of the eight women with whom I worked. As I have noted elsewhere (Glass-Coffin 1998), gender differences in healing strategies were most apparent for the women in my study who had not been apprenticed to male teachers. The two women discussed here both met that criterion. The gendered dimensions of healing discussed below suggest yet another reason why Koss-Chioino's concept of radical empathy is integral to spiritual transformation and healing. In addition to the emotional engagement and catharsis made possible by the awareness that the patient's suffering is shared with the healer, radical empathy can also be understood in terms of a patient's transpersonal engagement with his or her environment, social networks, and spiritual beliefs.

In this sense, radical empathy describes the shift in consciousness that accompanies a patient's awareness of profound connection with these elements, even in the face of imperfection. It encompasses the acceptance of, reconnection with, and surrender to outcomes beyond an individual's control that are integral to both spiritual transformation and to healing (Canda and Furman 1999, 161–66, 251–60; Hirshberg and Barasch 1995, 333; Siegel 1986, 112, 190–200). It is another term for the attitude that Christian scholars and devotees refer to as *grace*. As I argue here, patient awareness of radical empathy, or this realization of grace, is a therapeutic goal for healing shared by female healers in Peru. As I will also show below, this attitude of acceptance, connection, and emphasis on spirituality as "right-relation-with" rather than "transcendence-of" human experience is also fundamental to feminist theology and feminist philosophies of religion (Parsons 2002; Shepherd 2002).

Background

The literature of anthropology, psychotherapy, nursing, and—more recently—complementary and alternative medicine (CAM) have defined healing much more broadly than the process by which disease or injury is ameliorated or cured. More fundamental to the healing process has been the restoration of wholeness to the sufferer, which requires a kind of transformation in the sufferer's understanding and experience of suffering (Barasch 1993, 56–59; 1994, 54–63; Benor 2001, 29–38; Borysenko and Borysenko 1994, 71–88; Canda and Furman 1999, 161–66). This transformation involves cognitive or behavioral change as well as psychological or spiritual adjustment, or adaptation, on the part of the sufferer. It requires an adjustment that allows for the discovery of meaning in the experience of suffering, a restoration of a sense of balance between the sufferer and the various worlds with which the sufferer interacts (telluric, social, cosmic), and a deep acceptance of the material realities that inform suffering. Paradoxically, it is this resignation that transforms the experience of suffering into one of transcendence and empowerment as the sufferer experiences profound changes in his or her relationship with the sacred. As this transformation occurs, life-satisfaction increases

(Canda and Furman 1999, 162), and health and healing become associated more with this measure than with an absence of symptoms or pathologies. Additionally, there is growing support for the argument that an increase in life-satisfaction also contributes to a more responsive immune system and decreased pathogenic loads (Daruna 2004; Pert 1997; Sternberg 2000).

In her development of the concept of radical empathy, Koss-Chioino suggests that the experience of healing and spiritual transformation is facilitated in the ritual-context of shamanic healing when boundaries between healer and patient consciousness and experience are transcended or blurred. Empathy becomes radical when healers "capture" (vicariously experience) and then effectively communicate back to the patient the experience or consciousness of the patient's own suffering. Additionally—and critical to the shaman's ability to convince the patient that healing is certain—radical empathy implies the transcendence of these normally autonomous boundaries of consciousness and experience. According to Koss-Chioino, this blurring of self/other boundaries allows for the patient to be enfolded in the healer's own communion with the spirit world. As Koss-Chioino suggests, when individual boundaries between shamanic healer, patient, and what might be glossed as the divine are transcended through this mutuality of shared suffering and shared caring, intersubjective spaces are created that facilitate spiritual transformation and healing.

My studies with female *curanderas* in Peru suggest interesting correspondences and add an additional ethnographic example supporting Koss-Chioino's insights. In the paragraphs that follow, I discuss how shared suffering between these women and their patients illustrate this mutuality of suffering and care in a Peruvian context.

Ysabel and Yolanda

Ysabel was forty at the time I first met her in 1988, and Yolanda was forty-one when I met her in 1987. Ysabel lived in the northern city of Chiclayo, Peru, at the time of my study, and Yolanda lived on the outskirts of Cajamarca in Peru's northern highlands. Both had migrated there as young women from rural hamlets in the northern departments of Piura and Cajamarca, respectively. Yolanda was married, and Ysabel was divorced, but both were mothers. They were not destitute, but neither were they well-off financially. Yolanda and her husband lived in a brick house and ran a small dry-goods store to supplement their income. Ysabel lived in an adobe structure that had neither light nor running water, but she seemed always able to put food on the table for her two children.

At the time of my visits, both their healing ceremonies employed the *mesa* to heal their patients of sorcery-caused illness. The *mesa* (sometimes translated as "table" and sometimes as "Mass") is used to describe both the object-laden altar that is the focus of the curing ritual and the ritual performance itself. Both women also employed the hallucinogenic, mescaline-containing cactus San Pedro (*Trichocereus pachanoi*) to facilitate contact and intercession with the spirit world in order to heal their patients. They both claimed not to have learned their trade from other humans at all but to have had their abilities to heal revealed through personal experiences with God.

Both Ysabel and Yolanda claimed to personally experience the suffering of their patients as a preliminary part of the healing process. For Ysabel this shared suffering involved physical incorporation of the patient's pain as part of the healing ceremony. After ingestion of the San Pedro cactus, Ysabel would "see" the causes of the patient's affliction by traveling in time and space to the very moment when a sorcerer had stolen away the patient's shadow-soul, and by reliving the suffering experienced by the patient as the sorcerer's hex took hold. On numerous occasions while deep in trance and divining the cause of a patient's suffering, Ysabel would double up in pain or complain of extreme fever or cold as she relived the moment of the patient's bewitching. She would sometimes ask which of those present at the *mesa* was feeling nauseous, or cold, or stabbing pain, and one of those present would invariably recognize the described suffering as their own. On other occasions, she would relive emotional suffering with the patient, as occurred the first time I visited her *mesa* (Glass-Coffin 1998, 83–84). As she debriefed her patients or shouted out a command to "speak up" and claim the physical discomfort that was washing over her, the mutuality of suffering between healer and patient was painfully apparent.

For Yolanda, the patient's pain was experienced in more spiritual than physical terms. As she described it to me, those who had succumbed to hexes were like "trees grown crooked" and were in need of spiritual rehabilitation, whereas those who were close to God (and therefore morally pure) were immune to a sorcerer's attempts to capture their shadow-souls. And when describing how she suffered for her victims, she told me that the pain she felt was like that of Jesus being crucified on the cross. In one postsession interview, she told me that some of her patients had even been able to see the holes in her hands oozing blood like those of the Savior who suffered for all mankind at Calvary.

The "mutuality of care" or assurance of spirit-intervention on behalf of the patient that Koss-Chioino describes in chapter 4 was made clear in various ways to Ysabel's patients during her ritual ceremonies. Sometimes these assurances were verbal, as when her assistant would clarify to those present that they should enthusiastically heed Ysabel's actions and instructions during the ceremony because "it is the Spirit of God who is talking through her to you now." At other times, Ysabel would demonstrate her ability to command spirit-familiars in other ways, such as by convincing her patients that she had stopped the rain by making offerings of holy water to the spirits or by demonstrating her ability to illuminate the night sky as patients fervently prayed the Lord's Prayer on their knees before her altar. These demonstrations were awe-inspiring and must certainly have convinced patients of Ysabel's special relationship with beings whose powers could be invoked on behalf of those suffering. In postsession interviews about their experiences, patients often expressed their complete devotion and faith in Ysabel's power as a healer and their complete conviction that they had been healed because of her ministrations.

Yolanda's ability to be accepted as a channel of divine intervention was based at least in part on her uncanny ability to divine her patients' life histories. The one patient (a high-level political functionary) whose illness I followed most closely (Glass-Coffin 1998, 93–101) came to believe in Yolanda's power to heal him as a result of their first meeting. As he later described the experience, Yolanda came to see him while he was bedridden one afternoon after having been hospitalized with extreme abdominal pain. During the preliminary diagnosis, she simply looked at him. Her gaze was so steady that he felt very uncomfortable. After a while she began uttering Catholic prayers while turning always to the right and raising her arms to the ceiling. Then she stopped suddenly and began asking questions. She admonished him to answer only with a simple yes or no. Their conversation was as follows:

> *Y:* You manage many documents?
>
> *R:* Yes.
>
> *Y:* There is a tall, balding man in a jacket who wants to do daño [sorcery] to you. There is a tall, good-looking, female lawyer who wants to harm you. There is a mustached man from a ministry that also wants to harm you. There are two men that you helped to raise up, and now they want to do you in. . . . There is also a woman, who to your face is very sweet, but who stabs you in the back. . . . These people want to bind you, they want to tie you up, they want to rob your soul, and they have your life in the palm of their hands. The only thing left is to close their hands over it to kill you. (Glass-Coffin 1998, 94–95)

During that interview, Yolanda told the patient things about his personal life that surprised and impressed him. As he summarized it, "I was very surprised by so much coincidence and so much detail with which she precisely divined these things [about my life]. . . . She told me she could cure me. . . . After she left, I felt different . . . more at peace" (95).

Yolanda's abilities to instill her patients with both hope and faith in her authority to heal also stemmed from their experience of and participation in the *mesa* ceremony itself. These ceremonies closely replicated the Catholic Mass (even incorporating pre- and post-Communion hymns as part of the ritual process) and repeatedly invoked the same kind of reflective and reverent attitudes in patients (especially those who described themselves as "devout Catholics"), as did their participation in the Mass.

Radical Empathy and Acceptance beyond the Patient/Healer Dyad

In chapter 4, Koss-Chioino discusses the relationship between one's having been a "wounded healer" and being successful then at engaging in radical empathy with one's patients. This was certainly the case for Ysabel and Yolanda. For both these women, their ability to empathize with others was rooted in the fact that as wounded healers they had also traversed the depths of despair and suffering felt by their patients.

As I have described it elsewhere (Glass-Coffin 1998, 176–82), the particular suffering that Ysabel and Yolanda endured and overcame is the suffering that comes when one takes on the role of the victim. Specifically, their own entry into healing was preceded by periods in which they had been the victims of *love-magic*—a kind of sorcery that robbed them of the autonomy to choose mates willfully. Instead, they became like puppets acting at the behest of others, and as a result lived with men to whom they had been joined through sorcery. In this sense, although love-magic can be said to provide a socially appropriate outlet for both men and women who don't meet the appropriate role demands of macho virility (for men) or chastity and submissiveness (for women), "love-magic also creates victims rather than emphasizing agency and the bolstering of self" (178). By renouncing love-magic and truly accepting (rather than conquering) the misfortunes that cast them as victims, Ysabel and Yolanda provided a model for their patients and demonstrated how empowerment can come through acceptance—even the acceptance of socially structured inequalities like those that require different moral standards for men and women.

But in addition to providing this model of acceptance for their patients, these *curanderas*, as I have repeatedly suggested, employed therapeutic strategies that emphasized the spiritual transformation of patients' lives as an underlying principle that guides healing (Glass-Coffin 1996; 1998; 1999). Like the healing outcomes summarized above, the shamans with whom I studied also emphasized the relationship between healing and patient adaptation to the material circumstances of their suffering. Additionally, they emphasized the relationship between healing and patient responsibility for undergoing spiritual adjustment.

> [The female shamans'] cures are not transformative in the sense that patients can benefit vicariously from the mediatory action of the healer. . . . Instead of treating their clients as passive victims, dependent on the shaman's power to transform their suffering . . . these [shamanic healers] emphasized the need for the patient to

awaken to the [healing] power within himself . . . [not] through "overcoming" an unseen enemy but through acceptance, surrender, self-awareness, penance and purification. (Glass-Coffin 1996, 74)

This acceptance of responsibility requires patients to adapt to the circumstances of their suffering by embracing a basic connectedness with their lived realities whether cosmic, social, political, economic, or material. Viewed in this light, radical empathy is extended beyond the healer-patient dyad to describe how spiritual transformation works to create new intersubjective spaces between the suffering patient and the physical, social, and spiritual worlds in which they live.

This emphasis on adaptation to the circumstances of suffering, as well as the emphasis on connection between healer, patient, and the patient's own lived realities, finds resonance in accounts of terminal-cancer survivors (cf. Barasch 1993, 56–59; Borysenko and Borysenko 1994; Hirshberg and Barasch 1995, 333; Siegel 1986). A common theme emerging from these reports is the assertion that a patient's accepting attitude towards his or her illness may enhance the chance of remarkable recovery from neoplastic disease. The characteristics of the cancer survivors reported by these authors might be summarized as follows. First is the ability to accept or even surrender to their suffering by reinterpreting their pain as somehow meaningful or useful for personal growth rather than as the random consequence of an unjust universe. With this adjustment, patients find an ability to reconnect with others, as opposed to retreating into despair, by loving compassionately, forgiving completely, accepting imperfection (in themselves and in others) and choosing to be happy. They tend also to fully engage in life's joys with childlike playfulness even while dying of a terminal disease, and to act in accordance with their innermost feelings and desires rather than in accordance with the expectations of others—expressing rather than suppressing even negative emotion. Finally, these patients tend also to embrace lifestyle changes that prioritize health and healing, including activities that promote good nutrition and stress reduction and that encourage optimal immune responses. Thus, there may be physically measurable reasons, as well as psychodynamic reasons, to embrace these attitudes of acceptance, connection, and empathy.

According to Siegel, these characteristics are not only attributes of the survivor personality, but are the fundamental components of spirituality, whether or not a person believes in God or a higher power. As he puts it,

> If we become survivors, we realize that our deepest need is to love and be at peace, and our motivation becomes spiritual or selfless, not selfish. Living with the knowledge that we're going to die someday means that we may choose to give something to the world. In the process, we develop an inner sense of worth that helps us achieve goals that improve the quality of life. We find ourselves striving for the survivor's paradoxical goal—to have things work out well for ourselves *and* others. (1986, 169)

As Siegel continues, "Acceptance, forgiveness, peace, and love are the traits that define spirituality for me. These characteristics always appear in those who achieve unexpected healing of serious illness" (177–78).

The ability to transcend ego, to love compassionately (which includes sharing in the suffering of another), and to thus engage in a deep connection with the transpersonal seems at the heart of spiritual transformation. For Ysabel and Yolanda, the purpose of therapy is to produce this kind of spiritual change. The transformation that occurs involves awakening the patient's awareness while moving the patient toward wholeness. In this respect, their view of their work is strikingly similar to that expressed by social workers, nurses, and psychotherapists who define healing in terms of coming into a wholesome relationship "with self, other people, the universe, and the ground of being itself" (Canda and Furman 1999, 253).

Transcendence, Immanence, and Co-essence: Engendering the Discussion

In classic descriptions of biomedicine (where suffering is overcome and a cure is equated with the eradication of disease), of shamanism (where the healer undergoes a symbolic as well as physical "near-death" in order to gain the power to cure), and of some religious traditions (where life's temptations are rejected and the very limitations of being are transcended to achieve enlightenment or connection with the divine), this *relational* approach to spiritual connection is underdeveloped. Instead of this compassionate, deeply empathetic, or *coessent* approach (Glass-Coffin 1998, 184–94) to spirituality and healing, the transcendence of the day-to-day, and the mundane limitations of lived reality and of suffering are privileged as the path towards connection with the divine (cf. Glass-Coffin 1998, 139–63; Tedlock 2005, 72–75). But as Bynum noted twenty years ago (1986), as I noted in my comparisons of male and female shamans in Peru (1998), and as Tedlock recently demonstrated on a much wider scale (2005), religious and shamanic interpretations of spiritual connection are heavily influenced by our perception of those connections. And, as our experience of the world is gendered, so also is the interpretation that we bring to our understanding of spirituality. As Bynum put it,

> Men and women of a single tradition—when working with the same symbols and myths, writing in the same genre, and living in the same religious or professional circumstances—display certain consistent male/female differences in using symbols. Women's symbols and myths tend to build from social and biological experiences; men's symbols and myths tend to invert them. Women's mode of using symbols seems given to the muting of opposition, whether through paradox or through synthesis; men's mode seems characterized by emphasis on opposition, contradiction, inversion, and conversion. Women's myths and rituals tend to explore a state of being; men's tend to build elaborate and discrete stages between self and other. (1986, 13)

Whereas traditional Judeo-Christian definitions of the divine emphasize "God's own non-physicality" and divine connection as "otherworldly" (Ochs 1983, 21), an orientation towards connection, toward empathy, toward acceptance, and toward engagement with the "what is" of lived reality has informed much of the scholarship on feminist spirituality. As Carol Ochs has summarized it, feminist visions of spirituality are those that celebrate the process of "coming into a relationship with [lived] reality and must be tested continually against [the] actual experience of living in this world" (1983, 10–11). Or as Rosemary Radford Reuther has put it, "feminist theology affirms a vision of exodus, of liberation and new being, but emphasizes that these must be rooted in the foundations of being and body, rather than as an antithesis of nature and spirit" (1993, 67). And finally, as Joan Borysenko has noted, a woman's path towards psychospiritual development is more relational than transcendent, found "not somewhere above us . . . to which we ultimately ascend [but] . . . It is found within us, here and now" (1999, 69). In this light, radical empathy becomes another way of understanding feminist approaches to spiritual transformation, healing, and wholeness because of its engagement with, rather than renunciation of, "this world" in favor of an "otherworldly" awakening.

Key voices in feminist theology (e.g., Gross 1996; King 1995; Plaskow 1980; Reuther 1983; 1993; 1998; 2002; Saiving 1960; Schussler-Fiorenza 1983; Tamez 1989), feminist spirituality or feminist "thealogy" (e.g., Christ 1997; 2002; Christ and Plaskow 1979; Daly 1973; 1984; Spretnak 1982; Starhawk 1997; 1999), and feminist philosophy of religion (e.g., Anderson 1998; 2002; Bynum 1986; Fulkerson 1994; Jantzen 1998; Ulanov 1981) echo these assertions. In these related fields, most feminist scholars suggest a "this-life" orientation to spiritual connection. Furthermore, rather than seeing God as transcendent, as "somewhere 'out-there' separate and apart from the world" (Christ 2002, 87), and enlightenment as requiring a renunciation of the physical world (Ochs 1983, 21), "feminist theologians of all stripes argue that [this kind of] dualistic thinking must be replaced with more holistic models" (Christ 2002, 87). As Anderson has argued, "the monotheistic concept implicit [in a transcendent God] . . . seems an outmoded ideal to which Western men aspired . . . but . . . The *aspiration to be infinite* is distinct from *the craving for infinitude*" (2002, 53; italics in original). In other words, as Anderson explains, one does not need to transcend the limitations of this life in order to seek goodness, justice, or truth. One can seek perfection without requiring perfection in oneself. One can accept the imperfections of this world, even as evidence of the sacred.

In Judeo-Christian terms, the kingdom of heaven has been reformulated by feminist scholars as the here and now, and as evident in our lived experience of this world, rather than as that which must be expected at some distant moment marked by the ultimate end of humanity and creation. As Karras (2002) puts it, "Simultaneously, these feminist thinkers have shifted the thematic center from humanity, as the apex of creation, to creation itself, with humanity removed from centre stage to a supporting position as an interwoven, interdependent component of that creation" (243). And, as an interdependent component of that creation, it is these connections, with one another, with the natural world, and with the cosmos that make sacred every conscious moment of our lives.

These are the central features of what Ysabel describes as *gracia* and what Yolanda refers to as *conciencia*. Like the cancer survivors discussed above, both these women suggest that healing can only occur as a result of a profound reorientation to suffering that involves acceptance of all that life offers as sacred. According to Ysabel, illness has only occurred because the patient has been an empty vessel. When patients are able to connect with their life experience instead of feeling victimized by it, they become filled with the spirit of the divine. "[Ysabel] describes sorcery as the condition of being 'empty' [*vacío*], 'self-less' [*sin decisión propia* or *sin yo personal*] . . . or . . . of being in a state of 'non-being'" (Glass-Coffin 1996, 73). She calls this state *desgracia*, by which she means "a rejection of life, of Being, and of the experience . . . of living (which includes joy as well as suffering)" (78). Healing, for Ysabel, requires coming back into God's grace, accepting Being, accepting suffering, and accommodating imperfection rather than lamenting or disdaining it.

For Yolanda, the same idea is echoed in her discussion of sorcery as "the condition of being far from God, morally 'crooked' [*torcida*] and in need of 'spiritual rehabilitation. . . . The cure requires internal transformation and . . . a decision to come closer to God" (Glass-Coffin 1996, 73). Healing is not external to the patient, but "an immanent force, which is awakened in the patient through . . . a kind of 'getting right' with the forces of the Universe. The healer's role is only to guide the patient to a conscious understanding of this task" (74).

As do the scholars of feminist theology and spirituality referenced above, Ysabel and Yolanda describe wholeness and spiritual connection as a result of acceptance, rather than as a rejection of "what is." Spiritual development is embodied in this world, connecting self to other and individual desires to the requirements of social and cosmic order. Ysabel refers to the connection between her patients and the world of spirit using the metaphor of the umbilical cord (Glass-Coffin 1998, 189–203). Rather than being transcendent or immanent—which feminist scholars such Parsons (2002) and Shepherd (2002) complain are simply two halves of the false dichotomy of spiritual connection—the umbilical cord is inherently coessent. The umbilical cord is an apt metaphor for the relational, empathetic, nurturing approach to spirituality and healing described above. Like the more general metaphor of motherhood (which has also been associated with feminist approaches to spirituality [cf. Glass-Coffin 1996, 69–80; 1998, 186–203; Ochs 1983, 32; Tedlock 2005]), "it allows for a transfer of energy, blood, and life between two beings. But, although the animating essence is shared, mother and child are two separate beings, with different pasts, futures, and life-trajectories" (Glass-Coffin 1996, 80). As a uniquely shared space that nurtures, that embodies, and that connects, the umbilical cord as a metaphor for spiritual connection surely embodies the kind of radical empathy that Koss-Chioino suggests as an outcome of spiritual transformation and healing.

Conclusion

Obviously, there is much comparative work still to do before we can conclude that the concept of radical empathy is universal or near universal in ritual-healing processes. My work comparing and contrasting illness concepts and therapeutic strategies of male and female shamans in Peru makes me wonder, for example, about the degree to which gendered experience and consciousness facilitate the formation of this relationship between healer and patient. That database topic searches on the role of caring and empathy in healing find substantial discussion of both in the literature on nursing, social work, and complementary and alternative medicine (which all attract a majority of female practitioners) also makes me wonder about the influence of a gendered experience and consciousness on the establishment of this relationship. Ysabel and Yolanda emphasize healing in terms of this kind of coessent, emergent, embodied connection. The resemblance of their models of spirituality and healing to those of the feminist scholars described in brief above, suggests the importance of continued exploration into gender as a critical endeavor in the analysis of religious traditions, radical empathy, and healing (cf. King 1995; Glass-Coffin 1999).

I offer this contribution as one that is very preliminary and open to debate. But there are so many intriguing parallels between the literature on spiritual transformation and healing, feminist approaches to theology and spirituality, and my own comparative work with female and male shamans in Peru that I am convinced discussion of gendered consciousness and experience may provide a fruitful line of inquiry as scholars continue to explore the concept of radical empathy.

References

Anderson, S. 1998. *A Feminist Philosophy of Religion: The Rationality and Myths of Religious Belief.* Oxford: Blackwell.

———. 2002. Feminist theology as philosophy of religion. In *The Cambridge Companion to Feminist Theology,* ed. S. F. Parsons, 40–59. Cambridge: Cambridge University Press.

Barasch, M. I. 1993. *The Healing Path: A Soul Approach to Illness.* New York: Penguin.

———. 1994. A psychology of the miraculous. *Psychology Today* 27 (2): 54–63.

Benor, D. J. 2001. *Spiritual Healing: Scientific Validation of a Healing Revolution.* Southfield, Mich.: Vision.

Borysenko, J. 1999. *A Woman's Journey to God.* New York: Riverhead.

Borysenko, J., and M. Borysenko. 1994. *The Power of the Mind to Heal.* Carson, Calif.: Hayhouse.

Bynum, C. W. 1986. The complexity of religious symbols. In *Gender and Religion: On the Complexity of Symbols,* ed. C. W. Bynum, S. Harrell, and P. Richman. Boston: Beacon.

Canda, E., and L. D. Furman. 1999. *Spiritual Diversity in Social Work Practice: The Art of Helping.* New York: Free Press.

Christ, C. 1997. *Rebirth of the Goddess: Finding Meaning in Feminist Spirituality.* Reading, Mass.: Addison-Wesley.

———. 2002. Feminist theology as post-traditional theology. In *The Cambridge Companion to Feminist Theology,* ed. S. F. Parsons, 79–96. Cambridge: Cambridge University Press.

Christ, C., and J. Plaskow, eds. 1979. *Womanspirit Rising: A Feminist Reader in Religion.* San Francisco: Harper and Row.

Daly, M. 1973. *Beyond God the Father.* Boston: Beacon.

———. 1984. *Pure Lust: Elemental Feminist Philosophy.* Boston: Beacon.

Daruna, J. 2004. *Introduction to Psychoneuroimmunology.* Boston: Elsevier Academic.

Fulkerson, M. M. 1994. *Changing the Subject: Women's Discourses and Feminist Theology*. Minneapolis, Minn.: Fortress.

Glass-Coffin, B. 1996. Male and female healing in northern Peru: Metaphors, models and manifestations of difference. *Journal of Ritual Studies* 10 (1): 63–91.

———. 1998. *The Gift of Life: Female Spirituality and Healing in Northern Peru*. Albuquerque: University of New Mexico Press.

———. 1999. Engendering Peruvian shamanism through time: Insights from ethnohistory and ethnography. *Ethnohistory* 46 (2): 205–38.

Gross, R. M. 1996. *Feminism and Religion: An Introduction*. Boston: Beacon.

Hirshberg, C., and M. I. Barasch. 1995. *Remarkable Recovery: What Extraordinary Healings Tell Us about Getting and Staying Well*. New York: Riverhead Books.

Jantzen, G. M. 1998. *Becoming Divine: Towards a Feminist Philosophy of Religion*. Manchester: Manchester University Press.

Karras, V. 2002. Eschatology. In *The Cambridge Companion to Feminist Theology*, ed. S. F. Parsons, 243–60. Cambridge: Cambridge University Press.

King, U., ed. 1995. *Religion and Gender*. Oxford: Blackwell.

Ochs, C. 1983. *Women and Spirituality*. Totowa, N.J.: Rowman and Allanheld.

Parsons, S. F., ed. 2002. *The Cambridge Companion to Feminist Theology*. Cambridge: Cambridge University Press.

Pert, C. 1997. *Molecules of Emotion: Why You Feel the Way You Feel*. New York: Scribner.

Plaskow, J. 1980. *Sex, Sin and Grace: Women's Experience and the Theologies of Reinhold Niebuhr and Paul Tillich*. Washington, D.C.: University Press of America.

Reuther, R. R. 1983. *Sexism and God Talk*. Boston: Beacon.

———. 1993. Spirit and matter, public and private: The challenge of feminism to traditional dualisms. In *Embodied Love: Sensuality and Relationship as Feminist Values*, ed. P. M. Cooey, S. A. Farmer, and M. E. Ross, 65–76. San Francisco: Harper and Row.

———. 1998. *Women and Redemption: A Theological History*. Minneapolis, Minn.: Fortress.

———. 2002. The emergence of Christian feminist theology. In *The Cambridge Companion to Feminist Theology*, ed. S. F. Parsons, 3–22. Cambridge: Cambridge University Press.

Saiving, V. 1960. The human situation: A feminine view. *Journal of Religion* 40:100–12.

Schussler-Fiorenza, E. 1983. *In Memory of Her*. New York: Crossroads.

Shepherd, L. M. 2002. *Feminist Theologies for a Postmodern Church*. New York: Peter Lang.

Siegel, B. 1986. *Love, Medicine and Miracles: Lessons Learned about Self-healing from a Surgeon's Experience with Exceptional Patients*. New York: Harper and Row.

Spretnak, C. 1982. *The Politics of Women's Spirituality: Essays on the Rise of Spiritual Power within the Feminist Movement*. Garden City, N.Y.: Anchor Books.

Starhawk. 1997. *Dreaming the Dark: Magic, Sex, and Politics*. 15th anniversary edition. Boston: Beacon.

———. 1999. *The Spiral Dance: A Rebirth of the Ancient Religion of the Goddess*. 20th anniversary edition. San Francisco: Harper.

Sternberg, E. M. 2000. *The Balance Within: The Science Connecting Health and Emotions*. New York: W.H. Freeman.

Tamez, E., ed. 1989. *Through Her Eyes: Women's Theology from Latin America*. Maryknoll, N.Y.: Orbis.

Tedlock, B. 2005. *The Woman in the Shaman's Body: Reclaiming the Feminine in Religion and Medicine*. New York: Bantam Books.

Ulanov, A. B. 1981. *Receiving Woman: Studies in the Psychology and Theology of the Feminine*. Philadelphia: Westminster.

6

Sustainable Faith? Reconfiguring Shamanic Healing in Siberia

Marjorie Mandelstam Balzer

Nostalgia is currently rife in Siberia for the pre-Soviet days when powerful shamans, in control of a panoply of spirits traveling across multiple layers of the universe, could cure patients during deeply dramatic and transforming, community-wide séances. Poignant stories abound of lost knowledge: the shaman who died knowing where a special plant that could have cured his cancer was located, "just at the edge of the village airport," and just beyond the edge of our current medical practices and perceptions. Another story depicts the shaman who died several days before a repentant Soviet doctor returned to probe the healer's renowned, yet earlier rejected, understanding of an illness, known in the ethnographic literature by the infelicitous term *Arctic hysteria* (*ménérik* in Sakha and Russian). Such stories are told and retold with sorrow by the Sakha (Yakut) of the Russian Far East, from whom I have been learning since the early 1980s. These stories can be understood on multiple levels.[1]

For many elders and some youth of the Sakha, such accounts sustain their faith as well as place it in a distant temporal and spatial perspective. Many Sakha yearn for the reincarnation of named hero-shamans of previous generations who could recognize a medicinal plant from its life-force vibrations, who knew as well when to harvest the plant at its peak, how to prepare it, and, as important, how to ask permission from local spirits for the plant's removal by giving a token offering in return. Yet discourses of disaster are deceiving, for a strong and, I argue here, effective revitalization of shamanic healing has become a crucial part of larger processes of cultural recovery. The post-Soviet period has led to considerable personal and social transformation for many Sakha, as well as other Siberians.[2]

As a new generation of healers has turned to elders and spirits for guidance, exciting (for healers, patients, and ethnographers alike) accounts of miracle cures have begun to supplant the litanies of loss. This chapter features three sets of healers from two generations. Each set is imbued with human or spiritual kinship. All are well-known in the Sakha Republic, with varying degrees of controversy, rumor, and confidence swirling around them. In each case, I know or have worked with only the younger generation, since the generation of legendary hero-shamans has passed on in the biological sense, though not spiritually. Examination of generational differences enables us to analyze shamanic approaches to spiritual-healing processes and transformations using specific descriptions and epistemologies of cures in their cultural contexts over time (Crandon 1987). A key and often explicitly stated task of the healer is to stimulate a patient's own potential for self-cure, using an integrated body and mind approach, activating the "heart-soul-mind" that the Sakha term *kut-siur*. Sakha healers, through painful and patterned demands of spiritual initiation, are able to combine *kut-siur* with the *radical empathy* that is a hallmark of intuitive healers in many parts of the world (see chap. 4). I follow the suggestion of Thomas Csordas (2002) that in studying spiritual healing, anthropologists should understand embodied, emotional experience as "the starting point for analyzing human participation in a cultural world" (241).[3]

The first set of healers profiled here is the family of Konstantin Ivanovich Chirkov, who is also reverently called the "Elder of Abei region" and Konstantin *oiuun* (shaman). He is renowned for miracle cures and for his empathy and tact under the extreme conditions of Soviet repression. His daughter, Alexandra Chirkova, at his urging, became a Moscow-trained surgeon and the head doctor of her northern region. After age fifty, she returned to the shamanic healing traditions of her father, incorporating spirituality into her therapies selectively and creatively, depending on the patient. The second set or family of healers is that of Foma Petrovich Chashkin, whose two sons have increasingly and openly been seeing patients in their rural Tatta region after years of hiding their inherited shamanic gifts and the spirit-torture that constitutes Siberian shamanic initiation. The third set is linked by apprenticeship and spiritual communication, since the famed shaman Niikon (Nikon Alekseevich Vasilev, of the Viliuisk region) is said to have passed on his legendary abilities to a young shaman named Fedot Petrovich Ivanov. In this chapter I examine the interplay among Sakha principles of shamanic healing gifts that are inherited genetically, like musical talent, yet activated spiritually and cultivated with training. My data on the healers, their supplicants, and their communities derive from periodic fieldwork in the Sakha Republic (Yakutia) beginning in 1986, and continuing though many summers in the post-Soviet period.

Konstantin and Alexandra: Adapting the "Healing Gift" to Fit the Times

Alexandra Konstantinovna Chirkova shared with me in 2000 a curing event that she considered best illustrated her father's colossal talent as simultaneously a "white shaman" and a "psychotherapeutic master." She later featured the story, related by the son of the patient, in a memoir honoring her father (Chirkova 2002). I begin with Alexandra's voice, as she speaks with the authority of a licensed surgeon who later decided that cutting into people's heads was unbearable.

> One Spring a Sakha hunter who was a friend of father's went blind, probably from the glare of the sun on snow. Possibly the nerve endings in the brain that guide vision were affected, or it was a kind of spasm. In any case, nearly a year passed, and he requested Konstantin's help. Konstantin prepared him psychologically by asking the family to please find an Arctic white owl, within the next three days. Konstantin promised to return with his cloak, drum and assistants for a séance, if only the owl could be found. "How can we?" fretted the hunter's family, for he was inactive and his son was too young. "Do your best," said Konstantin. "Even if it is not alive, we will manage." Soon after, the

hunter's wife found that a frozen owl somehow had landed on their sled. They worried that the owl was dead, but when Konstantin arrived with his entourage and drank tea with the family, he said, "It will be fine." They prepared the room for the séance, placing the owl near the hearth. The old hunter sat near the fire as Konstantin began drumming, dancing, and calling his helper spirits. One moment, he was drumming close to the hunter's ear, and took his drumstick, *whooosh*, and made a whistling sound nearby. (211–13, confirming fieldnotes, 2000)

The account of the hunter's son, a witness, continues:

About midway through the séance, Konstantin took up the owl and put it on his knees, stroking it and saying incantations. I sat near him and with amazement watched his every move. I saw that the frozen owl had come to life, was scratching, and had taken flight. "Bai, what happened with that bird, look where it is flying," exclaimed Konstantin. The owl, flapping its wings, was flying around the cabin, and then flew up the chimney. Konstantin continued long in his singing [in Sakha, *kuturuu*]. His assistants took two frozen boards from the yard and hit him in the kidneys. They took an axe and beat him . . . As they held it, the shaman licked it, ran his hands over its blade. It was horrible. . . . The shaman licked hot strips of wood from the fire and licked the hunter's eyes, [then] . . . bound [them] with a dark cloth. [Konstantin] told him to open his eyes by slowly and carefully unbandaging himself only on the third day. . . . "You will at least see your feet. . . ." And on the third day, my father made it to the open door and took off the bandage. Opening his eyes, he cried several times, "I can see," and he wept for joy. (212–13, confirming fieldnotes, 2000)

Alexandra further explained that the Arctic white owl is sacred, not to be killed. Thus the hunter was primed to be thrilled that his family had avoided having to kill the bird: its appearance was a blessed sign. Its revival and flight during the séance created conditions for a still more intense epiphany for the hunter, who so wanted to see, and for his extended family, who all rejoiced at the sharp-eyed owl's recovery. They were in a state of spiritual astonishment—possibly group trance and certainly group solidarity—caused by the drama of the drumming, the rhythm of dancing, the poetic, mantra-like incantations evoking nature, as well as by the palpable presence of the

shaman's spirit helpers. All this was compounded by the adrena-
line- (and perhaps endorphin-)stirring excitement of the shaman's
exploits, aided by Konstantin's human helpers, his *kuturuk-sut*.[4] The
séance lasted well into the night and was perceived by its attendees
as a miracle, the epitome of a "benevolent spirit shaman" (*aiyy
oiuun*) in his negotiation with the spirit world. Alexandra for her
part wondered if the bird was really an owl, and if the group was
not under mass hypnosis. She noted that ophthalmologists recommend waiting three days after an eye injury before removing bandages, and she suggested that Konstantin's licking probably had a
medicinal, purifying value precisely because he licked a hot stick
first. Yet she too has had spiritual epiphanies, after moments of self-
doubt, followed by "shamanic illness" and a yearning to be guided
from the realms of the dead by her father, who was born in 1879 and
died in 1974.

In childhood, Alexandra had notorious symptoms of shamanic
illness, called in the Sakha language *éttéénii* and "the Sakha sickness" (*Sakha yald'ar*). A form of spirit-torture, it often results in the
painful feeling of being "sick all over" or of being torn apart and
remade from the inside out by snakes and other animal-like spirits.
The goal of this initiation is to feel a variety of pains that one's future patients are likely to feel and to gain enough empathy to become a true intuitive healer by tapping into the spiritual potency of
oneself and one's patients in a synergistic way. To recover, the potential healer must promise to cure others, in a literally and figura-
tively enlightening bargain with the spirits who will become the
healer's helpers.[5] Alexandra explained to me: "I was young when I
first felt the strength. I had visions, forebodings. But I was also
headstrong and emotional. . . . Father tried to tell me this was not
how to be. I had a dream that I was thrown into a pit with snakes.
I heard a voice that said, 'She will see it through. She will win.'"

Alexandra, confirming that various stages of transformation
are typical of Sakha shamans, describes in her memoir a later
episode.

> In 1985, something happened with me that is beyond explana-
> tion. It began with a headache and unstoppable vomiting. For
> three days, I was not able to get up from bed, and then I revived.
> The whole time I wanted fish. . . . My body was covered with red

hives. I had a terrible skin itch, as if worms were crawling all over my body. . . . A woman came to me and said that I was not curing myself correctly, that what I had was well-known. . . . She brought three kinds of herbs and said to burn them in the evening and purify myself with smoke. Also, that I should eat fish. . . . After feeling better, I decided to take the smell of smoke from my body. But again the headaches began, and I realized what I had to do. I had to put on my father's [shamanic] dress [bequeathed to her ten days short of three years after Konstantin's death, as he had directed]. . . . I put on the cloak and immediately felt a lightening. I even looked at myself in the mirror. I felt a tranquilizing of the soul, and with a great yawn I lost my footing, and fell into a deep dream. (Chirkova 2002, 100–101)

After taking sick leave, Alexandra continued to use her father's cloak to cure herself, as she gradually realized that what was happening was "the ritual of tearing apart." She explained in 2000 that this is "a ritual of suffering through which one is taught." Among her teachers were animal-spirit guides, including a bear. Significantly, one of her father Konstantin's most famed forms was that of a bear, the animal also associated with his "mother beast spirit," or *iié kyl* in Sakha. But Alexandra's suffering was far from over. During this period, she sang ancient Sakha songs with abandon in her sleep.

After three years a still greater trauma occurred, the one that led her away from being "the kind of doctor who cuts and sews," as her father used to say. Immediately after performing brain surgery, she reeled from the operating room, vomited, and was unconscious for three days. She was transferred to several hospitals, including one in the republic's capital, Yakutsk. Marks appeared on her face that some said resembled a cross on one side, and a drum on the other. She then envisioned the next hospital bed she was to have, and was later taken there, near patients who subsequently were amazed when she understood their illnesses without having been told their complaints. She hid her own dizziness, blurred vision, and mental state, however, in great fear that her colleagues would put her in one of the notorious Russian psychiatric clinics where she might be inappropriately drugged. Gradually she realized: "I had acquired a new gift, the ability to see through a person into their illness." She saved one woman from a kidney stone operation by willing the stones into sand. Another, who was to have a leg amputated, was saved when Alexandra "by thought, with intense gaze, cured her. Soon the woman stood, felt warmth, and itching in the leg." As Alexandra cured others, she improved herself, and was finally released, still wobbly, with the diagnosis "sickness uncertain" (Chirkova 2002, 105).

Back home, donning Konstantin's cloak, Alexandra finally felt the relief and calm that eventually led to her spiritual transformation from a surgeon to a healer, guided by the spirit of her father, who sometimes sent messages through an elderly mediator fondly named "Aunt Shura." Konstantin had once delivered Shura in a difficult birth, had accurately predicted her future family life, and later began sending her elaborate dreams as a way to contact Alexandra. Alexandra herself had saved Shura from going blind in 1991, by Shura's own account to me. When I first met Alexandra in 1992, she was head doctor of her region, with a large plant-filled room within the Belaia Gora hospital for those patients who wished to be cured in séances that included Sakha chants, incense purification, and mutually reinforcing group prayers. The enthusiastic testimonies of these patients in 1993 made me realize Alexandra's *étééníí* had fulfilled a powerful promise, though she still wore her white doctor's gown and inspired confidence in more "modern" ways as well. Within ten years Alexandra resigned as head doctor of the region and began receiving selected patients in her home, including those she helped occasionally by donning Konstantin's cloak and drumming by a fire, in a special healing hut in her backyard. Alexandra continues to be well-loved for dealing with the emergencies and the traumas of hunting accidents, as well as for curing nervous-system disorders and alcoholism. Nikolai, a patient with cancer, and several others say they have seen a man standing behind her while she chants, as she evokes the beauty of the northern mountains.[6]

The Chashkins: From Exploits to Tractors

In the central Sakha region called Tatta, renowned for producing many artists and writers, the family of Foma Petrovich Chashkin felt the same heat of Soviet repression that Konstantin's did. Foma and

Konstantin together spent time in jail in the 1930s for their illegal practice of "charlatan medicine," since in those days Soviet antireligious authorities considered the words *shaman* and *deceiver* to be synonymous. Foma first came to my attention not for his reputation for healing, though it was great, but for his exploits with the Soviet police. In one account, Foma invited a policeman who had come to arrest him to eat a cooked fish with him, but the fish wiggled on the policeman's plate, and the poor man fled. In another Foma had been arrested, but he kept showing himself in the surrounding fields and woods, as if he were everywhere at once. So Soviet authorities let him go because they could not be sure where he was. In a third account, Foma was being taken to be shot, but a policeman put the gun to his own temple instead. Finally, officials let Foma go home, where he married a girl he had cured of a skin disease.

Chaashka oiuun, as he is nicknamed in Tatta, became known for curing alcoholics in secret, after his performance of community-oriented Sakha drumming séances attracted too much attention and became too dangerous. One time, recalled a friend of his, Chaashka and he visited another friend, who was drunk. The drunk evicted them angrily, so Chaashka made himself invisible. Later, at a time chosen for maximum effect, he "scared the guy straight out of his drunkenness" and, implied the speaker, his addiction. In another case, two men showed up on Chaashka's doorstep asking to be cured of their vodka habit. But they were not entirely sure that they wanted to quit, so they had decided to test Chaashka by hiding a couple of bottles along the way. "If you really want to be cured," he told them, "then you must get rid of those two bottles that you hid along the way here." Impressed, the two men decided that Chaashka could see everything, and that they may as well agree to be cured. Chaashka's usual method was to get people to swear by a ritual oath that within a particular amount of time they would quit drinking. "If they violated this, they could be in big trouble," said one of Chaashka's elderly followers. "Sometimes people came back to him asking that the 'spell' be lifted, so that they could go to someone's wedding and drink for just a short period, say, three days. But, if they didn't get the ritual and tried this on their own, they had terrible repercussions—sickness, dizziness, and even death." Swearing and fear of spiritual enforcement enables emergence from addiction in these cases.[7]

Two of Chaashka's sons have continued the family healing traditions, one more publicly than the other. I traveled to meet a modest, somewhat jolly, middle-aged Mikhail Fomich Chashkin in his home village in 2003. Large and brawny, he has not given up his regular job as a tractor driver on an impoverished nearby farm that is part of a former Soviet collective, although he also regularly receives patients from the capital, a full eight hours' bumpy drive away. A local patient explained that Mikhail "has a strong tie to the land, and this is where he derives his strength, the human-natural connection that creates the context for the information he uses to heal. This includes deep knowledge of plants, of all their medicinal possibilities. But he doesn't pretend to cure everything."

Mikhail began our discussion with his ancestry. "Doimpo was my ancestor, one of the great shamans of this area. We all probably got our healing abilities from him." In answer to my question about using the heavily charged word *oiuun*, or "shaman," for the more recent generations, he replied:

> Yes, it is in our line to be *oiuun*. Foma certainly can be called an *oiuun*. He died at age seventy-eight, treated like an ordinary person, and was buried that way, not as the *oiuun* of the past were [on special tree platforms in sacred groves]. . . . There is a place named for Doimpo, and a sacred tree [*kérék mas*] associated with him. I sometimes go to Foma's grave for inspiration. He died quietly in his sleep. He knew when he was going.

As is Mikhail, Foma was perceived as *oiuun* by his patients because he went through the painful process of *éttéénii* to become a healer. While Foma probably had some inkling of spirit-torture in his childhood, the most striking bout in this process did not take place until Foma had reached the age that many Sakha claim is a key turning point in the revelation of creative and spiritual talent.

> When Foma was about forty, he became very sick and was tortured by spirits. He had *éttéénii* for about seven years. For three to four of those years, he could hardly walk. He sang at night. . . . I was born when he was around fifty, so I do not remember his *éttéénii*. He cured it the way Sakha shamans do—he drank milk as if it were his life's blood, used milk to purify his system.

Rather than stressing a pact with spirits, Mikhail chose to emphasize Foma's "rechanneling of his talents." He explained, "Since he could not use a drum . . . He used other instruments, for example horn tubes for bloodletting." With some sorrow, Mikhail said, "He didn't pass his healing implements to me; he didn't think his children should suffer [by becoming healers]."

Foma channeled his talent toward herbal knowledge and psychological understanding. Mikhail elaborated: "He used everything that was in his head, his brain. I myself can figure out who is coming and why. He did this too. It is possible when you are calm and connected. I think that telepathy was more needed then than now. Now we have the telephone." Unlike many rural Sakha, Foma did not keep cows or horses, but rather was a forest-oriented hunter. This helped him avoid too much contact with Soviet authorities in the village and, more importantly, gave him the spiritual connectedness he needed to open himself to appropriate cures for individual patients. Many of his patients were women with *ménérik*, meaning that they were perceived to have psychological problems collectively (mis-)labeled *Arctic hysteria*. Quite possibly, such women were themselves frustrated healers, unable to cure themselves by becoming openly respected *udagan*, the Sakha term for female shamans. Instead, their "nervous" bouts of dancing with wildly loosened hair, talking in tongues, and singing were perceived by their families and communities as frightening reminders of a "primitive past."[8] Mikhail said, "In those days, there were quite a few *ménérik*. Foma helped them, calmed them, and let blood out of them, from their temples. He also cured depression, back pain, osteochondrosis, stomach ulcers, and fertility problems."

Mikhail's practice is imbued with the faith that he will eventually learn to cure precisely forty-one illnesses. He got this from his own version of *éttéénii*, which he freely admits began with suffering from alcoholism. Mikhail recalled,

It was really through dissipation and disorientation. I was very out of it when I drank, and through this, I suffered *éttéénii* without at first understanding what it was. I too went through this struggle for about seven years. Papa died before he could help me in this [healing] life. He was an *oiuun* and accepted that fate for himself. But now I see him in my dreams. This is how he has helped me.

When I asked if he had any urge to take up drumming and perform séances, Mikhail hooted with laughter:

> How am I going to jump around like that? The most important thing is the results, the cures that you help people achieve, when people believe in you. You can use herbs and the words of a blessing [*algys*] the same way as the drum. The energy of the curing is in the herbs, in all of nature itself.

Mikhail's spirituality is inspirational and ad hoc, in that his intuition (*tagkha*) guides him to the right diagnoses, herbs, and prayer-chants to use. He explained, "The words just come to me, they come from nature, a kind of prayer. I can see a person and figure out their illness. But I only have strength for five to six people a day." In the Sakha language, the word for "nature," *aiylgkha*, stems from the root *aiyy*, meaning "benevolent spirit." Mikhail recognized this, yet hesitated to discuss its implication as his prayer source.

Mikhail distinguished between Sakha and Russian patients, noting that sometimes Russians are more receptive than Sakha, and had "softer internal structures," that is, were more adaptable and less prone to chronic ailments. With Sakha patients, he is particularly attuned to their three souls, thought by most Sakha to be an integral part of their being. The first and primary soul is the "mother soul," or *iié kut*. It is important not to scare the *iié kut*, but rather to let its life force refresh itself. "Most curing, however," said Mikhail, "takes place with the *salgyn kut* [the breath soul]. Nearly everyone has their breath soul spoiled to some degree." This is because of human exposure to the destruction of nature, and to human-made ecological imbalances. If a mother or breath soul wanders or is stolen, the task of the great shamans of old, including Foma and Konstantin, was to recover and control it. But Mikhail confessed he cannot do this, nor can he send his own soul in search of another's, as shamans are supposed to do. The third soul is the "earth soul," or *buor kut*, most often identified with a person's shadow, and possibly, in some interpretations, with a person's "aura." All three make up the full harmony of an integrated, healthy person, enabling a balanced *kut-siur* (heart-soul-mind) and a pure liver.[9]

On leaving Mikhail, I noticed patients were waiting. Mikhail apologized for not being able to personally reveal the local sacred tree where his father had gone to make spirit offerings and derive inspiration. Mikhail admitted he had not been there for a long time, and felt more comfortable at Foma's grave, rather than Doimpo's tree. To my surprise, he then encouraged a pilgrimage, probably because he was charmed by the woman I was with, the well-known Sakha sociologist, parliamentarian, and author Uliana Vinokurova. We searched for the tree in a nearby forest, where a stand of larch meets one of birch. But sadly, the most likely sacred tree (*kérék mas*) we could find was a prone larch, an enormous, once-living being lying on the forest floor, abandoned. Uliana, having been ready to make a prayerful offering, stared forlornly at it and, it developed later, expected me to photograph it as a symbol of cultural and spiritual decay.[10] We pondered the twenty-first-century irony of a milk-drinking, tractor-driving healer whose breath soul (*salgyn kut*) did not fly.

Niikon and Fedot: Transcending the Generations

In the Viliuisk and neighboring Suntar regions, a phenomenal number of shamans were once renowned for their healing, spirituality, and ability to counteract or at least hide from Soviet repression. In one almost unbelievable case, the head of a village council managed to cover up his continuing shamanic practice because he was protected by his loving community and was perceived by the outside world as a good Communist. But probably the greatest of all the Viliuisk shamans was Niikon, for whom a local curing center is now named. One legend about Niikon is that in the 1930s he was shot, having fled into the forest with a rebellious group of Evenk trying to avoid Soviet collectivization. Then when the activists who had shot him came to his body, they found only a dead dog, instead of Niikon.[11] Though hounded, humiliated, and forced to relinquish his drum and cloak, Niikon, who is believed to have lived 104 years (1880–1984), managed by the end of his lifetime to gain special official dispensation for aspects of his curing practice. F. Khonoruin described (in a special collection honoring Niikon) how Foma Chashkin himself had referred him to Niikon in 1971:

> Niikon was an open, warm and hospitable elder, who loved to chat and tell stories. He looked at me and said just what Foma

had: "Come next summer when the birches are budding." I came at the right time and found Niikon had moved to his summer camp. With other patients, he took us to a birch grove and had us gather large branches of young birches into a pile. He then instructed us to make a pit for a fire, and when there were only coals left, he lined the pit with them and put birch branches in a bed on top, covering the pit. He had us one by one lie on the branches naked. Then he asked what part of the body felt hot, and added more branches there. During this, he held our hands, taking our pulse, to check our heart. When he finished with one, he'd take another, adding coals and branches as needed. After this healing, I became well and for twenty years have had no illnesses. (Boeskorov 2001, 41–42)[12]

This frustratingly spare yet glowing testimony, by a man with multiple ailments when he first appealed to Niikon, is typical of many accounts given by Niikon's admirers. Niikon used prayer-chants (*algys*) during such purification sessions, made spirit offerings, and rarely discussed his own relationship with helper spirits, hard-won through shamanic initiation. In the darkest moments of his secret practice, fear of Soviet police vigilance constrained him from taking the life histories of patients, some of whom he barely knew. He occasionally told newcomers that he did not want to know their names, yet his loving empathy came through, especially as he lay his hot, gentle hands on their heads, softly blew across their fontanels and prayed for them. He modestly received all supplicants, taking from them only the gifts that they could afford to give. Thus his practice in retrospect is surrounded with the mystery of successful healing using a relatively narrow range of traditional therapies such as herbs, bloodletting, sucking, prayer-chants, purification, and counseling. His healing gifts were said by local Sakha and a few influential Russian patients to be "from nature" and inherited within his shamanic line. But to whom could he pass this precious yet dangerous gift? One of the many tragedies of the Soviet repression of shamans is that the shamans only with great difficulty found appropriate youths to whom to bequeath their secret knowledge and practice.

Niikon, however, had several apprentices in his lifetime, including one promising young man who landed in jail for alleged murder after working with Niikon for seven years. Late in his life,

Niikon learned of another extraordinary young man named Fedot, who was still in school in a neighboring village. By Fedot's own testimony,

> Niikon called me to him when I was sixteen. I felt the pull and resisted. I was ill [with *ётёёnii*]. I was confused. And I was different from the other kids and did not want to be. My mother was very upset. But Niikon found me. He sent me signals through dreams and sent me a letter asking me to come live with him, to train with him.

Fedot's mother, sitting nearby as we talked, confirmed that she had been vigorously against his leaving school and going to study with Niikon in 1981. But she could not stop him, and she became the only one who knew where he had gone; it was kept secret from the rest of the family. Fedot continued:

> Niikon taught me a lot. He taught me how to find healing herbs, and how to mix them in appropriate doses. He gave me my drum and instructed me in how to gather important components of my cloak [through spirit communication]. I worked with him for about a year. . . . [As he became infirm] he passed me on to his friend, another shaman.[13]

Since Niikon's death, Fedot has periodically visited his grave, known to special followers as a pilgrimage site. One aspect of Fedot's burgeoning reputation with intelligentsia members in the capital is that he spends time each year at Niikon's grave, something few have the courage to do. At the grave, Fedot occasionally has felt comfortable enough to spend the night, shyly saying in answer to a direct question, "Yes, I go to Niikon's grave. . . . I cannot go into details, but you can say we met each other there."

Fedot outlined more specifically some of the Sakha therapies that Niikon had taught him, while making clear that he was still learning and was still at a relatively early stage of his healing abilities. One of the most common of these therapies, which bears a striking resemblance to the healing practices of some Native Americans, is *bokhsuruii*, sucking illness from the body.[14] Another is a ritualized massage, *ilbiyii*, meaning "casting out illness," that includes lengthy incantations. More serious illnesses require *sullérdééhii*, a kind of telepathic operation without cutting the body, and *d'albyii*, removing and escorting ill-willed spirits (*abaahy*) from a patient, through a séance. For this, a shaman needs a darkened room with a hearth or an isolated spot in the forest where a fire can be lit. Prayer-chants (*algys*) are said to the fire spirit (*iot ichchi*), with offerings of white horsehair, Sakha pancakes, and butter, as is typical of many Sakha rituals. Then, early in the séance, while drumming and singing, Fedot evokes his helper spirits, a raven and a black dog.

> I use the same song always to start. I cry like a raven, to evoke Raven, and then call to Dog, like a dog. . . . I do not consider my spirits *abaahy*—they are *ichchi*. They are helpers, not evil spirits. I try to cure people, to be kind, not to hurt people. How effective I am partly depends on what kind of illness is being discussed.

One reason I had found Fedot, whose village is remote, and was received warmly, was that I was accompanied by a Sakha friend, Ivan Alekseev, who is a linguist from the region and a virtuoso player of the jaw harp (*khomus*, also called a mouth organ or Jew's harp). A deeply resonating instrument, the sculptural, forged-metal *khomus* is famed in the republic for creating calming, sometimes healing, effects, and has had an enormous revival of popularity in the last twenty years. Fedot too plays the *khomus* and welcomed Ivan with joy. Yet he was not ready to treat either of us for the specific complaints that we arrived with, for he had just performed a risky séance with his own brother the day before and admitted he was feeling unwell himself. He nonetheless managed through some sort of telepathy (called "clear-seeing," or *kéur-béuchur*) to discern what our needs and hopes were as potential patients before we explicitly mentioned them.[15] He also warned us that he could not simply sing and drum "for show," without immediately evoking his helper spirits. My respect for his effectiveness has increased over the years, as he has intermittently treated a mutual friend, the singer and songwriter Anastasiia Varlaamova, for chronic diabetes.

A less-successful case was mentioned by Fedot himself, who admitted that he could not use "clear-seeing" or a nonintrusive operation to cure patients from afar, although he had tried. One desperate family had brought him the clothing of a loved one dying of cancer. "It was too late," he recalled, "but I think I made the pain of the illness easier to bear." Interestingly, I first heard of Fedot because of a sensational story buzzing in the capital about a Russian woman doctor whom he had cured of cancer. This woman, knowing well the pitfalls of Soviet operations, secretly had gone to Fedot around 1990, after Japanese scanning technology revealed she had a tumor. Fedot worked with her during numerous séances in the forest near his home over the course of a month. When she returned to her hospital, her doctor-colleagues were furious that she had delayed her operation. But they were completely confounded when they found no tumor and learned where she had been.

Conclusions: Spiritual Transformation as a Social and Personal Process

The social and historical context of healing is integral to supplicants' potential abilities to respond to shamanic stimulation of their self-healing. Stories such as that of a remote, rural Sakha shaman curing a Russian woman doctor of cancer are just what a social doctor of a wounded post-Soviet society might have ordered. I have not been able to track the Russian doctor to confirm her recovery. But the account is at minimum a widespread affirmation of faith in traditional healing, in the revitalization of shamanic traditions, and in the spiritual transference of shamanic power to a new generation. Fedot in the post-Soviet period represents this and more, for his satisfied patient list has been growing, and in 2003, on a trip to Viliuisk, I heard from several of his followers that he had managed to put out a forest fire with a séance by evoking Niikon's help to create a storm. This is precisely the kind of legend told about the great hero-shamans of the past who used their abilities not only for healing but for community protection.

More than a decade of post-Soviet life has produced many changes in indigenous Siberian attitudes toward their healing legacies. Once associated with discredited "deceiver-shamans" in the Soviet period, Siberian spirituality has become more openly revered in the post-Soviet period by many Sakha and some Russians. However, zigzags of community support for shamanic cures have resulted in both openings and closings of some "traditional" healing centers. In the capital, Yakutsk, the Center of Traditional Medicine recently changed its name to the Center for Prophylactic and Sports Medicine, in keeping with a Russian Federation law that curtails the practice of "folk healing" without a license. The boom in post-Soviet healers of the early 1990s has given way to fewer practitioners a decade later, as patients learn for themselves who are effective healers with shamanic gifts and who are commercial "charlatans" trading on a new cultural credibility for religion. The Center for Folk Healing, founded by the shaman-historian Vladimir Kondakov, who uses Sakha therapies and Chinese medicine such as acupuncture, has had considerable success attracting healers and patients. Except for Kondakov himself, however, few of its healers are considered by either urban or rural Sakha to be full-fledged *oiuun* or *udagan*. For this, consultants say, one needs a shamanic lineage, spirit-torture inspiration through *éttéénii*, and a many-staged apprenticeship to a knowledgeable elder. While the proportions of these elements may vary individually, all three are desirable to create the personal synergism needed for curing through experience-rooted empathy (*ahynyy*). A wise, effective healer like Niikon literally and symbolically strips his patients naked to cleanse them of their fears and their community-defined sins, and to make them feel whole again, welcome, humble, and respectful in an imperfect world. Various kinds of empathy, intuition, and their resonance may be at work.

Sakha terminology concerning spiritual healing is revealing. A shaman (and a few others) is said to be "a person with an open body" (*ahaghas éttéékh kihi*), bravely open and heart-soul-minded to all experience. Perceptive healers have "eyes on the spine" (*kokhaugér kharataakh*), akin to the concept of a "third eye." All are adept at intuition-based diagnosis and at stimulating the life forces of *kut-siur* through mutually reinforcing blessings and prayer-chants (*algys*). But to reduce the healing process, and its transforming effects, to the power of prayer and purification misses the integration of many kinds of spirituality in shamanic practice, an integration derived from inner strength as well as from the outside, natural energies of the surrounding environment and the cosmos of a multilayered universe filled with named animate and active beings.

Tensions between individual- and community-oriented curing play out differently in diverse cases, especially given that many Siberian communities, as elsewhere, are multiethnic. The more cultural boundaries are blurred, the harder it becomes to identify fixed etiologies and philosophies of curing that can be linked to particular ethnic groups or specific language-based chants and mantras (Langford 2003).[16]

The healing and spiritual transformation processes that are illustrated here show several kinds of healing working at many social levels. First, the model of "healing the healer" through personal revelation is the classic shamanic pattern of spirit negotiation through suffering and its transcendence. Called *spirit initiation* in the ethnographic literature, it results in a radical empathy that brings results. Second, the cure of the blind hunter reveals the ability of a healer to communicate and enact compassion through elaborate ritual. The full power of a suspenseful, dramatic drumming séance, planned and executed with elaborate effort to appeal to higher spirit authorities, including the manipulation of the perfect symbol of a dead owl brought to sharp-eyed life, illustrates a cure enabled through a synergy of personal and community psychological persuasion, and perhaps more. The reality of spirits comes to life in the healing. Third, as Soviet repression curtailed such exuberance, the bare bones of traditional healing sustained faith: herbal knowledge tied to ecological care, massage, bone-setting, and counseling linked to close understanding of individual complaints. Especially for elderly supplicants, these techniques worked best when combined with spiritual endorsement and with accounts of shamans transcending persecution. With a new generation of healers, a fourth and exciting level has been added in the reemergence of spiritual healing into more open community practice. A few special healer-shamans are combining the poetic, inspirational, and creative chanting of previous generations into adapted rituals, guided by their dreams, by their intuitions, and by their acclaimed consultations with deceased yet spiritually alive hero-shamans. Far from being bound by specific chant formulas, healer-shamans are once again free to explore individual and community problems in interrelation with each other.

Returning to introductory themes, many in Russia too often have seen "folk healing" in terms of extremes: either disastrous or miraculous, either black or white. Soviet repression of shamans probably exacerbated already existing tendencies to project extreme images, hopes, and fears onto the shamans. As new generations of healers and their supplicants become comfortable with the creativity and energy of cultural (re)vitalization, they are also (re)kindling a vibrant and more pliant understanding of healing itself. To adapt the perspectives of Lewis Hyde (1998, 293–300) on cultural creativity, some gifted shamans can cross boundaries and become the creative tricksters of cultural revitalization. Thomas Csordas, however, warns that "healing is much more like planting a seed or nudging a rolling ball to slightly change its trajectory so that it ends up in a different place, than it is like lightning striking or mountains moving" (2002, 5). Combining these insights, we can see that the "nudge" of renewed faith in benevolent and active healers and in ancestral spirits may be making possible the effectiveness of newly revitalized shamanic therapies. Occasionally, when a few living shamans themselves evoke the sacred mountains, the rivers, the nine heavens, and the lightning of a culturally constructed Sakha cosmos in their prayer-chants, an incremental cure may occur so speedily as to seem miraculous.

Notes

1. I am indebted to Georgetown University, the International Research and Exchanges Board (IREX), the Social Science Research Council (SSRC), Yakutsk State University, the Academy of Sciences Humanities Institute, the Sakha Republic Ministry of Culture, and to the Kennan Institute of the Woodrow Wilson Center for fieldwork or research support. Fieldwork relevant to this paper was begun in 1986, continuing periodically from 1991 to 2003. I am deeply thankful to my Sakha language teacher, Klara Belkin, with whom I began studying in 1983, and to many Sakha friends and colleagues, especially Zinaida and the late Vladimir Ivanov for sharing their home; Albina Diachkova and Anatoly Gogolev for hosting me in 2003; Alexandra Chirkova for working with me periodically since 1992; Uliana Vinokurova for our long-term partnership, especially in the Tatta region in 2003; Ivan Alekseev and Anatoly Gogolev for guiding me in the Viliuisk region in 1991 and 2002 respectively; and to Eduard Alekseev for his perceptive critique of this chapter.

2. While acknowledging the seriousness of Soviet repression of shamans, analysts should also consider that mourning a previous generation's lost esoteric knowledge and spirituality may be a pattern that goes back to at least the nine-

teenth century, when shamans were hounded and denigrated by Russian Ortho-dox missionaries. For historical background, see Alekseev (1984), Balzer (1999), Il'iakov (1995), and Znamenski (1999). On shamans and definitions, see Balzer (1997), Narby and Huxley (2001), Schenk and Ratsch (1999), and Siikala and Hoppál (1992). While controversial for its generalizations and lack of directly experi-enced field data, see also the classic, Eliade (2004/1951).

3. On my eclectic approaches to healing and anthropology theory, see Balzer (1996).

4. On group dynamics, see Jakobsen (1999), Kendall (2001), and Ksenofontov (1992/1928). On séances as group therapy and the possible stimulation of endor-phins, see Balzer (1987; 1991).

5. See especially Basilov (1997), who stresses the shamanic call as being "cho-sen by the spirits." Compare Brown and Cousins (2001), Hultkranz (1992), and Mehl-Madrona (1997). Gender-sensitive aspects of shamanic healing are relevant. In Sakha, a male shaman is an *oiuun* (with a Turkic root), while a woman is called *udagan* (with a Mongolic root). Neither is considered by definition stronger than the other, but during the Soviet period more high-profile male shamans were ar-rested, causing a feminization of folk curing as healers went underground (Balzer 1999). On the significance of women shamans through history, see Tedlock (2005). See also Koss-Chioino (1992), and Perrone, Stockel, and Krueger (1989).

6. A patient who had never seen a picture of Konstantin recognized his pho-tograph, an identification that may have involved the "power of suggestion." An-other of Konstantin's children, Maria, has also become a healer in her home region of Belaia Gora. Alexandra has moved to the capital, where she works in one of several "traditional" healing centers, without using the cloak or drum. She briefly treated the former Sakha Republic president, M. E. Nikolaev.

7. This approach is also practiced by a healer-shaman I have visited twice, Vi-taly Nikiforov. It brings out some of the more negative, fear-inducing aspects of dealing with spirits, who can be vengeful if not appeased and respected. How-ever, a Sakha barrier to the misuse of spirit power is the widespread belief that in-voking ill-intentioned spirits or cursing can rebound against one's close family members. Compare Whitehead and Wright (2004).

8. On *ménérik*, see the Russian doctor S. I. Mitskevich (1929). For a social in-terpretation of similar phenomena, see I. M. Lewis (1971). The ethnomusicologist Eduard Alekseev is researching the inspirational singing of *ménérik* sufferers.

9. The body-purifying liver is considered as important in Sakha conceptions, if not more so, than the heart. For more on concepts of the three souls and health, see Kolodesnikov (2000), Kondakov (1992; 1999), and Kulakovskii (1979).

10. Off numerous dirt roads in the republic are sacred groves with large, im-posing trees—often larch—festooned with ribbons and other offerings. I was first taken to one in 1986, in secret, and have been to many since with Sakha friends honoring their local spirits.

11. This account is from a conversation with the ethnographer S. I. Nikolaev (Somogotto), fieldnotes July 1991.

12. This collection honoring Niikon (Boeskorov 2001) is typical of publications that have appeared recently to celebrate the lives of repressed shamans. I am

grateful to Zina Ivanova for insights into its meaning and for help with its translation.

13. I hope to work more with Fedot, and am grateful to Ivan Alekseev and
Anastasiia Varlaamova for helping me to connect with him in 1991.

14. See also Kondakov (1999). In addition, the stunning 1984 documentary film
Time of Dreams, by A. Slapinch with E. Alekseev and E. Novik as advisors, includes
a segment on Niikon. It is available through the Smithsonian museum's Arctic Research Center in Anchorage, Alaska, and was originally shot under the auspices
of the Soviet Academy of Sciences.

15. Shamans rarely heal family members, since family members are considered
too close and with too much at stake. Although Fedot rejected performing a
séance with me or Ivan, I have been a patient with several other Sakha healers, including one who "saw" an abnormality in my body (X-ray vision?) that I had only
just learned about with Western technology. My skepticism has been tested to the
point of considerable realignment and spiritual confusion, as I absorb information
about instances of relatively rapid spiritual healing, shamanic telepathy, uncanny
coincidences, predictive dreams, and "clear-seeing" into future events and into
patient's bodies.

16. See also Csordas (2000; 2002) and Davies (2004) on Navaho healing in new,
culturally mixed contexts.

References

Alekseev, N. A. 1984. *Shamanizm Tiurkoiazychnykh narodov Sibiri* [Shamanism of
Turkic Peoples of Siberia]. Novosibirsk: Nauka.

Balzer, M. M. 1987. Behind shamanism: Changing voices of Siberian Khanty cos-
mology and politics. *Social Science and Medicine* 24 (12): 1085–94.

———. 1991. Doctors or deceivers? The Siberian Khanty shaman and Soviet medicine. In *Anthropology and Medicine*, ed. L. Romanucci-Ross, D. Moerman, and L.
Tancredi. 2nd ed., 56–80. New York: Bergin and Garvey.

———. 1996 Flights of the sacred: Symbolism and theory in Siberian shamanism.
American Anthropologist 98 (2): 305–18.

———. ed. 1997. *Shamanic Worlds: Rituals and Lore of Siberia and Central Asia*. Armonk, N.Y.: North Castle Books.

———. 1999. Shamans in all guises: Exploring cultural repression and resilience in
Siberia. *Curare* 22 (2): 129–34.

Basilov, V. 1997. Chosen by the spirits. In *Shamanic Worlds: Rituals and Lore of
Siberia and Central Asia*, ed. M. M. Balzer. Armonk, N.Y.: North Castle Books.

Boeskorov, S. T. 2001. *N'iikon* [in Sakha]. Yakutsk: Bichik.

Brown, J. E., with E. Cousins. 2001. *Teaching Spirits: Understanding Native American
Religious Tradition*. New York: Oxford University Press.

Chirkova, A. K. 2002. *Shaman: Zhizn' i bessmertie* [Shaman: Life and immortality].
Yakutsk: Sakhapoligrafizdat.

Crandon, L., ed. 1987. Beyond the cure: Anthropological inquiries in medical theories and epistemologies. *Social Science and Medicine* 24 (12): 1011–1118.

Csordas, T. J., ed. 2000. The Navaho Healing Project. *Medical Anthropology Quarterly* 14 (4).

———. 2002. *Body/Meaning/Healing*. New York: Palgrave Macmillan.

Davies, W. 2004. Western medicine and Navaho healing. In *The Politics of Healing*, ed. R. D. Johnson, 83–94. New York: Routledge.

Eliade, M. 1951. *Shamanism: Archaic Techniques of Ecstasy*. 3rd ed. Princeton: Princeton University Press, 2004.

Hultkranz, A. 1992. *Shamanic Healing and Ritual Drama*. New York: Crossroad.

Hyde, L. 1998. *Trickster Makes This World: Mischief, Myth, and Art*. New York: Farrar, Straus and Giroux.

Il'iakov, N. 1995. *Bor'ba s shamanizmom v Yakutii (1920–30)* [Struggle against shamanism in Yakutia (1920–30)]. Yakutsk: Dom Narodnogo Tvorchestva.

Jakobsen, M. D. 1999. *Shamanism: Traditional and Contemporary Approaches to the Mastery of Spirits and Healing*. New York: Berghahn Books.

Kendall, L. 2001. Encounters with Korean ancestors. In *Ancestors in Post-contact Religion*, ed. S. Friesen, 135–56. Cambridge: Harvard University Press.

Kolodesnikov, S. K. 2000. The person in the traditional Yakut (Sakha) worldview. *Anthropology and Archeology of Eurasia* 39 (1): 42–79.

Kondakov, V. A. 1992. *Émtééhin kisténgnéritén* [About a few secrets of folk curing] (in Sakha). Yakutsk: Sakha Republic Association of Folk Medicine.

———. 1999. *Tainy sfery shamanizma* [The secret sphere of shamanism]. Yakutsk: Aiyy Archyta.

Koss-Chioino, J. 1992. *Women as Healers, Women as Patients: Mental Health Care and Traditional Healing in Puerto Rico*. Boulder, Colo.: Westview.

Ksenofontov, G. V. 1992. *Shamanizm: Izbrannye trudy* [Shamanism: Collected works], ed. A. N. Diachkova. Yakutsk: Sever-Iug. for Museum of Music and Folklore. (Orig. pub. 1928.)

Kulakovskii, A. E. 1979. *Nauchnyie trudy* [Scientific studies]. Yakutsk: AN.

Langford, J. 2003. Traces of folk medicine in Jaunpur. *Cultural Anthropology* 18 (3): 217–303.

Lewis, I. M. 1971. *Ecstatic Religion: An Anthropological Study of Spirit Possession and Shamanism*. New York: Penguin.

Mehl-Madrona, L. 1997. *Coyote Medicine*. New York: Scribner.

Mitskevich, S. I. 1929. *Ménérik i emiriachen'e* [*Ménérik* and sudden illness]. Leningrad: AN.

Narby, J., and F. Huxley, eds. 2001. *Shamans through Time: 500 Years on the Path to Knowledge*. New York: Putnam.

Perrone, B., H. H. Stockel, and V. Krueger. 1989. *Medicine Women, Curanderas, and Women Doctors*. Norman: University of Oklahoma Press.

Schenk, A., and C. Ratsch, eds. 1999. *What Is a Shaman? Shamans, Healers and Medicine Men from a Western Point of View*. Berlin: Verlag für Wissenschaft und Bildung.

Siikala, A., and M. Hoppál. 1992. *Studies on Shamanism*. Helsinki: Finnish Anthropological Society.

Tedlock, B. 2005. *The Woman in the Shaman's Body: Reclaiming the Feminine in Religion and Medicine*. New York: Bantam Dell.

Whitehead, N., and R. Wright, eds. 2004. *In Darkness and Secrecy: The Anthropology of Assault Sorcery and Witchcraft in Amazonia*. Durham, N.C.: Duke University Press.

Znamenski, A. 1999. *Shamanism and Christianity: Native Encounters with Russian Orthodox Missionaries in Siberia and Alaska, 1820–1917*. Westport, Conn.: Greenwood.

7

The Making of a Shaman: A Comparative Study of Inuit, African, and Nepalese Shaman Initiation

Edith L. B. Turner

According to the thinking of many societies, spiritual forces outside of ourselves exist. In our illnesses and breaks from normalcy, there then opens a space for something spiritual to "come through" to us. This is not a matter of mere belief, however; those who have had their lives transformed in this way insist they know from experience what is spiritual, owing to the work of a spirit or divine being who has taken the initiative. Their spiritual life crisis has been followed and supported by rituals, the help of a guru, or the comradeship of similar sufferers, as in Alcoholics Anonymous.

It is the character of these events, their typical episodes, their order, in which I am interested. Briefly, the spirit speaks first, commonly appealing to the person to become a healer and sometimes reaching no result at first, but then, through further strong demands—even through the person's illness—making connection. Finally, in the midst of illness or fear, comes the spiritual gift.

Compare a similar order of events as seen through the world-view of a psychologist or moralist. For example, an individual may fall into the habits of a bad lifestyle, or may commit breaches in the social order. Society tends to repudiate them, punish them, or require them to take treatment. They succumb to the pressure of society and, perhaps aided by the kindness of a psychologist, may contrive by their own efforts to suppress the bad actions. I posit that this theory of therapy flattens the process into something near-rational—however beautifully described.

In contrast, the life events of persons destined for the life of a spiritual healer or shaman may vary, but there is one distinguishable pattern that may be followed in many cultures. Healers' initiations are not planned for them by society; they are not a "social construction of society." Healers begin by "falling" into their initiations, initiations that are bestowed by spirit agencies. The novitiate healer feels the impending sense of something beyond his or her comprehension—that is, the shamanic gift-to-be—then suffers many troubles, and finally is granted a sense of opening, and with that the gift arrives. The pattern is evident, for example, in the case of the Pomo Indian woman healer Mabel McKay (Saris 1994), the Balinese woman healer Jero (Asch and Asch 1980), Roy Willis the Scottish anthropologist (Willis et al. 1999, 80), Sacin the Hindu (Samanta 1998, 37), the Inuit hunter Kehuq (E. Turner 1996, 207), Bhirendra of Nepal (Peters 1981, 79–110), Muchona of Zambia (V. Turner 1967, 131–45), in many Arabian and African stories, in stories about healers in the Western world, and in the books of the great religions, to name but a few of the people and sources.

This chapter discusses these features of shamanic initiation as evident in three major world regions: the New World Arctic, Old World Nepal, and Central Africa. Each case also tells of a central moment of wonder and realization. One may ask, why does this kind of visitation occur from without, why this fear and suffering before the gift is given? The days of suffering—a condition psychiatrists would probably term *fugue*—are quite recognizable in each case and are often diagnosed by medical authorities as episodes of mental disturbance and hallucination. But this phenomenon of suffering is rather *sparagmos*, the "break-up" of the personality in order to allow the formation of something much more powerful.[1] The suffering frees incipient shamans from the everyday world, an event which could not happen without the shamans being shaken to their depths. Then the shaman or healer has a new perception of a world of spirits where healing can happen. This experience is especially common in shamanic societies, and its details are too precise and similar in all the cases I present to be ignored. Taking the view of the experiencer, it is the spirits who have called the neophytes; they give the neophytes the faculty to see and know the spirit world. We learn from the spirits that we live in symbiosis with the spirit world, and we are beginning to understand that this spirit world is a real part of the natural world, and amenable to study by the natural historian.

Our first account of shamanic initiation approaches that initiation from two perspectives. One story describes the first hint of the shamanic faculty as experienced by an Alaskan Inuit hunter, whom I call "Kehuq," a man living at the beginning of the twentieth century. I will then give a recent example, the story of a modern Christian healer who would not call herself a shaman, but who had the same kind of experiences.

Kehuq's story is about the one-eyed ancestor spirit who gave him power. It represents a case typical of these initiations, the kind of decisive episode that can change a person and, indeed, the life of a village. His story records how he gained shamanic powers and taught these powers to his village. In my own time, in Kehuq's village in 1987, the Kehuq family kept a framed photograph of the shaman on the wall beside the dinner table in their prefabricated house. The photo shows Kehuq, a stocky man, wearing a parka with an enormous fur ruff. Looking at the photograph, you can feel the eyes in the somber face penetrating you and staring beyond you. The following narrative describes the key to the spirit-created shaman initiation. It is the story of Kehuq's flying boat and his strange vision.

The Story of Kehuq, the Inuit Hunter

When Kehuq was a young man, he was out on the tundra when he heard the sound above him like paddles dipping slowly into water. He looked up and saw a boat high in the air, circling around and around as if it were descending from the moon. Men were evidently in the boat paddling, but when it came nearer and landed on the ground in front of him, he couldn't see anyone. Soon a man stood up, Anguluk, a shaman of ancient times. He wore a fine parka and his mittens were decorated with pieces of copper. He had one big eye instead of two, with a protruding brow and the eye in the middle of it. The shaman danced and the copper ornaments on his mittens rattled, giving Kehuq pleasure. Here the vision ended. Kehuq looked about him but there was nobody to be seen. He took the trail home to his tent and on the way the event vanished from his mind.

Late that night he awoke and started up naked, about to leave the tent. His wife called, "Kehuq, come back, are you crazy?" She made him put on his clothes. The man was like a crazy person and kept wandering away. He continued crazy for four days, getting worse whenever he ate anything. After four days he began to improve.

When he recovered, Kehuq could dance. His spirit left him, and he was possessed by the strange shaman's spirit. Kehuq taught the people the shaman's songs and also taught them how to carve the shaman's face in wood. He was now gifted with shamanic powers. He taught them how to let their spirits go out from their bodies and come back in, pulling themselves back into their bodies as if they were pulling themselves backward into their underground igloos. The songs gave them power, power to heal the sick, to close up mortal wounds, to predict the future, bring animals to the hunter, change the weather, and speak with the dead. (see E. Turner 1996, 207)

This is just one of many Inuit accounts telling of a four-day "crazy" period, typically followed by a very successful hunting period, and also by healing gifts and other benefits.

The Story of Claire, the Inuit Healer

My Inuit healer-friend Claire belonged to an unspoken sisterhood of shamans (E. Turner 1996, 204–7), and experienced curious "time-out," or blanking-out, episodes. Claire, who was a Christian and a respected local healer, experienced at different stages of her life at least four gaps in ordinary consciousness that psychologists in our culture would diagnose as fugue or even psychosis—but these episodes did not derive from psychosis. They were irruptions of shamanic powers just as the ancient Inuit knew such irruptions, typically lasting four days. They involve meeting with something fearful, such as the spirit of a dead or dangerous animal, after which this entity, having first afflicted the budding shaman, then changes and becomes the shaman's helper.

Claire's first recorded chaotic state should not be given a psychological label, however, because we cannot regard it as an illness described by the *Diagnostic and Statistical Manual of Mental Disorders: DSM-IV* (American Psychiatric Association 1994). It appears that in 1970 Claire was in Anchorage in an expensive hotel, alone for four days, for reasons unknown. There she had some kind of transformation. A person who did not know Claire's powers would think she was crazy. Her condition was characterized by *glossolalia*, the phenomenon of "speaking in tongues."

That was one episode. Then in 1984, when Claire was not doing much healing, she had another visitation, a very disturbing one. Claire began to continually see a devil figure in her peripheral vision. In the negative phase of this episode, Claire uttered a torrent of nonsense words that nobody could understand. It was glossolalia again. This greatly upset her relatives. Claire told them irritably, "Don't be like that, you don't think I'm anything, do you? I can't help it, it comes to me." But at the end of the episode's four-day period Claire was able to pray again to Jesus, and afterward her healing power was stronger than before, as it was after each of these events. Jesus, of course, is the obverse of the devil, and if he were Clarie's helper spirit he would then be her guide in healing. This switch from dangerous to helpful is one that often manifests itself in spirits in precontact days.

Claire went through another encounter with her trouble, whatever it was—maybe the devil again. On Thursday January 14, 1988, I found her lying on her couch, very depressed. She had her eyes shut, and she blurted out words critical of her family and others. I was frightened. Was she angry with me? I put down beside her some ripe pears I had brought for her, and left. Four days later she was herself again. What I had seen had all the hallmarks of a shamanic episode.

During a visit I made in 1991, yet another repeat of this state seemed to occur. I heard that Claire had returned from the hospital where she had been a patient from May 28 to June 2. I went to her house with a gift. When she saw me she turned convulsively and flung herself into my arms. We were crying. I stroked her wild gray hair and haggard face. When we recovered she told me the doctor at the hospital had given her the wrong medicine. She was really mad at him. "I'll get an attorney," she said. Now she was off all medicine and feeling better by the minute. I wondered what ailment the doctor thought he had prescribed the medicine for.

Such is the way a shaman is made. The vision, the four-day crazy period, and the coming of the shaman's powers appear in all the stories of the creation of Inuit shamans. This is also the general pattern of the other shamanic initiations I describe here, though these are from altogether different societies. All three initiations, Inuit, African, and Nepalese, happen to the chosen person at the will of a spirit and are preceded by something like a near-death experience or a frightening depression. The three shamans who undergo these initiations learn that they must never renege on their craft, must never refuse to heal, must cause no harm by their power, and must not attribute the power to themselves. This is the shaman ethic, and it is commonly found wherever Shamanism exists.

In the journey I have made through the experiences of healers, I have encountered various understandings, not only of spirits but of the human soul. Among the Lungu of north-eastern Zambia, for example, *ngulu* spirits struggle with their human host so that their host will allow them to appear (Willis et al. 1999, 95), and for this reason there is blackness at first. Both Kehuq and Claire experienced similar cruel episodes outside of normalcy, without realizing there would be a gift at the end of it. Such episodes are a matter of the deepest being, a matter of that "thing" beyond value, the soul. These episodes fragment a person's ordinary existence, and afterward there follows the entry of a beneficent spirit of overwhelming power, causing shock and blackness at first—as with Saul (later Paul) on his horse (Acts 9:1–6).

The soul exists in reality, a sensitive living entity. When the breakthrough occurs, the heart fires up, the lungs suddenly spread wide with a kind of recognition—with a gasp, like the lungs of a newborn baby. The very pores quiver in goose bumps. It is one's consciousness that is changed, for it is set at-large, "with no fixed boundaries . . . There was a permeability and flexibility between self and other, an infinite flexibility," as the anthropologist Willis described it when he shared the change of consciousness with the Lungu of Zambia (1999, 103). This soul is not in our own hands. It does not operate by the laws of ordinary consciousness.

My next account of shamanic initiation, also full of similarities to the previous ones, is set in Nepal some six thousand miles away from northern Alaska, among stone huts straddling the mountain slopes of the Himalayas. The religion here is Shamanism and Animism, with a trace of Buddhism. In 1976 anthropologist Larry Peters was working in Nepal when he encountered the shaman Bhirendra. Bhirendra told Larry the story of how he became a shaman. The episodes of initiation Bhirendra described proceed in almost exactly the same manner as in the stories above: affliction, followed by benefits.

The Story of Bhirendra of Nepal: "How I Became a Shaman"

When I was thirteen, something came over me. I started shaking violently without knowing why. I couldn't stay still for a minute even when I wasn't trembling. My grandfather was making me mad through possession, and I ran off into the forest, naked, for three days. I found myself where three rivers cross, in the cemetery. The cemetery was terrifying. Out came a horde of demons with long crooked fangs, and others with no heads at all and eyes in the middle of their chests. Some of them carried death flags, and still others brought decaying corpses along with them. I ran. They chased me and leapt on me and started eating me. This was the end.

"Help, help!" I cried. "Help me, gods, I'm only a boy!"

I drew out my dagger to defend myself, but I dropped it. It fell on a rock and out came a long spark. Immediately everything changed. It was daytime and I was alive. The demons were gone.

When I got home I told my parents everything. They said, "Your grandfather saved you. It was his dagger that saved your life. You have to know that your grandfather went off to Tibet nine years ago and never returned."

My father said, "You're going to need a guru to train you in Shamanism." My shaman uncle started to teach me: rituals, prayers, everything. My good grandfather's spirit, the one who made me mad in the first place and who protected me, was with me all the time, inside of me, teaching me.

I had no choice in being a shaman. I was chosen. If I refused, I'd have gone completely mad and committed suicide. I'd never have been able to stop shaking. I was cured by becoming a shaman.

I learned to do healing. I learned the ritual to open the top of my head and let my spirit go out on a journey accompanied by my protecting spirit, in order to seek lost souls separated from their bodies.

The last stage was a ritual of vision in the cemetery, a climb to the highest heavens. For this the people went to the cemetery and erected a temporary shelter on stilts and decorated it with white soul flowers. For six days I played my drum alone, fasting. On the seventh day I saw myself walking into a beautiful garden with flowers of many colors. I saw a very tall building that reached up into the sky. It had a golden staircase of nine steps leading to the top. I climbed the nine steps and saw at the top Ghesar Gyalpo himself, the supreme god of the shamans, sitting on a white throne covered with soul flowers. He was dressed in white and his face was all white. He had long hair and a white crown. He gave me milk to drink and told me I would attain much power, *shakti*, to be used for the good of my people.

I left the sanctuary and returned to the village. The people and my guru were on the way out to meet me, and cheering they carried me back.

It's hard to explain this experience to you. It—it makes me cry. It was the most significant experience of my life, and from then on, my entire life changed. (paraphrased from Peters [1981, 79–110 passim])

The story shows precisely the same days of confusion and wild action as the "craziness" of Kehuq, even the scenes of running off naked, the not eating, the presence of an ancestor spirit who makes the first call and who is later felt to be inside the shaman teaching him, and the drumming. Here in addition is a ladder to heaven, a connection like the Iñupiat boat in the sky, the tunnel in a near-death experience, or, as in the story of Jacob's ladder (Gen. 28:11–19), the radiant path to the light. A curious similarity can be noted between Kehuq's vision of the shaman with one eye in the middle of his brow and Bhirendra's vision of demons with eyes in the middle of their chests. Another similarity is in the matter of the soul entering and exiting the body: with Kehuq, it is the way you let yourself down backwards into your igloo, and with Bhirendra, it is through the top of the head before going on a shaman journey.

Shamans are thus given the gift of healing through spirits, and their miracle medicine is beneficent power. Their call is to take up a different mode of being in the world, a mode taught them by the spirits and sometimes called the "shamanic state of consciousness." In this state, experienced shamans are able to release their souls from their bodies and to "fly out" to the place where the soul of a sick person is wandering, lost.

My final story of the initiation of a healing shaman describes how a Ndembu medicine man, Muchona, was caught up in the spirit's purpose. The Ndembu are a forest people of northwestern Zambia. This story tells of Muchona's first initiation into the work of spirit healing. His vocation as a spirit healer started with an affliction caused by the spirit of his dead mother, who herself had had illnesses and whose spirit, after her death, wanted Muchona to become a healer. This spirit attack and its cure began Muchona's career as a medicine man.

Muchona of Zambia Tells the Story of His Vocation

I kept getting ill. I was caught by a very heavy sickness in the body, and I found it hard to breathe. It was like being pricked by needles in my chest, and sometimes my chest felt as though it was blown up by a bicycle pump. I could only mutter, "*Boyi, boyi.*" My ears felt completely blocked up. I was like a drunken person and kept slipping to the ground in a fit. Then I kept dreaming of two of my mother's brothers and of my father. And I dreamed of my mother. My relatives went to a diviner to see what was wrong. When the diviner tossed the objects in his basket, the seed of the palm tree came up on top of the objects in the basket. This is the tree used for palm wine.

The diviner said, "That means you're suffering from the sickness of Kayong'u. It's the sickness that comes before the call to be a doctor and diviner. Those four spirits in your dreams have come out of the grave to catch you and enter you, because they want you to become a diviner and treat people's illnesses. I can't make out who that fourth spirit is, the image is too weak." It was the shadow of my mother.

So, I realized that four spirits were determined to make me take on this difficult job. And it's a dangerous one! I could tell the divination was true: it was my destiny to take this course; the spirits wanted it. The drum ritual for making a doctor began. All night long the elder doctors washed me with medicine. I kept shuddering convulsively to the Kayong'u drum rhythm; the spirits were doing whatever they liked with me. Every time I shuddered it was like being drunk or epileptic, as if I was suddenly struck in the liver by lightning or beaten with a hoe-handle and stopped up.

Early in the morning while it was still dark the doctors seated me before a new ritual fire of green wood. When it began to be light, the old doctor who was in charge, a hunter-diviner, came up to me holding a red rooster by its legs, wings, and at the top of its head. The rooster, who crows in the morning, was there to end my sleep, to wake me up. The Kayong'u spirit also wakes up people it has caught. It makes them breathe hoarsely, like a rooster or a goat. The same thing happens when an initiated diviner is about to shake the basket full of divining objects: the person's voice changes and the person doesn't use the Lunda language anymore, but speaks hoarsely in another tongue. Diviners sometimes make a deep wheezing noise in the course of ordinary conversation. I can't help doing it myself when I talk. It's the voice of the Kayong'u spirit inside me.

Faced with the rooster I saw its color was red, the color of the shedding of blood. My mother used it in her women's rituals. It came to me. Blood!

I sprang forward in a sudden spasm, in a trance. My teeth snapped, and the rooster's head lay apart from its body. What had I done? I had beheaded it. I seemed crazy. Blood was pouring out of the head, so I took it up as it bled and beat it on my heart to quiet my mind. Then the big doctor ordered a goat to be beheaded. Its blood poured out on the ground—and the blood was also for the spirit in me. I lapped it up where it puddled.

They took the rooster's head and put it on a pole made from the tree of the ancestor's tears. My dead rooster was up there in contact with the ancestors, with the spirits. All was opened, now that the rooster was killed. The openings of my body that had been stopped up, my nostrils, ears, and eyes, were released and became supersensitive. From the killed animal I obtained wakefulness and sharpened senses, necessary for a diviner who needs to seek out hidden things.

Now the sun was rising. The doctors kept me quietly waiting while they went on some strange business in the bush. This is what they were doing: the old doctor took a hoe, a cupful of the goat's blood, the hearts of the rooster and goat, and a collection of special sharp objects. The old doctor led a procession of men and women doctors out of the village into the bush. Soon the path forked. Usually people make a choice which fork to take because they know the way, but these people were diviners. They didn't take either of the forks but went straight on into wild bush. They were seeking a certain path to a secret place. They knew more than other people; they had secret knowledge. That's how they found a *kapwipu* tree, a hard wood, a sign of misfortune to begin with followed by success. They hunkered down and prayed to the spirits who were burdening me, then started to hoe up a mound of earth at the foot of the tree in the shape of a crocodile, with legs and a tail. Next they took the hearts of the rooster and goat and used some of the special sharp objects, a needle and razor, to prick the hearts. The pricking was the pain that sick people feel before they're healed. Now that the hearts were pricked, the sick person wouldn't feel it again because it was already done. They hid all these objects, including a knife, a bracelet, and a string of beads, in various places under the soil of the crocodile mound. Then they brought the drums and beat out the Kayong'u drum rhythm. They were ready.

They came for me. They led me to the crocodile in the bush and seated me on its neck.

"Okay," said the old doctor. "What have you come here for, eh? Speak up."

"To look for divination," I said. "To be healed. To be a healer. I'm looking for my spirit."

"Now, divine! Find the objects."

A great power came upon me. My hands went out over the mound and a fierce pricking entered my fingers. My fingers plunged in, pushed by the spirit, and in a flash I found everything except the needle, and I snatched up the needle an instant later. I could divine. Now, whenever I work at divining, the sense of that pricking returns. It's the thing that tells the diviner how to scan the objects tossed in the basket and see the cause of the client's illness or bad luck, or see whether someone's death was brought about by a witch or sorcerer. The diviner will gain the sharpness of the needle and the cutting power of the knife and of the sharp teeth of a human or crocodile. The diviner goes straight to the point in hidden matters. He sees the right ritual to use by shaking the basket, and his fingers see by the sharpness of the needle. The divining objects and sharpness help one another.

Because I found all the objects the doctors praised me and the women trilled aloud. I was extraordinarily happy. We danced home. I was cured of my illness, which had completely disappeared, and I was protected. The very spirit that had made me sick cured me and immediately entered my body to aid me in making correct decisions. As the saying goes: Making a new healer starts by the healer getting sick. *Kutachika wakata.*

Shortly after the ritual I sought out an experienced diviner and apprenticed myself to him. Now I could learn the difficult craft operations and interpretations needed for the profession. I learned all the herbs; I even learned how to cure a woman who was suffering from delusions as a result of puerperal fever. For that cure I had to venture alone into the graveyard, full of ghosts and far from the firelight. Only there could I exorcize the agencies of evil at work on the poor woman, making her writhe and babble nonsense. I had to subdue my fear to my curative vocation. (paraphrased from V. Turner [1967, 131–45])

Here are the same themes of sickness, falling in a fit as if drunk, an ancestor spirit's intention that the chosen person become a diviner, the moment of opening up, and the shamanic gifts: healing, second sight, and happiness. All these healers-to-be know the dream-like state, the falling (or falling into forgetfulness), and in the case of the last two, Bhirendra and Muchona, the sense of being beaten and tormented. Muchona's voice becomes "different" after his experience; his life too changes. These healers knew happiness and helped their people, and we note how the teaching of the power enters all of their stories. The basic features of spontaneous spirit initiation are all here, in these initiations in Arctic America, Nepal, and Africa. The similarities of these stories from cultures so distant from each other are obvious, and the significance of this cannot be denied. One has to accept that humans anywhere may go through the same processes, and that the processes are spiritual ones. It dawns on us that this tendency toward religion is inborn, an endowment, a biological predisposition, existing for the purpose of just such a communication with spirits, and that perhaps the only common human process to which it can be compared is childbirth, a biological event. The practice of religious healing is the most generally beneficent activity in which anyone can engage, for it is a matter of full consciousness and the expansion of being.

Conclusion

This chapter is not written from the point of view of regular anthropology—which itself is in need of expanding its field of study and correcting what is now termed its "cognocentrism"—nor does it follow the complex philosophy that plumbs the mystery of the individual, a separate, solitary being who is likely to create his or her own imaginary life. What it does do is present facts about the mystery of human permeability. Humans are permeated by each other and by spirits. Willis among the Lungu of northern Zambia made a bridge to this discovery when he experienced *communitas*, the prime, natural, unstructured social sense (1999, 117–19). This may be the same sense felt among the Pentecostals and in many sacred communities. The Iñupiat tribe, in order to survive in their fearsome land, needed a battery of power from their ancestors. They surely needed to know how to switch it on more than they would need to know in later years how to switch on the furnace in their prefabricated houses.

Peters (1981) documented how the good grandfather of Bhirendra, the man who had been a shaman, came back from his grave in Tibet. Yet a dead shaman is not truly a dead shaman, but rather a shaman all the more powerful over time and space. In the case of Bhirendra's grandfather, it was a matter of the passing of ten years and of a distance of a thousand miles. So Bhirendra was to learn. The spirit of his grandfather entered into his body and rooted itself there, in all benevolence, giving the young shaman its own powers to overcome the illnesses and fears of his patients and to point them to the beauty of the healing that came from the heavenly throne of Bhirendra's vision.

My old friend Muchona is dead, and his son now stands as elder in the Christian Fellowship church—a church related to the Apostles of Maranke, the Assemblies of God, and the Pentecostals. There Muchona the younger gives healing through the Holy Spirit, and the brethren also fall in the spirit and remember nothing.

So the threads weave back and forth. Muchona still lives. The Pentecostals draw down the power. Healers throughout America—little by little—learn the power. That peculiar language of the spiritual world is heard. Healers of different persuasions stare at each other in conferences, suddenly recognizing they are talking about the same thing, something very hard to put into words. The hands of the healers can feel it. Is the spirit pricking? Truthful accounts from all over the world—accounts of actual experiences—do succeed in saying it, just as William James found when he took on a similar task in assembling *The Varieties of Religious Experience* (1958/1902). He let the spirit flow in his words describing the many religious conversions. He did not adopt a cold objective style, and his book has never been equaled.

As for talking about what spirits are, I have found this cannot be done without "listening," without a kind of prayer or an "invocation" to the spirits, as it is grandly called. But it's more like pleading, "C'mon, give, give. *Please.*" Could people—*possibly*—know what spirits are? One gets the sense that the drive to analyze according to ordinary comprehension has never and will never learn the language of such matters. But through stories, for some reason, one can understand. This is a very serious business, this matter of stories. One asks, why does the inquiry work through stories? It is because of human permeability, because other people's experience may become actually "one's own." One sees *through* such a story—as Victor Turner said of the spontaneous social drama—right into the experience of the person who experienced it and it becomes one's own, "whole cloth." Stories touch on a very spiritual matter, they slip under one's skin, so to speak, they cause one spirit to slide into another in the same way that healing works, by the coming-into-concrete-reality of sympathy—*sym-pathy*, which has the literal meaning "feeling with."

This very sympathy is needed in order to grasp the idea that humans are contacting other entities and are in active relationship with them, and that there is a spiritual world "out there" that has its own patterns and its own ways of acting. In our stories about spirits, that world appears to be not so hard to describe, because the spirits come visually, unlike energy or power, which are not visually experienced. People experience possession by spirits, incorporation by them. All this makes the psyche look much simpler than what many of today's psychologists and psychiatrists have concluded when they say that spirits are a condition of the mind. Furthermore, up comes in 3-D an understanding of the soul, very much a spirit, wedded deep to the human body and spreading in an aura outside, creating it, the permeable organ itself, and everything that *shakti*, or power, says it is, and what Jacob Levy Moreno says it is, and just as Lévi-Bruhl put it, even Jung: it is the unlimited psyche, connected with everything else in mystical participation.

The theory, then, is that *there is a soul*, and that the work of examining it will add to the knowledge of humanity—which is anthropology. This prime claim, the existence of the soul, is accepted by the mass of humanity. But it is philosophically unhealthy for scholars who have no sense of the soul—because they have been trained otherwise—to describe healing in reductive language (as if we took our food in the form of carbon, nitrogen, and calcium atoms). Furthermore, the principle of human rights is involved. All societies have a right to the knowledge of the spiritual experiences of their sister-societies, each story set out with respect and honor, and dealt with in accordance to the people's own accounts.

Note

1. *Sparagmos* once meant the tearing to pieces of a live victim in a Dionysian orgy. Mircea Eliade describes this tearing apart in the making of a shaman (1972, 43–45).

References

American Psychiatric Association. 1994. *Diagnostic and Statistical Manual of Mental Disorders: DSM-IV.* 4th ed. Washington, D.C.: American Psychiatric Association.

Asch, T., and P. Asch. 1980. *Jero on Jero* (film). Ipswich, U.K.: Royal Anthropological Institute Video Library.

Eliade, M. 1972. *Shamanism: Archaic Techniques of Ecstasy.* Princeton, N.J.: Princeton University Press.

James, W. 1902. *The Varieties of Religious Experience: A Study in Human Nature.* New York: Mentor, 1958.

Peters, L. 1981. Ecstasy and healing in Nepal: An ethnopsychiatric study of Tamany shamanism. *Other Realities* 4:37–54.

Samanta, S. 1998. The powers of the guru: Sakti, "mind," and miracle in narratives of Bengali religious experience. *Anthropology and Humanism* 23 (1): 30–50.

Saris, G. 1994. *Mabel McKay: Weaving the Dream.* Berkeley: University of California Press.

Turner, E. 1996. The Hands Feel It: Healing and Spirit Presence among a Northern Alaskan People. DeKalb: Northern Illinois University Press.

Turner, V. 1967. *The Forest of Symbols: Aspects of Ndembu Ritual.* Ithaca, N.Y.: Cornell University Press.

Willis, R., with K. B. S. Chisanga, H. M. K Sikazwe, K. B. Sikazwe, and S. Nanyangwe. 1999. *Some Spirits Heal, Others Only Dance: A Journey into Human Selfhood in an African Village.* Oxford: Berg.

PART III

SPIRITUAL TRANSFORMATION AND HEALING FROM RELIGIOUS PERSPECTIVES

8

Spiritual Transformation and Healing: An Encounter with the Sacred

Philip Hefner

Spiritual transformation and healing pose a great challenge for our research and interpretation—in both science and religion. Understanding spiritual transformation and healing at the depth that is required will elude us unless we properly acknowledge this challenge and respond to it with sophistication. The challenge arises in large part because our study and reflection inevitably encounter the dimension of the sacred, or the holy. Kenneth Pargament appropriately reminds us of this fact in chapter 2. He speaks of the limitations of social-scientific methods in the face of the sacred. Since these methods are also at work (whether explicitly or implicitly) in religion's approach to the sacred, his admonition applies in that domain as well. In this chapter, I elaborate my understanding of the sacred and its significance for spiritual transformation and healing, and I insist that neither science nor religion can be comfortable with these methodological limitations. If we are to claim adequacy for our explorations of these phenomena, we must imagine methodologies more adequate than those we presently have at our disposal. Fashioning such methodologies is not only essential, but is also an exciting frontier for us as we explore this area of human experience.

New Testament Usage:
The Double Entendre of Healing

A study of the Christian scriptures points to the sacred element in spiritual transformation and healing. Three terms are important for interpreting the texts in the Christian New Testament that are most relevant to our theme. The terms (from the Greek) are *hiamoai*, "heal or cure"; *therapeuo*, "serve or care for"; and *sothesomai*, "make whole." These terms all share the character of the double entendre, that is, they refer to curing, caring, and wholeness as purely physical but also at the same time spiritually transcendent. The point I wish to make in noting this phenomenon in the New Testament is that this same polysemic character of language pervades all Christian language about health and healing down to the present time. I provide an example for each term.

Hiamoai, heal or cure. Matthew 8:8 uses this term in the story of a centurion asking Jesus to heal his favorite servant. The centurion says, "Only speak the word, and my servant will be healed."[1] This is purely physical healing. Matthew 13:15 places the term in a traditional maxim in which Jesus says that even though the "people's heart has grown dull and their ears hard of hearing . . . I would heal them." This is clearly spiritual healing at the hand of God, in a situation that indicates no physical ailment at all.

Therapeuo, serve or care for. Luke 9:11 speaks of the crowds that followed Jesus at Bethesda: Jesus spoke to them, and "healed those who needed to be cared for"—this is purely physical. The same author, in Acts 17:24–25, reports that St. Paul preached that God "does not live in shrines made by human hands, nor is he served by human hands." The word translated here as "served" is the Greek *therapeuo*, from which we derive the word *therapy*, but here used in a spiritual sense to apply to one's relationship to God.

Sothesomai, make whole. A cognate of this verb is the noun for "savior." Matthew 9:31 tells the story of a woman "who had been suffering from hemorrhages for twelve years [and who] came up behind him and touched the fringe of his cloak. . . . Jesus turned, and seeing her he said, 'Take heart daughter; your faith has made you whole.' And instantly the woman was made whole." This is a physical healing of a designated ailment. Matthew 16:25, however, contains Jesus's teaching "For those who want to save their life will lose it, and those who lose their life for my sake will find it." The phrase "save their life" contains the Greek word in question, and here it has a transcendent, spiritual meaning.

The Double Entendre of Healing in Sacrament and Belief

What I call the double entendre of the physical and the transcendent occurs not only in the sacred texts, but also in Christian practice and belief. Two useful examples are the sacramental view of healing and belief in eternal life, or life after death.

Healing as sacrament. A sacramental perspective holds that material objects and processes signify transcendent realities. This applies to health and healing in that a Christian outlook holds that health and healing are part of God's action in the world and that they prefigure the final human condition. God wills healing, and the final outcome of our history will be eternal health and healing. The sacramental prefiguring is, of course, fragmentary. But, even though healing does not always result from our human efforts, and even though all physical healing is something of a short-term proposition, Christians nevertheless believe that health is an image of what God intends for us and of what we will finally enjoy. Consequently, the healing arts and practices also carry the double entendre character of the Christian vocabulary. Healthcare professionals are not the only actors in the healing process; God is also at work in ways that we cannot exhaustively measure or understand. As I will note, this sacramental perspective is important for understanding the role of empathy in healing.

Belief in eternal life. Belief in the hereafter, as it is commonly expressed, is one of the most enduring and widespread elements of Christian faith. Although secularizing trends have displaced this belief among many Christians, on this point the formal public stance of the churches is reinforced by popular belief and practice. This belief is also held by orthodox Jews and Muslims.

Belief in eternal life is important to our consideration of healing for at least two reasons. First of all, in an ironic sense, it introduces a realism into our thinking about curing and healing. Curing simply does not happen in much of the healthcare process because illnesses are often incurable or chronic. As we observe friends and relatives succumbing to cancer or other lethal diseases, or as we read about SARS (severe acute respiratory syndrome) and other diseases, we know deep-down that human life is fragile, that it hangs by a thread; death is fearful. All curing is provisional, at best enduring to the day of our death. Belief in life after death provides a way of dealing with this fragility and uncertainty. It is a way of reminding us that death is never far away. As I discuss below, this belief is a response to the sacred and relativizes the healthcare process by placing it in a larger context. This relativizing impact can be noted in a contemporary Christian denominational statement, "Caring for Health: Our Shared Endeavor":

> Health is a blessing from God. It is good and proper that we attend to our health and healing; however, we show sin's power when we become unduly absorbed in our own selves and make health an idol by denying our own mortality. The temptation to make health our god may show itself in excessive preoccupation with physical appearance and a denial of aging or the inevitability of death. It may also lead us to demand unlimited resources or services that go beyond responsible stewardship of good health. . . . Health is good for its own sake; it is also good for living abundantly in relationship with God and in loving service to our neighbor in the vocations to which God has called us. (Evangelical Lutheran Church in America 2003)

This statement relativizes health by placing it in the context of a purposeful life in vocations. It also relates those vocations to the will of God. Since a life spent in God-given vocations bestows eternal value on human life and work, this perspective flows naturally into beliefs about eternal life. The sacramental nuance reinforces this set of ideas. Sacramental actions are not viewed primarily in the terms of their literal empiricism, but rather as symbolic actions that prefigure the transcendent. All healing activity, whether it results in immediate cure or not, can be viewed in this way—its character as prefigurement is as significant as its immediate success or failure. When healthcare professionals care for and attempt to heal sick people, their action is viewed sacramentally as a respect for the eternal worth of the patient.

The point to be made from these examples is that this double layer of meaning, referring to the physical and the transcendently spiritual, is intrinsic to the Christian vocabulary. Further study, which cannot be undertaken here, will reveal that Christian language is not unique in this respect.

Spirit and Spiritual: The Importance of Mihaly Csikszentmihalyi

The double-layered character of meaning is also inherent in both the words and the ideas contained in the basic vocabulary of our theme: the words *spirit* and *spiritual*. This is exemplified even in literary history. When translating the Hebrew scriptures into Greek (250–130 BCE), scholars chose to render the Hebrew *ruach* with the Greek *pneuma* (Isaacs 1976, 69ff.). *Ruach* is the word for both "wind" and the "spirit" of God; it figures in Genesis 1:1 as the agency of the world's creation. *Spirit* refers in the ancient Hebrew, Jewish, and Christian traditions to the creative power and presence of God in the world, accomplishing his divine purpose (Jacob 1958, 365). The double-layered character of the Hebrew word is reinforced in the Greek, since *pneuma* is a relentlessly material term, referring to breathing. It was a common word in medical texts (Schweizer 1961, 30–45), since a person's pneuma could be a cause of a disease or its healing, and the absence of pneuma was considered a sign of death. (The "mirror test," holding a mirror to a person's mouth to check for the absence of breath, was once a criterion for judging that person to be dead.)

In my opinion, a most useful discussion of spirit and spiritual is that of psychologist Mihaly Csikszentmihalyi, who reflects that it is not possible to live adequately only with descriptions and explanations of what is empirically discernible. We also require visions of what the empirical present can become, what its possibilities are. When we envision these possibilities, we are in the domain of spirituality. Csikszentmihalyi writes, "Spiritual values, spiritual ideas, symbols, beliefs, and instructions for action . . .

point to possibilities to which our biological inheritance is not yet sensitive. The sensate deals with what *is*, the spiritual deals with what *could be*" (1991, 17–18). Spirituality is the focus in our stories and in our myths on *something more* that goes beyond the here and now and tells us what the here and now can become. The spiritual does not contradict the material world, and it is not necessarily another, supernatural world. The spiritual offers a vision of a world whose truth is not empirically necessitated, but without which the material world has no meaning or vision for us. Csikszentmihalyi goes on to write,

> The realm of the sacred contains memes that refer to things we intuitively believe to be important but do not understand, and instructions about how we should behave with reference to them. But for spirituality to exist, it is essential that material values should not have jurisdiction over what is sacred. (19)

The spiritual refers to the way in which our *consciousness is organized* (another of Csikszentmihalyi's ideas), so as to enable us to put our knowledge and experience of the world together in coherent ways that support values, viable lifestyles, and moral behavior. Spirituality refers to the organization of our consciousness that makes richness of life possible, for individuals and communities.

The challenge to reason is the challenge to understand the world rationally, to comprehend its causal relations. The challenge to spirituality is to understand what the world can become. This is not the same as predicting the future by methods of extrapolation from the past and present. Rather it is a matter of attending to the possibilities of the present and imagining what they are capable of becoming.

A word is in order about the work of Mihaly Csikszentmihalyi. His work is important for the way in which it deals with the methodological challenges that form a major theme of this chapter. Csikszentmihalyi has been able to frame the concept of spirituality in ways that acknowledge the integrity of the transcendent element of the double entendre that I speak of, and he integrates it into his approach. At the same time, his framing of the concept renders it fully suitable for empirical research and theory formation based on that research (1991; 1993, 238–51; 1996, 315–16). Csikszentmihalyi is an important guide for how research into spiritual transformation and healing should advance.

A Surplus of Meaning, Overbelief, and a Challenge to Methodology

From a scientific point of view, the double-layered character or double entendre quality that is exemplified in the biblical passages above and in the sacrament of healing will appear to be *a surplus of belief and meaning*. This surplus of belief may be frustrating to the scientific perspective, and it may also be subject to reductionist interpretation, a reductionism that I define as those methods that break down a phenomenon or process into its component parts and functions (Raman 2005, 2). This frustration is understandable, and reductionist interpretations are to be respected for the valuable insights they often provide. However, we must also acknowledge that this *overbelief*, to use William James's terminology (1902, 485–519), will not be dissipated by scientific method or interpretation. The overbelief will remain both an important element and a surd. For example, belief in eternal life and in God's transcendent love is utterly intrinsic to the process of healing for many people, even though, as such, these elements of belief are indigestible to scientific scrutiny. I suggest that this indigestible character makes our theme all the more interesting. We must find ways to factor it into any credible study of spiritual transformation and healing. At the same time, reductionist interpretations can throw light on the processes and function of this overbelief for the persons involved. Consequently, we must develop methodologies that maintain the integrity of the overbelief and the surplus of meaning it entails, and at the same time take seriously the partial meanings provided by reductionist interpretations. I go so far as to say that this emerging field we are observing, the field of science and spiritual transformation, will be recognized as a mature field only when it can demonstrate this bifocal methodology that integrates materialist functional interpretations with the phenomenological presentations of overbelief.

The Sacred and the Profane: Two Tectonic Plates

This double-layered meaning or overbelief is an indicator that spiritual transformation and healing are an encounter with the sacred in our experience. It is appropriate that Pargament defines spirituality as "a search for the sacred" and describes spiritual transformation as "a fundamental change in the place of the sacred or the character of the sacred in the life of the individual" (see chap. 2). The sacred, or the holy, and the profane point to a basic divide in human experience between two faces we perceive in reality: the rough, unpredictable, uncontrollable face, not only uncomfortable but inspiring terror and dread; and that which is comfortable, manageable, and replicable. Akin to the classical Apollonian and Dionysian dichotomy, these two faces may be seen as powerful experiential tectonic plates that grind against each other. This grinding exposes us to a bottomless chasm out of which raw power surges over us, with apparently little regard for right and wrong, individual worth, or past accomplishment.

Rudolf Otto's *The Idea of the Holy* is a basic book on the sacred; it was informed by his lifetime of engaging the world's religions (1923/1917). Otto's subtitle is "An Inquiry into the Non-Rational Factor in the Idea of the Divine and Its Relation to the Rational." For Otto, the holy represents the "non-rational" or "supra-rational" aspect of religion, which we experience in two ways: first, it shakes us to the very core of our being—he called this the *mysterium tremendum*—and second, it exerts an irresistible fascination upon us. He summed this up in a term he himself coined, *numinous* (from the Latin *numen*, meaning "god," "spirit," or "divine"); for experience of the sacred, according to Otto, is experience of the numinous. It includes the element of what he called "creature-feeling," in which we are aware of our smallness and are overwhelmed by reality. It also includes "awefulness," [*sic*] "overpoweringness," and "energy" or "urgency" (5–40).

Forty years later, Mircea Eliade wrote an equally significant book, *The Sacred and the Profane: The Nature of Religion* (1959). Eliade emphasizes that the sacred embraces both the rational and nonrational. The sacred presents the paradox that its concrete manifestations become *sacred "otherness"* (as in Otto) and yet never cease to be the *concrete forms* that they are. A sacred stone never ceases to be a stone, even though it is a transcendent reality for the person who experiences it as sacred (Eliade 1959, 11–12). Spiritual transformation and healing never cease to be the psychological and physical processes that they are, while at the same time they transcend these processes. Precisely because spiritual transformation and healing are fully concrete, empirical processes, they are available to science for study and interpretation, as well as to religion in its practices of spiritual formation and healing. At the same time, because these same empirical processes may be bearers of sacredness and cosmic otherness for the persons involved, neither science nor religion can take their measure.

Much of our lives is spent devising strategies for taming the uncontrollable elements of our experience. Like Moses confronting the burning bush or the threatening face of God at Sinai, we try to distance ourselves from these elements; when we call them "holy" or "sacred," we declare them set apart, or "off-limits," and surround them with taboos. At the same time we pay our respects to these elements, to the sacred, even to the point of worshipping the sacred, mostly from a safe distance. Or we engage in denial, pretending that if we do not acknowledge the reality of the sacred, it will not touch us. This tension between the unmanageable and our attempts to tame it is inevitable and inescapable. It must be integrated into our ways of knowing.

The relationship between science and the sacred challenges our understanding in important ways. Kenneth Pargament writes in chapter 2,

> It is important to stress that the reality of the sacred cannot be determined from a social-scientific perspective. We have no tools to measure God, nor can we assess the authenticity of miraculous healings. However, we can study perceptions of sacredness and their implications for people's lives. In fact, there is growing evidence that people who see the world through a sacred lens experience life quite differently than do their more secular counterparts.

The question then arises whether scientific study of spiritual transformation and healing turns the limitation of which Pargament speaks to a search for an enhanced method or whether the limitation becomes itself a strategy of denial, an attempt to tame the untamable in our experience.

When we speak of spiritual transformation and healing we are asserting that uncontrollable power has entered our lives and changed us—in other words, that the grinding of the tectonic plates is at work in our individual experience. This change is not uniform, and it can take many shapes. We may say that a life-threatening illness has been cured, or that an addiction that was driving us to destruction has been tamed, or that the fundamental goals and values of our lives have been changed, or that we have been converted from one way of life, perhaps a religion, to another. Or, we may describe the change as our coming to terms with our incurable condition, our mortality.

Strategies of Response to Spiritual Transformation and Healing

Both science and religion are concerned with spiritual transformation and healing, but in different ways. Both want to see it happen. In fact, transformation is the centerpiece of every religion that I am familiar with (Hefner 2002, 177–96). Society employs scientific knowledge to bring about the transformations it considers to be most important—for example, in medical healing, addiction control, mental illness, and education. Religion also devotes itself to bringing about transformation; its traditions are vast repositories of interpretations, procedures, routines, and rituals for overcoming obstacles to transformation. If we recall the two faces of Apollo and Dionysius, the controllable and the uncontrollable, it appears that both science and religion may devote themselves to taming that which stands in the way of transformation. Both seek knowledge, describe phenomena, look for causes, and devise responses.

Religion, however, in contrast to science, is born in the experience of the holy, or sacred. Every religion and every basic religious practice or ritual is a response to some primordial experience of the holy. As a result, while both religion and science try to understand what obstructs transformation and what responses can enable it, religion is also focused on the originating abyss of transformation—the mysterium that shakes us and fascinates us. Religion bears witness—incessantly and with a sense of accountability—to the vulnerability and fragility of the transformational experience, the uncertainty and unpredictability of that experience. Religion takes account of our fear of death even in the midst of our hoping for healing and, ironically, religion knows full well how that fear makes us turn away from the demands of our mortality and follow instead the allure of superficial substitutes for transformation and healing.

Consequently, religion adopts three different strategies vis-à-vis spiritual transformation and healing. I have already mentioned the first strategy (and it is the subject of the other discussions in this chapter): cultivating transformation and healing, preserving older methods and rituals that serve transformation and healing, and developing new ones. Science may on occasion share this strategy, albeit with significant differences from religion.

Religion's second strategy aims at sustaining the members of its community in the face of the terror and uncertainty of this encounter with the sacred. No matter how fervently we pray for transformation and healing, no matter how many hours and days and years we seek to prepare for them, no matter how experienced and competent the agents, transformation and healing do not always happen. In fact, most of the time the sought-after transformation and healing elude our experience. Furthermore, transformation and healing may come to the one we deem unworthy and shun the saint. Or, they may be so full of terror and pain that intensive efforts at care and support are called for. Terror and pain may manifest themselves in the endless waiting for results, in the misery of chemotherapy and radiation therapy, and in the agony even of folk practices, as the experiences of Latin-American *curanderas*, spirit healers, and shamans exemplify. Transformation and healing may carry consequences that are at best ambiguous and at worst disruptive of our previous relationships and lifestyles. Although transformation and healing happen within the community, transformed persons may feel called to renounce previous relationships. The community that sustains them during their quest for transformation and healing may not be the community to which their future belongs. They may believe themselves called to a totally different way of life. The power of the sacred at work in human lives is neither tame nor manageable nor manipulatable; it cannot be controlled. It cannot be called forth at will, and it cannot be banished from experience by a simple word.

The third strategy of religion is vigilance in the face of ersatz spiritual transformation and healing, that is, skepticism toward claims and experiences that appear to be too easy and comfortable or that claim to control and manipulate transformation and healing. Superficial claims for transformation and healing are frequently made in order to deceive their seekers and make an easy profit. Easy transformation and healing are in fact denials of the sacred and its consequences for our experience. In a self-help culture, such as is found in the United States today—which also embraces the myth of control through technology, and whose medical practice is increasingly devoted to beautification and improvement of the human body rather than the healing of disease, a society in which nothing is exempt from the profit-seeking of the market—in such a society, religion finds its task all the more concerned with making the distinction between profound transformation and healing on the one hand and ersatz substitutes on the other. The task facing science is daunting and difficult, but the task of religion in pursuing the threefold strategy I have sketched is also exceedingly complex and full of tension, if not contradiction.

When science and religion enter the terrain of spiritual transformation and healing, they find themselves in a minefield. This territory will test both religion and science, separately, and together. They must be willing to learn from each other as they confront the challenges posed by the sacred and also by the need to find the most appropriate methodology to guide their efforts. Religion must learn confidence from science, the recognition that even the domain of the sacred is not impervious to our search for understanding. As Pargament instructs us, we may not be able to explore the sacred itself or take its measure, but "we can study perceptions of sacredness and their implications for people's lives" (see chap. 2). Religion must also learn from science to appreciate reductionism. Reductionist methods cannot exhaust this subject of inquiry, but they do nevertheless give us considerable knowledge and a better understanding of how even the sacred is at work under the conditions of our human experience. As V. V. Raman observes, reductionist and holistic methods are complementary (2005, 5).

Science in turn must learn from religion that even though the ships that science builds are huge and impressive, the sea is even bigger and rougher. The "perfect storm" may blow upon the ship of science at any moment and break it to pieces. Well-conceived and well-intentioned efforts produce unwanted consequences, even when smart people carry out those efforts with flawless expertise. Many a successful surgery has not prevented the patient from dying, just as many well-reasoned therapeutic interventions have produced little lasting effect or even worsened the conditions of life; and pharmaceutical wonder drugs sometimes go awry, contrary to our best knowledge. Vulnerability and uncertainty in our sailing over rough water are to be expected and acknowledged. Religion is dedicated to celebrating such voyages. It is an indication that the sacred accompanies us on our travels.

Both religion and science can trivialize the territory of the sacred, and both regularly do. The God who is manipulated in the sports arena, the God to whom both sides in every war pray for victory, the God whose blessings are tied to the free-market economy—these and much more are the scandal of religion. The spiritual transformation that fits in nicely with anyone's preferred style of living, and the healing that equates to Botox, body sculpting, and clear financial profits to those who organize and support similar healing efforts—these too are scandals.

Empathy and Healing

Empathy lies just below the surface of all of the foregoing reflection (see chap. 4). Caregiver and care receiver stand together within a process that is larger than both of them. This larger process may be related to the sacred and to the fundamental purposes for living.

The core of empathy is mutual identification of one or more persons with each other. Ronald Green has spoken of "human equality and the primacy of a generic human identity" (1988, 139). We are all made of the same clay, no matter what our differences may be. If activities of healing are grounded in a transcendent agency and interpretation of life, those activities embrace the giver and the receiver equally and together. The worth that the healer affirms of the receiver's life is the same worth the healer shares. The healer participates in the process of affirming that, in a profound sense, life is about healing and being healed, for the healer as well as for the patient. When the healer recognizes that his or her activity touches the patient at the patient's point of vulnerability and fragility, the healer also recognizes that vulnerability and fragility are shared qualities of life. When the healer engages the patient's deep desire for health in both the short-term and the long-term, the healer engages his or her own desire for health. Comparable statements made here about the healer apply also to the one who receives healing care.

The empathic relationship of mutuality that is essential for healing also shares in the reality of the sacred. The healer shares with the patient vulnerability in the face of the unknown and the uncontrollable, along with an accompanying sense of dread. The healer is also tempted to deny the elements of the uncontrollable and unpredictable. Further, along with the patient, the healer can also be taken in by the desire for easy and superficial versions of healing. The healer today may well feel the burdens of both science and religion. The healer is called upon to gain the knowledge, technical competence, and clinical experience that scientific healing requires, but at the same time cannot avoid the reality of the mysterium that shakes us to the core, and must remain vigilant against the temptation to engage in denial or to accept too easy or superficial a cure. It may also come to pass that in the relationship of reciprocity and empathy, the healer must share this burden and its consequences with the one who is seeking healing. Both healer and receiver must take care to avoid the denial of empathy that comes to us so easily. As they acknowledge together the reality of the sacred and the struggles of science, healer and patient may find an even deeper level of empathic community.

Conclusion

I conclude by reiterating the significance of the experience of the holy for spiritual transformation and healing. Recognizing the holy is important for two reasons. First, we have not properly perceived spiritual transformation and healing if we do not take note of the dimension of the holy in human experience. Second, this field of research cannot attain maturity until it fashions methodologies sophisticated enough to encompass both the unmanageable element of the holy and the reductionist techniques that can provide knowledge about human "perceptions of sacredness and their implications for people's lives" (see chap. 2).

Note

1. For this and all references to the Bible, see the New Oxford Annotated Bible, Revised Standard Version.

References

Csikszentmihalyi, M. 1991. Consciousness for the twenty-first century. *Zygon* 26, no. 1 (March), 7–26.

———. 1993. *The Evolving Self: A Psychology for the Third Millennium*. New York: HarperCollins.

———. 1996. *Creativity: Flow and the Psychology of Discovery and Invention*. New York: HarperCollins.

Eliade, M. 1959. *The Sacred and the Profane: The Nature of Religion*, trans. W. Trask. New York: Harper.

Evangelical Lutheran Church in America. 2003. *Caring for Health: Our Shared Endeavor*. Chicago: Evangelical Lutheran Church in America.

Green, R. 1988. *Religion and Moral Reason: A New Method for Comparative Study*. New York: Oxford University Press.

Hefner, P. 2002. Transformation as mission. In *For All People*, ed. E. M. W. Pedersen, H. Lam, and P. Lodberg, 177–96. Grand Rapids, Mich.: Eerdmans.

Isaacs, M. E. 1976. *The Concept of Spirit: A Study of Pneuma in Hellenistic Judaism and Its Bearing on the New Testament*. Huddersfield, U.K.: H. Charlesworth.

Jacob, E. 1958. *Theology of the Old Testament*, trans. A. W. Heathcote and P. J. Allcock. New York: Harper.

James, W. 1902. *The Varieties of Religious Experience: A Study in Human Nature*. London: Longmans, Green.

Otto, R. 1923. *The Idea of the Holy*, trans. J. W. Harvey. New York: Oxford University Press. (Orig. pub. 1917.)

Raman, V. V. 2005. *Reductionism and Holism: Two Sides of the Perception of Reality*. Retrieved July 15, 2005, from www.metanexus.net/digest/2005_07_15.htm

Schweizer, E. 1961. Spirit of God. In *Bible Key Words*, ed. and trans. D. M. Barton, R. Ackroyd, and A. E. Harvey, vol. 3. New York: Harper.

9

Spiritual Transformation and Healing in Light of an Evolutionary Theology

Karl E. Peters

Once while teaching a course on religious and philosophical issues in medicine, I came across a startling idea: a person could be healthy even in the midst of disease. This idea was prompted by the following passage about the goals of medicine in relation to the meaning of "health":

> An ancient and positive etymological link exists between "holy," "healing," and "making whole"; between "salve" and "salvation." Leon Kass emphasizes health as the determinative goal of medicine, which he defines in its classical sense as the well-working of an organism as a whole [Kass 1975]. To promote this "well-working" is the healer's fundamental goal. It emphasizes preventive and rehabilitative care as well as crisis intervention. Edmund Pellegrino rightly contends that health cannot be the exclusive goal of [the physician's] practice without undercutting the physician's responsibility for care in the midst of a patient's failing health. The organism may never work well again as a whole, but the physician still must "heal" in the sense of helping keep the distracted patient whole in the face of ineliminable adversity. Either way, the tasks of the healer define themselves positively. (May 1983, 130–31)

In this chapter I want to explore how health can be maintained when a person is seriously ill, even terminally ill. An individual may not be completely healthy in the sense of "the well-working of an organism as a whole." However, in many ways an individual may still be healthy.

My discussion of how this can happen is grounded in my experiences during the dying of my first wife, Carol Peters. A few days before her fifty-seventh birthday, Carol was diagnosed with a rare form of untreatable stomach cancer. She was given less than a 1 percent chance of living longer than six months. The diagnosis was the beginning of a medical-spiritual journey that lasted fifteen months. During that time I learned that it was possible to have health in the midst of dying from "ineliminable adversity."

One of the many things that helped me cope with the dying of my wife was the evolutionary theology that I had been developing for more than two decades. This theology helped me to understand cancer in a way that was meaningful in the general scheme of things. It also helped Carol and me to live effectively in the midst of a terminal illness. In this chapter I would like to suggest how an evolutionary theology can shed light on understanding how spiritual transformation can enable one to be healthy in the midst of disease.

What Is Spiritual Transformation?

One working definition of *spiritual transformation* is "dramatic changes in world and self views, purposes, religious beliefs, attitudes, and behavior" (Metanexus Institute on Religion and Science 2004, 5). Ken Pargament refines this understanding by suggesting that religion involves "a search for significance in ways related to the sacred" (Pargament 1997, 32). In keeping with this definition of religion, "spiritual transformation refers primarily to a fundamental change in the place of the sacred or the character of the sacred as an object of significance in the life of the individual, and secondarily to a fundamental change in the pathways the individual takes to the sacred" (Metanexus Institute on Religion and Science 2004, 8).[1]

Humanity's religions exhibit many different ways of thinking about the sacred. Sometimes it is thought of as many personal spiritual beings that underlie the workings of nature and human life.

Sometimes the sacred is thought of as one supreme reality—the God of Western theism. Sometimes it is thought of in nonpersonal terms as the Way of Heaven and Earth, or the Tao, in Chinese thought. The sacred can also be seen as the total system of creative forces of nature and human history. In all these concepts, however, two things seem to be present. Whether it is thought of as many or one, personal or nonpersonal, the sacred is the source of all existence, and it is that in relation to which our lives become meaningful.

One way to understand the sacred as the source of existence is by distinguishing between creator and created. This is an important distinction in Judaism, Christianity, and Islam. In these religions, all of God's creation is good, but God as the creator, the source of the world, is the greatest good. Genesis 1 affirms this when, after each phase of creation, God looks at what has been created and sees that it is good.[2] Augustine, a Christian theologian of the fourth century CE, developed this idea in contrast to a powerful form of dualism present in his day, Manichaeism. Manichaeism held that the world is a battleground between two opposing forces, one good and one evil. Instead of this, Augustine, following the thinking of the neo-Platonists, argued that all existence is good, that evil is only a negative concept, and that the source of all existence, God, is the highest good. So humans should not become addicted to the goods of this world (should not live in bondage to these goods) but should turn toward a relationship with the highest good—God (1961, bk. 7).

This distinction between all of creation as good and the creator as the greatest good is also advanced by the twentieth-century philosopher of religion Henry Nelson Wieman. In his book *The Source of Human Good* (1946), Wieman does not present God as a being who creates the world but, instead, as the process of creative transformation. Everything in the world is to some degree instrumentally or intrinsically good, or both at the same time. Wieman uses the idea of relations of mutual support as a way of generally characterizing what is good. When things are in mutually supporting relationships, they are good. One example is health, as when all parts of an organism work well together as a whole. Another example is meaning, that is, a system of ideas and experiences that are mutually supportive and in terms of which a human being can see his or her place in the larger scheme of things. Love also is such a good because it represents the mutually supporting relationships of feelings and behaviors between two people. And families and communities of all kinds are still other examples; whenever their members live and work together in supportive ways, good is present.

Still greater than any of these kinds of relations of mutual support is the process that creates health, meaning, love, and community. Wieman calls this "creative good," and also "creative process," "creative interchange," and "creative transformation." Because it is the source of all intrinsic and instrumental good, Wieman calls this process God (1946, 54–58). It is this understanding of God as a process that I'll be developing further as my evolutionary theology.

What Is Evolutionary Theology?

Evolutionary theology thinks of the sacred, or God, in relation to a scientific understanding of the evolution of the universe, life on earth, human society, and even individual lives. It is therefore, first, historical. Second, evolutionary theology is a form of process thought. In contrast to some older Western ways of thinking in which everything is thought of as entities and substance, process thought thinks of everything in terms of events, processes, and relational systems. Third, as a form of process thought, evolutionary theology focuses on how everything in the world is constantly becoming. Change, as well as stability, is a fundamental feature of the world.

Fourth, evolutionary theology focuses on the sacred within the natural world, and it sees the sacred manifested in small and large changes or in transformations to new forms of matter, life, and society. In keeping with the first law of thermodynamics, energy or matter is neither created nor destroyed, but it is transformed from potential energy into subatomic particles and simple atoms as the universe expands and cools after the "big bang" that marked its beginning. Energy or matter is then further transformed from simple elements to heavier elements in the supernovae of massive stars. These heavier elements (such as oxygen, nitrogen, carbon, phosphorus, and iron) form molecules, and simpler molecules are transformed into more complex, self-replicating molecules. Further, through processes of Darwinian evolution, organisms with simple nervous systems are transformed into those with nervous systems complex enough to think with symbols—the human symbolic species. Human communities that evolved biologically to care for genetically related kin are transformed into larger social communities guided by religions and morality. And religions themselves are created through processes of transformation, for example, when tribes of nomads enslaved in Egypt are liberated to become the people of Yahweh; when the Buddha discovers the middle way of the eight-fold path between extreme asceticism and extreme indulgence; or when Jesus, proclaiming the coming kingdom of God and universal love, is transformed though crucifixion and resurrection into a living presence in a new religion.

The sacred is also understood to be present in major transformative events in the lives of individuals, as evident in the rituals of transformation associated with birth, puberty, marriage, and death. In all these rituals of transformation, an individual becomes a new creature—dying to an old way of living to take on new understandings and roles as to what it means to be human. This can happen even as one approaches death. A few years ago a friend of mine, a priest, became transformed with a new self-understanding as he entered the care of a hospice in the final days of his cancer. He wrote that in allowing himself to be cared for by others, he now had a new kind of ministry. Evolutionary theology sees all these transformations in the history of the natural world, human history, and the lives of individual humans as locations for the presence of the sacred.

Ways of Understanding the Sacred in Evolutionary Theology

Various kinds of evolutionary theology share the above characteristics. One way they differ is in how they characterize the sacred, understood in Western religious thought as God. One kind of evolutionary theology, represented by Philip Hefner, does not attempt to address questions about the nature of God directly. Hefner focuses on how, by attending to the evolutionary processes of the natural world, we can understand the purposes of God as creator and our relation to God as "created-cocreators" (Hefner 1993). Another kind of evolutionary theology, stemming from the thinking of Alfred North Whitehead, identifies God as a personal system that includes the universe but is more than the universe (i.e., panentheism). One scholar who supports this type of evolutionary theology is Arthur Peacocke, who uses a musical metaphor to express the process idea that God is the cosmic symphony composer-conductor who begins the universe as a simple tune, and then unfolds the God-given potentialities of the universe much the way one develops a Bach fugue, or even a piece of jazz (Peacocke 1979, 105–6; 1993, 173–77). A third kind of evolutionary theologian sees the sacred or God in nonpersonal terms as the creativity of the universe itself (Kaufman 2004; Peters 2002). In this view, God is more a verb than a noun, a kind of activity or a type of interaction. Rather than saying that God creatively transforms the universe, this form of evolutionary theology suggests that the sacred is the process of creative transformation itself.

Evolutionary Theology and the Spirit

Since this chapter is on the topic of spiritual transformation and healing, it might be helpful to explore how this third form of evolutionary theology understands the idea of spirit. In Genesis 1, the wind or spirit (*ruach*) of God moves over the waters, which represent a formless void, in the first phase of creation. *Spirit* then also comes to mean that which animates or gives life. Like the wind, it can come to mean presences that are not seen but whose effectiveness can be felt in the world. Sometimes these presences are understood as forces or powers and at other times as personal, nonmaterial beings.

Much traditional Western philosophy has thought of spirit in terms of nonmaterial substance. Process and relational thinking suggests a different way of characterizing spirit and spirits—as events or interactions. Thus, in the third kind of evolutionary theology, God as spirit is not understood as an invisible, nonmaterial substance that continually creates the evolving universe. Rather *spirit*, here, refers to the interactions taking place as energy or matter evolve into more complex states of being.

One way to illustrate this is to return to the root meaning of *spirit* in the physical phenomenon of wind. In substantive thinking, wind is thought of as an entity in its own right that acts in our world. However, if one asks scientifically, how does wind come about, one discovers that it actually is the product of the interaction between warmer and colder air. The formation of winds on our planet is complex. Yet, in a simple example, diurnal winds are caused by the fact that land heats up faster than water during the day. In the morning, when colder offshore air comes in contact with the warmer air along a more quickly warming coastline, gravity pulls the colder air under the hotter air and thus pushes the lighter, hotter air upwards, causing lateral winds. Likewise on a global scale, prevailing winds are created when warm air resting on the tropical seas is displaced by colder, heavier air from more northerly latitudes (Cashman 2005).

So even the wind we feel is not a substance in its own right. It is the movement of air molecules as a result of complex interactions of geography, temperature, and gravity. What I want to suggest is that, when we use the word *spirit* to talk about the sacred reality that creates the universe, we can think of divine spirit as a set of interactions that are creative.

A Darwinian Model of Sacred Interaction

One way of modeling creative interaction is with a Darwinian *variation-selection* model. This model can be generalized to a universal pattern in which new possibilities for existence emerge (variation) and some of these are then selected to continue. The particular kinds of interaction operative in this universal pattern vary in the course of the history of the universe. In the formation of stars in a particular part of a galaxy, atoms of hydrogen and helium randomly combine under the influence of gravity. If enough atoms are available in a particular region to form a critical mass, nuclear fusion begins. The creation of stars occurs through the chance interactions of atoms, on the one hand, and through the laws of the universe on the other. Likewise in the evolution of life on our planet, the same pattern of new possibilities emerging and of some being selected for continuation occurs with different kinds of interactions. Copying errors in germ-line cells, random interactions with outside factors such as radiation and chemicals, and sexual recombination create genetic variations that give rise to a variety of organisms in a particular species. Interactions between the complete organism and its environment determine the organism's success in passing on new genetic variations to future generations. An analogous variation-selection pattern of creativity occurs in human culture, for example, in the recombination of ideas to form new ways of thinking and living, and then in the selection of ideas and behaviors by pressures in a particular discipline or wider culture.

The specific kinds of interaction that produce and select ideas and behaviors in society are different from the kinds of interactions that create stars and new species. But this twofold pattern of generating new possibilities and then allowing some to continue seems to be universal (see Peters 2002, 38–59). It is this universal, twofold pattern of interactions that is the source of our existence. And as the source of our existence, it fulfills one of the requirements we described above as making something sacred. The other requirement is that we can find meaning for our lives in relation to it. I'll discuss this below as I further develop my evolutionary theology in relation to disease. But first, let us look at how evolutionary theology regards human beings.

Human Beings as Relational Selves

Evolutionary theology sees human beings as *relational selves*, that is, selves constituted out of interacting cosmic, biological, and sociocultural parts that have been created during the history of the universe (Peters 2002, 68–73). Our bodies and the bodies of all living things on earth are constituted out of elements (such as oxygen, nitrogen, carbon, calcium, and iron) created in the deaths of massive stars, in supernovae. We are "star stuff"—creatures of the cosmos. We are also biological creatures. On earth, the elements created in stars have formed molecules and then self-replicating molecules that have evolved through natural selection into human DNA. Our genetic code is the blueprint for the kind of organism we are. This code and these biological processes shape us to be creatures with big and complex brains, creatures capable of language and of communicating through language such things as our beliefs about the world and the values we live by. In other words, we also are cultural creatures. As relational selves, we are constituted as complex systems out of atoms born in stars, genetic codes that have evolved on earth, and language, ideas, and values we inherit from our culture. We are multilevel cosmic, biological, and cultural systems.

As complex cosmic, biological, and cultural systems, we have, according to Antonio Damasio, three selves, each made possible by the activity of different regions of our brains (Damasio 1999, 174–75, 199). Each self is relational in that it is involved in interactions. The first is the *proto-self*. The proto-self is an interconnected, moment-by-moment coherent collection of neural patterns that represent and regulate the internal state of the organism. It is unconscious; we are not aware of our proto-selves. The second is the *core self*. The core self is generated when a human being interacts with an object, which can be either outside or inside the person. This object-organism interaction generates a nonverbal account of the object and its relation to the individual. This account includes the person's feeling of him- or herself knowing the object. It is a present-moment experience of awareness of self and other—a feeling of oneself in the process of feeling what happens. Damasio's third self is what he calls the *autobiographical self*. The autobiographical self is based on memories of multiple past experiences in images that are recalled or reconstructed. As we remember narratives of ourselves from the past, we gain a sense of our identity over time.

All these selves, along with the rest of our bodies, are in process. As the environment with which we interact constantly changes, we also are constantly changing in ways that maintain the integrity of our bodies and our brains and minds. We live our lives in states of dynamic equilibrium. When our blood sugar drops, a process takes place that gives rise to feelings of hunger, and we eat. When a bacterium or virus enters our bodies and succeeds in making us ill, our immune system responds to try to overcome the foreign organism and to restore us to health. When we learn about new ideas that are different from what we already believe, our brain works to either find reasons to reject these ideas or to find ways to incorporate them into revised ways of thinking. These are just commonplace examples of how we as complex systems maintain our chemical, biological, and ideational equilibrium. As we do this, we can say we are systems that maintain health, defined by Leon Kass as "the well-working of an organism as a whole."

The Challenge of Disease to our Complex Selves

There are times, however, as Edmund Pellegrino points out, when our complex systems are challenged to such an extent that they will never work well as a whole in the way they worked before (see May 1983, 130–31). Catastrophic events and diseases that leave people physically paralyzed, psychologically traumatized, or terminally ill are examples of such challenges. Likewise the dynamic equilibrium of families may be challenged when a child is born with major birth defects, or when a loved one is slowly dying of disease or has suddenly died in an accident.

When such events happen, a person is confronted "with death, and not because the patient has nearly died, though he or she may have, but because the catastrophe attacks the patient's basic identity as a human being" (May 1991, 9). William May goes on to say that this attack on identity—I would say on one's autobiographical self—occurs in three dimensions. The first is that of the self in relation to his or her own body. When it is healthy, the body is the way in which a person effectively experiences, acts on, and discloses him- or herself to the wider world. However, when illness occurs, we may no longer sense things effectively. We may be impaired in our actions. And our body discloses us to others as debilitated rather than healthy. We are no longer the same; we have significantly changed.

A second dimension of our identity lies in relation to others, to family and community. As we develop as autobiographical selves, a part of our identity is the roles we have in these relations with others in our families, professions, and community organizations. A health catastrophe can transform our identity to that of cancer victim, paraplegic, or AIDS patient in our relationships with others (May 1991, 11).

The third dimension in which illness challenges the identity of our autobiographical selves is in relation to the transcendent. May writes that "most people connect with the transcendent or express their 'ultimate concern' chiefly through rituals" (1991, 12). These may include the rituals of organized religion, and they also include

> a whole range of repeated actions that conform to and represent the foundational events and the patterns of meaning in people's lives. How one rises to challenge, eats, cleanses oneself, greets one's fellows, and shuts down the day—these repeated actions signal the way one connects with the ultimate" (12).

When disease or trauma force an alteration in these fundamental rhythms of life, a person is driven far from equilibrium, both in how they act and experience their own body, and in their relationships with others—and may never be physically healthy again.

When my wife was dying of cancer, I saw how her identity changed from that of a physically healthy woman in control of her life to a person largely dependent on others. I also remember how my identity changed as I became a full-time caregiver and also an advocate regarding certain aspects of the healthcare system. At the same time, my wife and I became healthy in new, nonphysical ways as we underwent a spiritual transformation in which new possibilities for good emerged in creative interactions between ourselves and others.

The Meaning of Disease in an Evolutionary Theology

A first step in this spiritual transformation, at least for me, was a new understanding of the meaning of disease. One of our capacities as evolved cosmic, biological, cultural beings with big brains is that we can give symbolic meaning to the events of our lives and worlds. The meaning we give to disease can have an effect on how we respond to it and live with it.

One of the common systems of meaning in regard to disease is a *dualistic-warfare* understanding. As human beings we are at war with all that threatens our wholeness as dynamically integrated creatures. This understanding captures how we feel when we are threatened by anything from a cold to a major life-threatening illness such as cancer. We feel we are under attack. And this supports our desire to do what we can to totally eradicate the threat to our lives. However, in light of what I have been saying in this chapter, I am able to suggest another understanding of disease. This understanding sees disease as threatening human beings, who are created goods, but it also recognizes that disease may be involved in the work of creative good, or God. As created goods, humans are valuable as dynamic systems interacting with other dynamic systems and with the wider ecological systems of our planet. Yet in an evolutionary theology, as well as in much traditional religious thought, there is a still greater good than humans, or any other created good for that matter. It is that which creates the world and all in it—the creative good, the sacred, or God.

If we place primacy on creative rather than created good, what then is the meaning of disease? One aspect of its meaning is that disease is sometimes part of the evolutionary process. This is the picture one gets in reading *Why We Get Sick: The New Science of Darwinian Medicine* (1996), by Randolph Nesse and George Williams. Nesse and Williams acknowledge that we must indeed do all we can to combat disease, usually by finding out the immediate causes of disease and trying to eliminate or remedy them. However, they are also interested in setting human diseases in relation to what they call the "ultimate cause" of disease, evolution itself. They ask how the maladies that make human beings so miserable and take human lives could have evolved in the first place.

They give five reasons for disease from an evolutionary perspective. The following summary is taken from Nesse and Williams (1996, 236). First, there are genetic defects. Some defects are new mutations that affect a particular individual. Others are inherited because they do not interfere with reproduction and hence have not been selected against. An example is a gene that predisposes people to late-life cancer. Still other genetic defects are actively maintained because they offer benefits that outweigh the costs. For example, when malaria is present, people with one copy of the gene for sickle-cell anemia are protected against malaria, while people with no copies are not. However, those that inherit two copies suffer from sickle-cell disease and, in the past, died before reproducing.

Finally, some genetic defects are quirks that show adverse effects only when they occur in a novel environment.

Second, according to Nesse and Williams's evolutionary perspective, diseases result from novel factors that were not present when human beings first evolved. New viruses and bacteria are examples. Ironically, sometimes we help create these new agents, when the improper use of antibiotics acts as a selection pressure for producing more virulent strains of bacteria. Third, diseases such as lower-back problems may be the result of "design" compromises (in this case, upright posture). Fourth, some diseases result from historical legacies. We are not created fresh from nothing but are built in bricolage fashion from older designs that themselves may have evolved with defects.[3] Finally, while we are a remarkable, evolved species, so are other species. We eat other forms of life for food. Likewise, organisms that cause disease are using us as sustenance in order to maintain and continue their own life forms. Also like us, such organisms have evolved and continue to evolve through interactions that I have called the creative process or the sacred. Nesse and Williams conclude their list of five evolutionary reasons for disease by saying:

> The human body turns out to be both fragile and robust. Like all products of organic evolution, it is a bundle of compromises, each of which offers an advantage, but often at the price of susceptibility to disease. These susceptibilities cannot be eliminated by any duration of natural selection, for it is the very power of natural selection that created them. (1996, 236)

When I reflect on the meaning of disease in my own evolutionary theology, I am led to conclude that the sacred is ambivalent. In the creating of new good, it also creates what is bad—at least bad from our point of view. My understanding echoes that of the prophet Isaiah, through whom the God of Israel states that God alone is the creator of nature and the controller of history: "There is no one besides me; I am the Lord, and there is no other. I form light and create darkness, I make weal and create woe; I the Lord do all these things" (Isaiah 45:6–7). Similarly, in Hindu religious tradition, the god Shiva is both creator and destroyer, only to create again as the Lord of the Dance of Creation. As Rudolf Otto suggests, this ambivalence of the sacred may be universal in world religions (1990). Traditional religious thought and my evolutionary theology affirm that the ultimate creative reality underlying and working through the entire universe and in human life is responsible for good and evil, health and disease.

Such thinking does not take away the experience of suffering, which we feel as evil when our own intrinsic good is threatened. Naturally, we struggle to fight with our body's immune system the threat of disease. We also fight disease with our minds when we try to understand the specific causes of a disease and ways to prevent it, cure it, or reduce its effects. However, when all our efforts do not relieve the physical consequences of disease, there is still something that we can do. In terms of an evolutionary theology, we can view disease as part of the natural course of events in a constantly changing universe. We can also try to discern new opportunities for living in the midst of suffering, even in the midst of dying.

Discerning new opportunities for living in the midst of disease becomes possible when we recognize that humans have evolved to be more than just physical organisms. Because we are complex relational systems, there are other dimensions to our living than simply maintaining physical health. One of those dimensions is that of our intellect, with which we can engage in interaction with other people and their ideas to create systems of meaning. These systems can include the evolutionary meaning of disease, which I have just attempted to formulate. However, there are still other dimensions of our living—all involving relationships with others. This first became clear to me when, in a support group at the M. D. Anderson Cancer Center of Orlando, Florida, Carol and I learned about the dimensions of wellness: physical, intellectual, emotional, social, occupational, environmental, and spiritual.[4] Physically, Carol's body was deteriorating, and she would never be whole again. And we could no longer think of future occupations or avocations, such as the worldwide travel she enjoyed. However in other dimensions, especially in developing social relationships with others, in growing in our own love for one another, and in exploring new spiritual depths, we became healthier than we had ever been. In these ways we underwent a spiritual transformation regarding what was most meaningful for living in the midst of dying.

Living Well with Disease

The key to this spiritual transformation was moving from a focus in our lives on our existing created goods to a focus on creative good and how it might bring about new good. In part this meant letting go of aspects of our autobiographical selves and living more completely in what Damasio would call our core selves (1999).

I'm not sure whether Damasio's core self is the same as the state of being mindfully present as found in Buddhist meditation. Damasio's core self involves a present-moment experience of awareness of self and other—a feeling of oneself in the process of feeling what happens. Again I don't know whether the parts of the brain operative in this experience are the same as those recorded, for example, by Newberg, d'Aquili, and Rause with Tibetan meditators (2001, 1–5). A scientific comparison would be interesting. Still, I think that when we are in a present-moment state of experience that unifies self and other, when we are in a state of letting go of created goods that make up the autobiographical self, we are open to the possibilities of new good emerging.

Psychotherapist Richard Schwartz calls this state "being in self" (1995, 27–60). It is a state of being mindful of all parts of oneself—painful parts, fearful parts, angry parts, self-critical parts—parts that often become accentuated in the course of disease. It is a state of compassionately accepting these feelings while not letting them take over. It is a state of trusting oneself and one's interactions with others, of trusting that in such interactions new good can come. In this state one lives by God's grace, flows with the Tao, and is united with one's own Buddha nature.

I'm not saying that this is easy either for the one who is ill or for those who are the caregivers, family, and friends. But I know from my experience that when one is in this state, one's autobiographical self can be transformed. First, more aspects of the past can be present when, for example, a dying loved one and his or her spouse reflect on their lives together, accept the bad with the good, and allow the past to be transformed in the light of mutually accepting and forgiving love. Second, new and unforeseen events can be more easily accepted as parts of our stories, so that the course of a disease becomes an arduous journey of discovery, analogous to hiking difficult terrain in high mountains. Third, sometimes it is even possible to enlist the disease itself as a means of focusing on the present so that new relations of mutual support—new created goods—in one's life story can emerge.

Circumstances were such in my own experience that this happened. As the great intrinsic good of my wife's life was fading, and as our own physical relationship was coming to an end, Carol and I were pressed by the disease of cancer to focus on the day-to-day, hour-to-hour, even minute-to-minute moments of our existence. Whether it was getting up in the morning, changing bandages in the middle of the night, eating, moving about the house, responding to breakthrough pain, going to church, having friends over to visit—we were called by our disease to be in the present. In present moments we were called to be open to whatever new good might come our way, no matter how small. And new good did come—new ideas from books we read out loud together, the expertise of our compassionate oncologist who helped us control pain while maintaining Carol's intellectual clear-headedness, loving care from visiting nurses and healthcare aids, the completion of Carol's last watercolor by a newfound friend, food from a neighbor we hardly knew, and seeing an eagle swoop down from the sky to catch fish near the shore of our lake.

Looking back on this experience, I realize that in its own way this disease facilitated the same thing that various forms of meditation, prayer, or psychotherapy may accomplish—the giving up of our attachment to the things of this world and experiencing fully in the present whatever our lives had to offer. We were living by the grace of God, who creates both woe and weal. We were dancing with the creator-destroyer Shiva. While physical disease ran its course to death, we became more intellectually, emotionally, socially, and spiritually healthy.

In this process Carol was transformed into a person with a new identity. At her memorial service, when those present were invited to share their memories, an older man stood and said, "Once the great actress Sarah Bernhardt was asked what the most difficult thing about acting was. She replied, 'Making a graceful exit.'" Then the man said, "Carol Peters knew how to make a graceful exit." So Carol became the lady who died of cancer and in so doing, gracefully exited life. And as she died, I learned new ways to be healthy in the midst of disease.

Notes

1. This understanding of spiritual transformation is consistent with a model for the comparison of world religions developed by John Fenton. The model suggests that religions respond to basic human needs by relating human beings to what is sacred, that this relationship involves human transformations, and that symbols of the sacred and transformative processes, among other elements, are transmitted culturally from one generation to the next (Fenton et al. 1993, 4–16).

2. For this and subsequent biblical references, see the *New Oxford Annotated Bible*, New Revised Standard Version (1991).

3. Ursula Goodenough discusses why bricolage is an apt metaphor for how evolution works (1998, 71–72).

4. I now find these on some university web sites used to educate students in the "dimensions of wellness." See for example the site of the North Dakota State University Wellness Center, http://wellness.ndsu.nodak.edu/education/dimensions .shtml (last accessed December 13, 2005).

References

Augustine. 1961. *Confessions*. New York: Penguin.

Cashman, T. 2005. Evolutionary theology. Message posted to Nature-God list serve, March 28. Institute on Religion in an Age of Science. www.metanexus .net/other/otherfs.asp?page=irasng (last accessed December 13, 2005).

Damasio, A. 1999. *The Feeling of What Happens: Body and Emotion in the Making of Consciousness*. New York: Harcourt Brace.

Fenton, J. Y., N. Heim, F. E. Reynolds, A. L. Miller, N. C. Nielsen Jr., and G. G. Burford et al. 1993. *Religions of Asia*. 3rd ed. New York: St. Martin's.

Goodenough, U. 1998. *The Sacred Depths of Nature*. New York: Oxford University Press.

Hefner, P. 1993. *The Human Factor: Evolution, Culture, and Religion*. Minneapolis, Minn.: Fortress.

Kass, Leon, R. (1975). Regarding the end of medicine and the pursuit of health. *The Public Interest* 40 (Summer): 27–29.

Kaufman, G. D. 2004. *In the Beginning . . . Creativity*. Minneapolis, Minn.: Fortress.

May, W. F. 1983. *The Physician's Covenant: Images of the Healer in Medical Ethics*. Philadelphia: Westminster.

———. 1991. *The Patient's Ordeal*. Bloomington: Indiana University Press.

Metanexus Institute on Religion and Science. 2004. *The Spiritual Transformation Scientific Research Program*. Philadelphia: Metanexus Institute on Religion and Science.

Nesse, R. M., and G. C. Williams. 1996. *Why We Get Sick: The New Science of Darwinian Medicine*. New York: Random House.

Newberg, A., E. G. d'Aquili, and V. Rause. 2001. *Why God Won't Go Away: Brain Science and the Biology of Belief*. New York: Ballantine.

Otto, R. 1990. *The Idea of the Holy*. New York: Oxford University Press.

Pargament, K. I. 1997. *The Psychology of Religion and Coping: Theory, Research, Practice*. New York: Guilford.

Peacocke, A. 1979. *Creation and the World of Science*. Oxford: Clarendon.

———. 1993. *Theology for a Scientific Age: Being and Becoming—Natural, Divine, and Human*. Minneapolis, Minn.: Fortress.

Peters, K. 2002. *Dancing with the Sacred: Evolution, Ecology, God*. Harrisburg, Pa.: Trinity Press International.

Schwartz, R. C. 1995. *Internal Family Systems Therapy*. New York: Guilford.

Wieman, H. N. 1946. *The Source of Human Good*. Carbondale: Southern Illinois University Press.

10

Personal Transformation: Perspectives from Psychology and Christianity

Fraser Watts

Both Christian theology and contemporary psychology are, in their different ways, concerned with personal transformation. The purpose of this chapter is to explore the similarities and differences in how they approach this. It is a contribution to the broad project of developing the dialogue between theology and psychology (Watts 2002a).

It is right to acknowledge at the outset that both psychology and theology are very diverse traditions, and that it would be misleading to present either of them as monolithic. Psychology as a whole is largely concerned with investigating human psychological functioning and has no particular commitment to personal change. However, the diverse approaches to psychological therapy that developed in the twentieth century focus explicitly on personal transformation. These approaches range from that of B. F. Skinner, who sees people as transformed by the rewards and punishments of operant conditioning, to C. G. Jung, who sees people as transformed through their engagement with the archetypes of the collective unconscious. In their different ways, these various psychological approaches all provide us with both theories of personal change and technologies for achieving it.

The Christian tradition is also relevant to personal transformation, but it has dealt with it less explicitly. For example, I will suggest that the Christian Gospels are concerned with personal transformation, and that modern psychology can serve as a useful exegetical tool in elucidating this. It would be misleading to suggest that the Gospels deal with personal transformation as explicitly as it has been dealt with in the twentieth century. However in recent centuries, reformed, evangelical, and charismatic traditions of Christianity have all dealt with personal transformation with increasing explicitness. It seems likely that reformed Christianity in its various manifestations has both contributed to a contemporary Western concern with personal transformation and has itself been further influenced by that general cultural preoccupation.

A significant difference in how therapeutic psychology and Christian thinking have approached personal transformation concerns how narrowly focused they have been. Although, as we will see, Jesus promised transformation to particular people, this occurred within the broader context of the coming of the kingdom and the transformation of society. Though some versions of Christianity in contemporary society have become increasingly individualistic, the mainstream tradition has always wanted to contextualize the implications of the Christian message for the individual within a broader social framework. Therapeutic psychology, in contrast, has been more inclined to see things in purely individualistic terms, though there are exceptions to that. For example, there have been movements such as family therapy and social psychiatry that have maintained a social approach and suggested that how people function is often affected more significantly by their social context than by purely personal changes. There is a difference of emphasis here between psychology and Christianity, but not an irreconcilable one.

The first section of this chapter will use contemporary therapeutic psychology to elucidate the process of transformation that arises from the encounters of Jesus of Nazareth with various individuals as recorded in the Gospels. The second will compare the various events or processes that lead to personal transformation in religious and psychological contexts. That will lead to an examination, from the perspectives of both psychology and theology, of the role of reframing the personal story in personal transformation. The next section will look at the different use that is made of attributions in religious and psychological transformation. Then forgiveness will be taken as the basis of a case study of how religion and psychology approach personal transformation. Finally, some general perspectives of theology and psychology with regard to the transformation of personality will be compared.

Personal Transformation in the Gospels

The promise of personal transformation is implicit in many of Jesus's encounters with people, and the phrase "follow me and you . . . " is completed in different ways for different listeners. As I have discussed more fully elsewhere, the Gospels present Jesus as having an interesting and distinctive approach to the personal transformation of those whom he encounters, and one that can be explicated within the framework of contemporary psychology (Watts, forthcoming).

Jesus's approach begins with a promise of change and renewal, with encouraging people to entertain extravagant hopes of how things can be very different. For example, in the early chapters of the Gospel according to John, Jesus tells Nathanael about how, if he follows him, Nathanael will see the heavens open (John 1:51); Jesus talks to Nicodemus about being born again (John 3:5); and he tells the woman at the well that he can give her living water that will well up within her (John 4:14).[1] The journey of personal transformation exemplified in the encounters of these people with Jesus thus seems to begin with their being encouraged to take seriously their dreams of how life can be radically different and better.

This kind of message speaks powerfully to a contemporary sense of depletion, in which we often seem to experience a certain dryness in life. The things that are most important to us are easily drowned out by a welter of demands, obligations, and responsibilities. That leaves us wondering what benefit there is in "gaining the whole world" but "losing your own soul" (Matthew 16:26). For many, the dream that things can be different and radically better never completely goes away, and Jesus seems to be encouraging those he encounters to take their dream seriously again. The message is that this sense of depletion is not the inevitable lot of humans.

It is also an approach to personal transformation that can be understood within the relationship between ego and Self in Jungian psychology. Though the ego is the center of conscious life and can engage effectively with external reality, it is subject to severe limitations. If one is to embark on the journey to something higher and fuller that Jung calls "individuation," the ego needs to reconnect with the Self. The Self holds out the promise of wholeness towards which the ego can move, provided a healthy axis is maintained between ego and Self. In Jungian terms, Jesus's approach to personal transformation seems to begin by encouraging people to attend to the Self (the whole person that they can become) and to reconnect with it.

However, as one would expect in a psychologically healthy approach to personal transformation, this very positive initial emphasis on promise and possibility is balanced by a more negative strand emphasizing sacrifice. The Gospels call this "repentance." Jesus tells those whom he calls to follow him that they must give up almost everything for his sake (Matthew 10:37–39). There is also a very stark sense of priorities in which the "kingdom" (of which personal transformation is one aspect) needs to be an overwhelming priority. This negative strand, focusing on repentance or renunciation, finds an obvious parallel in the emphasis of modern cognitive-behavior therapy on abandoning limited or maladaptive patterns of behavior and thinking if there is to be any significant progress towards personal transformation. Similar concerns with renunciation can be found, albeit less explicitly, in other modes of therapy.

There is a third strand in Jesus's message, which emphasizes that his listeners are not embarking on this demanding personal journey on their own, but are joining in something that is already under way. Jesus emphasizes that the kingdom has already begun. Moreover, his followers pursue their journeys of discipleship with the support of a company of believers, and in relationship with the Holy Spirit. Similarly in modern psychology, there is usually an emphasis on the social context in which a journey of personal transformation can be pursued, whether that is a one-to-one relationship with a therapist or the more systemic approach of a therapeutic community.

Though it can be helpful to identify such common themes between the encounters of Jesus and the emphases of contemporary psychotherapy, it would be misleading to claim that Jesus was really a psychotherapist. The new way of being and living that he sought to inaugurate was for a society (Israel), and indeed for the whole body of humanity, as well as for the particular individuals that he encountered. He was not making the distinction that we might make in the twenty-first century between personal transformation and social transformation. Also, he was not working within professional boundaries but was taking opportunities as they arose to bring personal transformation to those he encountered.

All this is of contemporary relevance and is not just a contribution to the exegesis of two-thousand-year-old texts. Many people are still familiar with stories about Jesus and feel that he is a living presence in their lives. The kind of personal transformation that apparently took place in those whom Jesus encountered in Palestine is paralleled in the experience of contemporary men and women as they apply those encounters to themselves.

Transformative Encounters

As we have seen, the Gospels provide interesting examples of transforming encounters. In evaluating the nature of these encounters, however, we are handicapped by their being recounted only very briefly in the Gospels and with little background information. But the impression given by these Gospel stories is that relatively brief meetings, with few words exchanged, can be powerfully transformative. This contrasts rather markedly with how personal change takes place through psychotherapy in the contemporary world, where the process of transformation arises from patient and laborious self-exploration and through a relationship with the therapist that develops only gradually.

The transforming events with which the psychology of religion has been most concerned are those of *conversion*. The distinction between sudden and gradual conversion goes back to the early days of the psychology of religion and has stood the test of time (Spilka et al. 2003). However, despite the appearance of suddenness in many conversions, the possibility cannot be ruled out that there has been a gradual period of gestation leading up to the decisive moment. Conversion needs to be understood psychologically in terms of a preparatory period leading up to conversion and of a subsequent period in which the implications of conversion are assimilated. Understood in this way, religious conversion may be less unusual in its suddenness than at first appears. The distinction may be not so much about whether or not there has been a long period of preparation, but about whether or not that period of preparation reaches a specific and dramatic climax in one particular event or encounter.

Equally, there are probably examples of sudden change that occur in nonreligious contexts that are in some ways like religious conversion and could usefully be understood by analogy with it. For example, someone who has made repeated but not very successful attempts to overcome an addiction (alcohol, cigarettes, etc.) may have a crucial life-experience that leads to an immediate and sustained change in behavior in this regard. It would be fruitful for psychology to pay more attention to conversion-like experiences outside the sphere of religion.

Contemporary psychotherapy specializes in the patient preparatory work that underpins stable and radical personal change. However, it is not always very good at bringing this preparatory work to fruition. Religious traditions, in contrast, tend to focus on the brief and sudden moment that gives rise to radical personal transformation. However, without careful preparation and assimilation, the impact of a sudden, powerful, brief experience may be less dramatic than is often supposed. It is often assumed that conversions are permanent. Certainly that is implicit in the concept of conversion, but the reality can be very different. There are some people whose repeated but unsustained religious conversions are comparable to repeated but unsuccessful attempts to overcome an addiction.

These reflections suggest that there could be a fruitful synthesis of the approaches to personal change found in secular psychotherapy and in religious practice. Though the decisive experiences that lead to conversion sometimes arise spontaneously, Christianity (like many other faith traditions) has developed ways of creating experiences that may have this kind of dramatic impact. Some of these experiences arise through exposure to preaching. Others arise through sacramental actions such as confession, the laying on of hands for healing, or the ministry of deliverance (or exorcism).

For example, someone who has long been troubled by guilt and who eventually makes a sacramental confession may be deeply moved by hearing absolution proclaimed. Similarly, to receive the laying on of hands may crystallize in the recipient a potential for healing that may otherwise have remained dormant. Most dramatically, deliverance or exorcism may provide the opportunity for decisive change. The patient preparatory work of secular psychotherapy can sometimes be significantly augmented in such ways.

On the other hand, there is an increasing recognition that Christian practices are most effective when preceded by a careful preparation. For example, there has been a growing tendency, at least in denominations such as the Church of England, for those who wish to make a sacramental confession to talk to the priest as a counselor first and to explore the issues that they feel require confession. In this way the priest ensures that some of the necessary preparatory work is done before the use of sacramental resources.

Retelling the Personal Story

Though personal transformation often starts with a particular event, it also involves a process of reconstruction. The slow business of transformation that takes place in psychotherapy depends on learning to tell the personal story differently. Indeed, the task of discovering a more balanced and helpful version of the personal story is the core process in psychotherapy around which personal transformation is built. In contrast, the briefer but more dramatic events that characteristically lead to personal transformation in religious contexts leave a lot of the process of retelling the personal story to be done subsequently. It seems likely that the durability of religiously grounded personal change depends on how thoroughly people reconstrue themselves.

For some time, there has been much scientific interest in what most distinguishes human beings from other species. There are several plausible distinctions, such as our capacity for language and our capacity for empathic adoption of the perspective of other creatures. However, there is now quite widespread agreement that it is the human capacity for reflective self-consciousness that is the most fundamental distinctive feature of *Homo sapiens*. The story in Genesis 3 about the development of "knowledge of good and evil" seems to be, in part, about this developing self-consciousness. It is a capacity that is most evident in the way human beings reflect on their situation and, above all, reflect on their life story.

The social sciences have also, in different ways, recognized how much people are involved in telling their personal story. As life has become more complicated, the range of alternative personal stories widens, and the process of sifting, constructing, and selecting from among the available possibilities becomes a major preoccupation. Complexity also means that a single story line is seldom sufficient; increasingly we need to operate with multiple narratives that are to be used in different contexts. However, that is not to take an extreme relativist stance about personal narratives by assuming that there is nothing to choose between them. It is still possible for us to regard some narratives as more authentic than others and some as more fruitful than others for personal growth and transformation. What has happened to people cannot be changed, but how they tell their story is open to modification, and changes in how that story is told can have far-reaching consequences.

It is important to recognize that personal narratives are often embedded in broader social narratives. When we are part of a broader social group, national or otherwise, we tend to tell our stories in relation to that of the group we identify with. There are many examples of this in the religious traditions. It seems that Moses reconstrued himself as the Israelite who was to lead his people out of their slavery in Egypt. Similarly, Christians are inclined to reconstrue their personal story in relation to the ongoing work of Christ, and to claim that there is something particularly appropriate and helpful about seeing themselves in that context. Nevertheless, from a psychological point of view, some balance is needed, and the broader narrative should be used in a way that enhances personal identity rather than buries it.

There is an important issue here about the level at which this work of retelling the personal story is carried out. In recent theoretical work on the psychology of religion (Watts 2002b), I have employed a model of *interacting cognitive subsystems* that distinguishes two central cognitive subsystems. One subsystem deals with meanings that are general and thematic, and are closely linked to somatic and emotional processes, but which cannot be articulated directly. The other deals with meanings that are more narrowly cognitive, but which can more readily be articulated. Talk of personal "narratives" may suggest that the work of reconstrual that underpins much personal transformation is carried on at a level that can readily be articulated, whereas I would suggest that a good deal of the really fruitful work is carried on at subarticulate cognitive levels.

Attributions in Religious and Psychological Change

One of the most dramatic differences between religious and psychological approaches to personal transformation concerns the attributional frameworks used. There has been increasing emphasis on the importance of attributions in psychological approaches to conditions such as depression, and on the value of modes of therapy that seek to correct them. The most important distinction here is between internal and external attributions, remembering that people often have a different pattern of attributions for positive and negative events. Depressed people tend to see failures as due to their own limitations, and successes as mere chance; the nondepressed see successes as reflecting their ability, and failures as bad luck. It is now clear that such attributions have far-reaching consequences for adjustment.

Similarly, there has recently been increasing interest in the use of attribution theory in the psychology of religion (Spilka and McIntosh 1997). Attributions to God involve a distinctive and interesting attributional framework, in which God comes into play as an attribution alongside the more usual ones. I have suggested elsewhere that God defies the usual distinction between internal and external attributions (Watts, Nye, and Savage 2002, 9–11). I also suggest that attributions to God are normally (and properly) used in conjunction with other more usual attributions, rather than as an alternative to them. So, recovery from illness can properly be attributed both to God and to medical treatment.

It might initially be tempting to make a distinction between psychological and religious approaches to personal change in terms of the attributions that are appropriate. Psychological change might be seen as calling for ordinary human attributions, and religious change as calling for attributions to God. However, there are several reasons why that would not be the right approach (Watts, Nye, and Savage 2002). First, it has become almost a cliché of theology that God is not to be seen as one more cause in a series of causal factors, but as a different kind of causal agent. In a similar way, I would suggest that God is not to be seen as one more possible attribution in a series of available attributions, but as a different kind of attribution. The implication is that attributions to God are not an alternative to human attributions but are to be used in a complementary way, alongside other human attributions, to open up the attributional space to a broader range of factors.

It is also important not to imagine that because psychotherapy normally proceeds outside a religious attributional framework (i.e., outside theology), it proceeds outside the providence of God. The difference between religious and secular approaches to personal transformation in how religious attributions are used may thus be a relatively subtle one. By theological assumption, creation owes its existence to God, and all personal healing reflects his purposes in a particular way. That is true of both medical practice and psychotherapy. It is not that religious attributions are appropriate in one case and not the other. In addition, religious attributions may well be used in secular forms of therapy, though often privately. The difference may lie in how explicitly and publicly religious attributions are used, either by the therapist or client, and in the degree of particularity with which they are elaborated.

Nevertheless, how explicitly religious attributions are used may have far-reaching consequences. Many human actions lend themselves to multiple narratives. However, one story is often primary in the sense that it is the controlling account that guides the actions of the participants. Following this analysis, I would suggest that in religious approaches to personal transformation, religious attributions are central to the controlling account of what is going on. God is named and invoked with a degree of explicitness and particularity in religious practices that is not found in their secular counterparts.

Some may be inclined to see this difference as relatively unimportant and to suppose that religious attributions are an incidental "add-on" that does not fundamentally change what is happening. However, I suggest that there is good reason to suppose that naming and invoking God in religious approaches to personal transformation can open the door to a form of divine action that might not be possible otherwise. Theologically, I would make the assumption that God usually chooses to act along with human cooperation, rather than independently of it. So, invoking God may open the way for God to act within the limits of God's self-denying ordinance in a way that would not otherwise be possible.

Following an earlier suggestion from John Polkinghorne, I have developed the view that the efficacy of prayer may involve the development of a kind of three-way "resonance" or "attunement" between God, the person who prays, and the person who is prayed for (Watts 2002a). It seems reasonable to suppose that the explicit invocation of God sets up a resonance that opens the way for the transforming power of God to operate. Exactly how that resonance operates is a question that goes beyond what is currently scientifically explicable, though I would be rash to claim that it could never, in principle, be understood scientifically. It is certainly possible to take analogies from science, such as the nuclear resonance that John Polkinghorne had in mind, and to use those to illustrate how this mode of divine action might work (Polkinghorne 1989).

In developing this kind of view, I would want to resist any sharp dualism between the natural and the spiritual. Some religious practices, such as the laying on of hands for healing, may be the occasion for a form of healing that is properly and appropriately called *spiritual*. However, to call healing *spiritual* only excludes natural processes if you operate with a sharply dualistic view of the relationship between the natural and the spiritual. That kind of dualism has been widely held since the Enlightenment. Miracles have come to be seen as overturning the laws of nature, while naturalism has been pushed to the limit, with the intention of making it the sole explanatory framework. However, I would prefer to operate with an enhanced naturalism that does not exclude the spiritual, but allows for a mutually interpenetrating symbiosis of natural and spiritual factors. Such a view is still rather unfashionable, and a dualistic approach to the natural and the spiritual is proving harder to overcome than a dualism of mind and body.

Forgiveness: Religious and Psychological Approaches

The practice of forgiveness provides a particularly interesting context in which to examine the relationship between religious and psychological approaches to personal transformation (Watts and Gulliford 2004). Forgiveness has long been central to religious practice and is a key element in the Judeo-Christian tradition. Recently, secular approaches to therapy have become aware of the potential human benefit of procedures designed to promote forgiveness, and there has been a notable migration of interest in forgiveness from the religious to the secular domains of contemporary culture. That raises in a particularly interesting and acute form the question of what the relationship is, or should be, between religious and psychological approaches to personal transformation.

There has been surprisingly little interest, on either the part of psychology or religion, in maintaining a dialogue about forgiveness. Having raided the religious treasury, psychology has largely established its own approach to forgiveness and is getting on with things in a spirit of independence. Substantial progress has been made, and there is now an impressive body of psychological research and practice on forgiveness. Equally, there is little interest among religious thinkers in the way in which forgiveness has been developed in secular therapy. On the contrary, therapeutic forgiveness has sometimes been regarded with suspicion, as a form of cheap forgiveness that does not adequately grapple with important, though difficult, issues.

One major complaint about the psychological approach to forgiveness is that it ignores the need for repentance. However, the Christian tradition is far from unanimous in thinking that repentance is a necessary precondition for forgiveness. Certainly, there is the recognition that forgiveness and repentance need to go hand in hand, and it is a fair complaint that the link between repentance and forgiveness has not been adequately recognized in psychological forgiveness. However, in the early Christian centuries, there was a significant debate about the order in which repentance and forgiveness should arise, with some arguing that repentance can (or perhaps even should) follow forgiveness rather than precede it.

Though the difference between religious and psychological approaches is thus perhaps not quite as sharp as is sometimes supposed, it is a reasonable complaint about psychological approaches to forgiveness that they give insufficient emphasis to painful and difficult issues that need to be confronted in the context of forgiveness. However, I suggest that there is no fundamental clash here between religious and psychological approaches. Indeed, if psychological approaches to forgiveness were more receptive to the religious tradition on this point, they would be offering a sounder and more balanced psychology of forgiveness.

Another way in which there has been a difference of emphasis between psychological and Christian approaches to forgiveness concerns a relative emphasis on antecedents or consequences. The psychology of forgiveness focuses almost entirely on the act of forgiveness and the benefits that flow from it. Christian thinking on forgiveness emphasizes context and antecedents much more, and understands how demanding forgiveness can be. For example, it recognizes that human forgiveness arises from the prior forgiveness of God and that our ability to forgive depends on our spiritual maturity and moral development.

In as far as there is an imbalance here, it is one that could, with profit, be corrected. The psychology of forgiveness has probably not underestimated the degree to which forgiveness requires a degree of psychological development, such as in our being able to see the good and bad aspects of the same situation. But it has not adequately recognized that there are situations, such as child abuse, where forgiveness is very difficult and where an implicit requirement to forgive may just add extra, unhelpful pressure. However, there is nothing in the psychological approach that precludes those perspectives; on the contrary, it would enrich the psychological approach to take them more fully on board.

The Christian approach to forgiveness, in turn, might deal more explicitly with the benefits of forgiveness. There has been an understandable concern that to undertake forgiveness solely for the benefits that it will bring is to diminish it in some important way. From a Christian point of view, forgiveness is costly and may simply be right even if the costs exceed the benefits. However, taking that line too strongly has often resulted in religious forgiveness being presented solely in terms of moral imperatives, in terms of what *should* be done, with a strange concealment of the fact that people are being invited to do something from which they will benefit. The promise and potential of forgiveness has become eclipsed by a more negative message about costs.

In examining the relationship between what the psychological and Christian traditions have to say about forgiveness, it is important not to make the mistake of thinking that the Christian tradition is un-psychological (let alone anti-psychological). In contrast, I would suggest that the psychology in the Christian approach to forgiveness is implicit rather than explicit. Making it explicit allows psychology to see more clearly the richness of the Christian tradition and to draw on it more fully.

Personality: Old and New

One of the most important issues of personal transformation is the degree of continuity that we find between the transformed and untransformed person. Psychology is fairly unanimous in stressing this continuity, though there can be a degree of transformation, by which the "new" person grows directly out of the old person. The Christian tradition is more varied in its view of this matter. There are some strands of Christian tradition that share this view of the extent to which the new person is grounded in the old, but other strands emphasize that the transformation is so radical that there is real discontinuity.

Psychology is bound to view the idea of radical discontinuity with some skepticism. The difference concerns not so much the extent of the change that is believed possible as how much the new person is rooted in the old. From a psychological point of view, the idea that people can make a completely fresh start in their personality is likely to be seen as some kind of "flight into health," or as a "flight into faith," and to be inherently unstable. More secure and durable personal change depends on transformation, or redemption, of a previous personality.

Again, there are different theological traditions. Some, especially those that place a strong emphasis on repentance, are inclined to emphasize leaving behind negative aspects of the previous personality. However other traditions emphasize redemption. Within psychology, Jung placed a particularly strong emphasis on the incorporation of the shadow in a complete, healed personality, and was very much on the side of redemption, rather than renunciation, in this debate.

Another crucial theological issue here concerns the link that is drawn between personal fulfillment and the purposes of God. In some traditions, there can be a radical disjunction between the two, with personal fulfillment seen as essentially self-centered. However, some Christian thinkers such as Thomas Merton assume that we find personal fulfillment in becoming the people that God intended us to be (Morea 1997). Fulfilling that God-given vocation involves overcoming obstacles to its realization rather than eradicating the more negative aspects of personality. Seen in this way, there is no radical opposition to the psychological and Christian approaches to personal transformation. But awareness of the psychological dimension is likely to lead to an emphasis on the strand of Christian thinking that emphasizes redemption rather than renunciation.

The basic assumption of this chapter has been that both Christianity and psychology have rich contributions to make to the elucidation of the process of personal transformation, and that it is fruitful to bring them into dialogue. A psychological perspective can make clearer what is often only implicit in the Christian tradition, for example by using psychology to elucidate the processes of transformation described in the Gospels. Equally, the rich tradition of Christian thinking can open up issues and perspectives that may be ignored in psychology, for example by using Christian thinking about forgiveness to enrich psychological approaches. There is also a fruitful comparison to be made of the somewhat different processes of personal transformation with which psychology and Christianity are primarily concerned, as in an examination of the similarities and differences between religious conversion and therapeutic change. Personal transformation is thus better understood with the binocular vision that comes from drawing on both these perspectives, rather than with the monocular vision that results from using either one on its own.

Note

1. For these and subsequent biblical references, see the New Revised Standard Version.

References

Morea, P. 1997. *In Search of Personality: Christianity and Modern Psychology*. London: SCM.

Polkinghorne, J. 1989. *Science and Providence*. London: SPCK.

Spilka, B., R. W. Hood, B. Hunsberger, and R. Gorsuch. 2003. *The Psychology of Religion: An Empirical Approach*. 3rd ed. New York: Guilford.

Spilka, B., and D. N. McIntosh, eds. 1997. *The Psychology of Religion: Theoretical Approaches*. Boulder, Colo.: Westview.

Watts, F. 2002a. *Theology and Psychology*. Aldershot, U.K.: Ashgate.

———. 2002b. Interacting cognitive subsystems and religious meanings. In *Neurotheology: Brain, Science, Spirituality, Religious Experience*, ed. R. Joseph, 183–88. San Jose, Calif.: University Press.

———. Forthcoming. Personal transformation. In *Jesus and Psychology*, ed. F. Watts. London: Darton, Longman and Todd.

Watts, F., and L. Gulliford, eds. 2004. *Forgiveness in Context*. London: T & T Clark.

Watts, F., R. Nye, and S. Savage. 2002. *Psychology for Christian Ministry*. London: Routledge.

11

Spiritual Growth, Cognition, and Complexity: Faith as a Dynamic Process

Carol Rausch Albright

As its central contribution, this chapter suggests that spiritual transformation and spiritual growth may be understood within the context of a scientific theory that has extremely broad applicability within both natural and social processes: the paradigm that comprises self-organization, complexity, and emergence. This paradigm is gaining broad acceptance at every level of scientific thought, from subatomic physics to zoology to group behavior. For clarity, this analysis begins with a discussion of spiritual growth and transformation based on the work of James Fowler and his colleagues. Next, spiritual growth and transformation are contextualized within contemporary neuroscience. The third theme, complexity theory, is then introduced, and there follows a trial integration of all three of these understandings. Finally some theological questions are briefly explored.

Theories of Spiritual Transformation and Spiritual Growth

Historically many scholars have described spiritual transformation and growth as stepwise processes, including both one-time, major personality reorganization and sequential development. Here I refer mainly to the work of James Fowler and his colleagues.[1] Fowler and his colleagues developed a questionnaire format to classify respondents by stage of spiritual development, and they refined this research instrument so that inter-interviewer agreement exceeded 90 percent. They described each stage of faith as a complex, holistic way of perceiving and organizing life.

What causes a shift from one stage to another? In childhood, brain maturation appears to be an important factor. In adults, new knowledge, changed conditions, or personal crisis may be the drivers. Certain faith traditions emphasize a one-time conversion, while others encourage development over a lifetime, with or without an initial transformative experience. Many writers, from Saint Augustine through Kierkegaard (2000), William James (1997/1902), and Chicago theologian Henry Nelson Wieman (1946), have noted that periods of personal struggle and upheaval tend to precede religious and personal "breakthroughs," after which new stages of personal organization emerge and new goals and abilities appear. However for various reasons, these periods of turmoil may also lead to deterioration.

Such experiences are not universal. A person may remain relatively oblivious to spiritual life or may remain in spiritual stasis, especially when conditions are comfortable and unchallenging. Indeed, some resist and condemn spiritual change, in much the same way that paradigm shifts in science are resisted by those invested in established viewpoints. And in fact, everything that is new is not always also good.

According to the findings of Fowler and his colleagues (1995/1981), spiritual development typically follows the sequence outlined below.

Stage 1, Intuitive-Projective Faith, is characteristic of young children at an age when they have many fantasies and learn by imitation. Children at this age can be powerfully and permanently influenced by examples, moods, actions, and stories, including those related to the faith of their caregivers. Fowler observes:

> Young children do not understand cause and effect relations well. . . . There is in this stage the possibility of aligning powerful religious symbols and images with deep feelings of terror and guilt, as well as of love and companionship. Such possibilities give this stage the potential for forming deep-going and long-lasting emotional and imaginal orientations—both for good and for ill. (2001, 3)

Stage 2, Mythic-Literal Faith, develops at a time when brain maturation enables the child to grasp cause and effect and see the world as a somewhat sensible and predictable place. Narrative is the main way of understanding symbols, and concepts are fairly concrete and literal. The focus is on fairness and moral reciprocity.

Stage 3, Synthetic Conventional Faith, appears when the maturing brain supports the ability to use abstract concepts and also to see things in interpersonal perspective, so that others are known to have agendas and feelings separate from one's own. God can be understood in terms of such personal qualities as accepting love, understanding, loyalty, and as offering support during times of crisis. An ideology or worldview is lived and asserted rather than reflected upon. Many adults remain in stage 3 for the remainder of their lives. It can be a comforting and comfortable stopping point. Shared values and group support can make life seem worthwhile and cushion some of the difficulties that life brings.

Stage 4, Individuative-Reflective Faith, involves a relocation of authority from the external group to the self. The individual begins to take seriously the burden of responsibility for commitments, lifestyle, beliefs, and attitudes. Roles in and commitments to the faith community may remain important, but they no longer define reality. Through critical reflection, the individual may now "demythologize" symbols, rituals, and myths. Although persons in this stage have confidence in their own thinking, they tend to remain relatively unaware of unconscious factors that may influence their judgment and behavior. Many find this a good basis on which to reach equilibrium.

Stage 5, Conjunctive Faith, characterizes many persons who begin to perceive that there are mysteries beyond any intellectual framework that they may discover or construct, and appreciate that there are various paths to understanding. To face the realization that no system of human understanding can integrate all the realities of life may require considerable courage. The result may be what Paul Ricœur has called a "second" or "willed" naïveté, a "readiness to enter the rich dwellings of meaning that true symbols, ritual and myth offer" (Fowler 2001, 5). These insights are seen for what they are: suggestions of the nature of mysteries that lie beyond knowing. Venturing into such uncharted depths, many persons in stage 5 take on characteristics, projects, or views that might not have been predicted on the basis of the personality previously evident. As they approach stage 6, their courage seems to increase.

Stage 6, Universalizing Faith. Fowler and his colleagues say they have never met a person who fully characterizes stage 6, only persons who mix traits from stages 5 and 6. To describe this final stage, Fowler and his colleagues have synthesized traits observed in various people, concluding that

> the structuring of this stage derives from the radical completion of a process of de-centration from self. . . . Each progressive stage marks a steady widening in social perspective taking. Gradually the circle of "those who count" in faith, meaning-making, and justice has expanded until, at the Conjunctive stage, it extends well beyond the bounds of social class, nationality, race, gender, ideological affinity, and religious tradition. . . . Psychodynamically, the self in this . . . stage moves beyond usual forms of defensiveness and exhibits an openness based on groundedness in the being, love, and regard of God. . . . Their approaches to personal and social reform are as concerned with the redemption and transformation of those they oppose as with bringing about justice and reform. (2001, 6–7)

Those who are in stage 6 still have flaws—blind spots and inconsistencies—and their relations with others retain some old problems. But stage 6 persons love life dearly, even while holding on to life loosely. Their central priority is no longer the survival of the self but the advancement of the human project, the widest possible set of concerns, the deepest possible vision. Stage 6 is, clearly, a rough equivalent of sainthood.

Spiritual Transformation and the Brain

Personality reorganization inevitably reflects—and is reflected by—changes in the organization of the brain. To discuss these changes requires a little information about brain structure and function. In the three pounds of tissue between our ears are roughly 100 billion tiny cells called neurons, which govern the operation of the body (including the brain), receive and process data, experience emotion, store and retrieve information, sometimes reach new conclusions, design courses of action, and help communicate information to other neurons and other persons.

Many neurons communicate primarily with other neurons in their local group, which in turn are linked with other groups, and with the somatic nervous system and the endocrine system as well. Directly or indirectly, each neuron is connected with between one thousand and ten thousand other neurons via links called axons and dendrites, which transmit electrochemical signals. The total number of interneural connections is estimated at about 1 quadrillion, and the total length of this "wiring" is roughly 62,000 miles, or 100,000 kilometers (Coveney and Highfield 1995, 285). In 2001, Merlin Donald estimated that an individual's data-processing capacity exceeded that of the entire worldwide electronic highway (2001, 103).

How is this information system organized? The human genome has some thirty thousand genes that set general patterns for the entire body, including its neuronal organization. Obviously, the fraction of genes concerned with brain development (as opposed to, say, eye color or toe length) cannot convey enough information to do the job. While genes do play an important design role, specifics depend on activation of genes. Various kinds of activation are triggered by the social environment, imposed or selected; the physical environment, external and internal; and behavior, including the actions of muscles and glands. Neuroscientist Jerre Levy describes the process of gene activation by analogy: "Genes are like library books—useless unless checked out and read" (Levy 2005).

Development of neuronal patterns is most active in early childhood. A baby is born with a plethora of neurons, which are programmed to self-destruct unless they are recruited for use. By age five, important features of neuronal architecture are in place. However, the interconnectivity of the brain is subject to development and modification throughout life, providing the brain remains healthy (Diamond 1998, 91–114). This openness to modification is called *plasticity*.

For optimal functioning, various sectors of the brain must collaborate. For example, Antonio Damasio has found that persons whose emotional and logical capacities do not collaborate tend not to make good decisions. Emotions communicate a sense of whether an option is good or bad, depending on past experience; emotions also help us empathize and motivate us to act. Logical analysis provides a different sort of reality check (cf. Damasio 1999, 254).

All parts of the brain obviously cannot be conscious at once. Not only would that be extremely confusing, but this much activity would probably use up all a person's available energy and more. As it is, the three-pound brain, on average, uses some 20 percent of total bodily energy. However, a good deal of brain activity does go on beneath the level of consciousness: "probably 90 percent of the work of the brain is carried out automatically" (Levy 2005). Unconscious activity, for example, speeds up the heartbeat in response to perceived danger, enables us to run and walk without thinking about it, and in general frees up the mind for activity that must be handled consciously. Consciousness is usually brought in when a person is faced with decision making. Without it, we cannot evaluate appropriately.

Heavy usage of neuronal links strengthens them; lack of activation vitiates them. Thus the brain self-organizes. Brain functions become *"constrained by the structure they have created through this self-organizing process. . . .* This provides for stability of the emergent mind. . . . If one's mind is made up, this mind 'set' could very well limit communication between individual neurons that may be necessary to form competing thoughts and beliefs" (Kahn, forthcoming; italics in original). Under such conditions, spiritual growth may remain fixed at a given stage. On the other hand, self-organizing dynamics can also help to

> dissolve pre-existing mind patterns . . . when changes occur that are sufficiently large to cause the existing brain activity to become unstable. A transition to a new mind state that is stable in the changed environment may then occur. . . . After the existing thought patterns dissolve, the mind is then able to take on new learning through subsequent self-organizing brain processes. (Kahn, forthcoming)

Thus, spiritual transformation may result in semipermanent change, or it may prime the mind to remain open to continuing spiritual development.

Mind and Brain

I am assuming that changes in the mind and brain are companion processes—that, in fact, the mind is what the brain *does*—and that the brain becomes what the mind *is*. In this view, the brain is a thing, a "noun," while the mind is a process, a "verb" (cf. Ashbrook and Albright 1997). To be more precise, I should note that the mind is in fact a function of both brain and body, since brain and body are continually interacting and influencing one another. We could say that the brain is the principal organ of the nervous system, and the mind is the action of the entire embodied nervous system. Personality changes, including changes in spiritual organization, are thus correlated with changes in the organization of the nervous system, and particularly of the brain.

Many people find such physicalism simply unacceptable; to them, it not only implies determinism but also seems to deny human dignity and value. But perhaps the opposite is true. To identify mind with brain may seem threatening because it implies that our sense of self-determination is an illusion: if our neurons actually control us, then we do not really control ourselves. This belief has not entirely disappeared, even within neuroscience, but it is in fact a gross oversimplification of what goes on.

Top Down and Bottom Up

It is true that signals from primitive centers of the brain have an effect on the higher centers of the brain, so that, for example, a sense of endangerment will alert the analytical brain to evaluate the nature of a possible threat (LeDoux 2002, 216). However, the reverse is true as well. The brain takes note of outcomes and therefore modifies the way it responds to similar experiences and the value it places upon them. These modifications, in turn, influence future thought and behavior (cf. Brown 1999, 24). In more technical terms, "subjective experiences are causally potent emergent properties of the adaptive brain"; and consciousness, which "evolved in the service of adaptive function, [has] potent top-down regulation over less complex neuronal processes" (Levy 2005).

Top-down brain activity based upon learning is important to both personal survival and the persistence of human culture. Effective learned behavior improves one's odds of living and reproducing, and the thought patterns underlying such behaviors are therefore most apt to be culturally transmitted to future generations.

From such cultural learning we glean habitual thoughts and central motivations. As Joseph LeDoux has shown, those goals on which we "set our hearts" continually influence the organization of the neurons (2002, 319). Over time, this process supports individualization. Each person's specific gifts, personal interests, and responsibilities become more clearly defined. The individualizing personality is *emergent*, and it becomes increasingly effective through synergies of various sorts. In theological terms, one's particular calling in the world at the time becomes more evident, and optimally, spiritual growth and transformation proceed on this basis.

These observations bear on issues of freedom and determinism. A person cannot exercise every choice that is theoretically available. Realistically, choices depend not only upon external options but also upon who we have become. Over time our choices affect the abilities we develop and the values and perceptions that become embedded in our personalities. The personalities we build, together with immediate decisions, collaborate in self-determination.

Embodiment

On this account, our mind and brain can be said to *embody* our spirit, as biblical tradition has long recognized. The New Testament, like the Old, emphasizes the essential unity of the person, as what we might call a psycho-somato-spiritual entity. Malcolm Jeeves (1994, 130) therefore concludes that spirit may be regarded as a functional outcome of the human journey, not a separate structural entity.

Valuation or Devaluation?

It is difficult to conclude that one devalues the human person by recognizing such dynamism. Instead, this way of looking at the personality and its physical substrate can only underline the incredible value of the human person (Damasio 1994, xvi, cited in Goodenough 1998, 109). Far from feeling demeaned by having such brains, we may see these organs as hallmarks of our remarkableness. For the human brain is in fact the most complex system, for its size, that we know of in the universe.

Complexity Theory

As noted in the opening lines of this chapter, the process of spiritual growth and its neurological substrate seem embedded within a much broader process that appears to characterize the universe in a multiplicity of ways. This process is usually described under the rubric of *complexity theory*, which is rapidly gaining acceptance in a significant paradigm shift.

Very basically, complexity theory asserts that a tendency to self-organization pervades natural systems, from the basic building blocks of the universe to the most sophisticated forms of human social interaction. Furthermore, once certain levels of organization are reached, a shift in identity takes place. As a very simple example, when hydrogen and oxygen form water, they no longer resemble the gases they had been; in fact, the nature of water could not be inferred from the nature of oxygen and hydrogen. Similarly, the nature of slime mold, one of the simplest of living organisms, could not be inferred from the organic molecules that constitute it. Such surprises—known as *emergents*—are a hallmark of complexity. Emergents have properties unknown in their predecessors because new types of organization now characterize their constituent ingredients. This phenomenon is known as *synergy*, and it too characterizes complexification. (Scientists have not, in general, agreed upon a neat definition of complexification; rather, they recognize it by the hallmarks that I have just discussed and which I will describe in more detail below.)

Details of such processes have been uncovered rapidly since the 1985 founding of the Santa Fe Institute in New Mexico. The institute's founders, including Nobel Prize winners in a variety of disciplines, were convinced they were onto something important, and they established this center as a place to develop their understandings on an interdisciplinary level. The increasing power of computers has also helped enable research into complex systems.

Complexity theory is a subset of thermodynamics, and to discuss it in context requires a brief introduction to the second law of thermodynamics, in which it is embedded. First proposed by Rudolf Clausius in 1850, the second law today is foundational to almost every scientific discipline. It states that in closed systems— ranging in size from small enclosures to the entire universe— energy will be distributed more and more evenly. This takes place as areas or entities with more than average energy (e.g., warm objects) transfer energy (e.g., heat) to areas or entities with less energy (e.g., colder objects). This leveling-out of energy levels is known as *the increase of entropy*. In a small system, uniformity may develop rather quickly. But in a system the size of the universe, the process may take billions of years. During the periods intermediate between the big bang and the end of time, such as the one we live in now, for example, there remains a great deal of energy differential. Since energy transfer is what accomplishes all change and all work, we naturally live in a dynamic time.

Finally however, according to the second law of thermodynamics, all forms of energy will be equally distributed. At that point, no further exchange of energy can take place, and absolutely nothing more can happen. The predicted outcome is a completely uniform, static universe. All activity will cease, and time as we know it will end, "Not with a bang but a whimper," in the words of the poet T. S. Eliot (1980/1925, 59).

This belief in an ultimately dying universe has pervaded scientific thought for more than a century and has contributed to the ennui that Eliot poetically expressed. It has also been intuitively apparent, since Darwin's time and earlier, that processes that promote organization are concurrently operative. The direction of change between the big bang and the present day does not actually look like a one-way ticket to decay. Instead, many arrangements have become more and more complex.

After the big bang, it is said, matter clumped together in "clouds," and within them, matter coalesced to form stars. Within these stars, the light gases of the big bang were transformed into heavier elements, such as carbon and metals, through atomic fusion. Some of these stars exploded, sprinkling the cosmos with both light and heavy elements. (All known life requires these heavy elements, which once were stardust.) These elements joined together to form compounds, and some eventually formed large organic molecules. Finally, life itself appeared, on earth and probably elsewhere. Many compounds and simple life forms remained stable or changed into comparably simple entities, but others went on to form new and progressively more complex combinations. On our planet, these more complex combinations include multicellular plants and animals and intelligent life. And one can easily extend the process to include the evolution of culture and its feedback relationship with biological evolution, together known as *biocultural evolution*.

The sort of process described here—the progressive joining together of simpler compounds to form more complex entities—is self-organizing. All such reorganization involves the operation of many self-modifying feedback loops (as Warren Brown has pointed out in regard to mental complexification [1999, 24]). By definition, systems featuring feedback are nonlinear. And, in fact, all complexifying systems are nonlinear. That is, they do not behave in the straightforward manner of cause-and-effect.

In his massive work *The Structure of Evolutionary Theory* (2002), Stephen Jay Gould argues that complexification is only one of many sorts of "punctuated change" seen in natural evolution. In Gould's view, systems remain stable in the face of changing circumstance until events push them "over the edge." At this point, change occurs relatively suddenly. While complexification is one option, "horizontal" change and actual "de-complexification" can also occur (cf. 928ff.). However, according to Gould, complex entities often have an evolutionary advantage, and so they have persisted and proliferated. One could argue that human spiritual insights, for example, seem in general to be more complex than those reached in the distant past of humankind; that the changes in complexity have been partially driven by changing circumstances; and that in some but not all cases, they have been adaptive. Spiritual practice and its related interpersonal community are apparently key variables in health and longevity (Koenig 2004).

Conditions Supporting Complexification

It is important to emphasize that complexification as described here seems to occur only when neither order nor chaos prevails—

that is, when some features of the environment behave predictably and lawfully, while others vary stochastically, that is to say, with apparent randomness (Gell-Mann 1994, 115; Kaufman 1995, 91). Too much order produces only stasis; too much chaos prevents any sort of stable outcome. Our epoch provides both order and openness to change, and it supports dynamic complexification in spirituality as in other realms. (For this reason, it is erroneous to equate order with virtue and chaos with evil; both are necessary to dynamic life.)

Dynamic complexification gives rise to entities, including thought forms, that are genuinely new and more complex than their predecessors. Their qualities cannot be predicted on the basis of their constituent parts. Some of these emergent phenomena survive and persist, and in the nature of things, they in turn give rise to emergents that are more complex still.[2] Thus the world in which we live is a dynamic place, both physically and culturally, and fosters unpredictable outcomes.

Recognizing Complexity

As you can imagine, mathematically oriented scientists have tried to devise ways to quantify degrees of complexity. One way to do so is to measure the length of nonrecursive computer code necessary to describe something (Gell-Mann 1994, 50). A repetitive pattern of code (or a repetitive physical pattern, as in fractals) does not signify complexity no matter how long it continues. Rather, the pattern must be nonrepetitive, and the longer the nonrepetitive code, the more complexity it indicates.

Nonmathematicians may understand complexity through images. Complex organization involves multiple connections among its elements, and these connections need to be convergent. A honeycomb or a fishnet has many connections, but they are repetitive and not convergent. Therefore these patterns are not very complex. A spiderweb, on the other hand, has a pattern of convergent connections with cross-webbing. Many lines of communication come together in one spot: the center of the web. Now, suppose many webs hang in the same tree, and all of them are linked by spider silks. Furthermore, these linking silks all converge into a "master" spiderweb center. This pattern represents a second level of complexity. If more of these convergent centers were linked again into a third convergence, there would be a third level of complexity.[3]

Of course, this is only a model for real systems. In a biological system there are organizational levels including atoms, molecules, compounds, cells, cell assemblies, and so on. At each level, new characteristics unexpectedly emerge, and synergies increase. For example, a rabbit is much more complex than an equal weight of protozoa, and it has many more kinds of abilities.

Not only can the rabbit run and find food, it can also interact with other rabbits (and usually does), thus creating more rabbits. In their own interactions human beings breed, but they also develop and transmit cultural learning, and this activity enhances human synergies so much that culture is thought to be a defining human characteristic. In fact in every culture, one's personal effectiveness depends strongly on one's interactions with other persons and organizations. The relationships and organizations themselves may be seen as emergents. (Thus complexity theory becomes descriptive of cultural change, including religious change, and of individual spiritual development within a culture.)

A synergistic system accomplishes more, and it does so using fewer resources. A synergistic business system is therefore more likely to succeed. And scans show that the brain of a person who is working effectively to solve a problem metabolizes less energy than the brain of someone who is ineffectually casting about for solutions. We can assume then that the brain of the problem solver is organized with more complexity. It is for reasons such as these that Robert Wright referred to the process of complexification as a "non-zero-sum process" (2000, 252) with an outcome greater than the sum of its parts.

Complexity, the Brain, and Spiritual Growth

Let us pause here to recapitulate some of the ground we have covered. First, we saw that spiritual growth may be seen as a stepwise process. In childhood and youth, steps of spiritual growth are heavily dependent not only on genetic endowment but also on brain maturation and social learning. Later in life new experiences and opportunities, or life crises, may provide an impetus toward reorganization. The transition here often involves a period of turmoil.

We have also seen that changes in personality organization and changes in brain organization probably mirror one another. Brain imaging cannot be performed in enough detail to prove that this assertion is true, but current evidence supports it. Noted neuroscientist Jean-Pierre Changeux observes, "I have also much insisted upon the cleavage between levels of organization of the nervous system, which it seems legitimate to see as corresponding to levels of mental representation that become more and more integrated the higher one rises in the hierarchy" (Changeux and Ricœur 2000, 247). In this case, each stage of spiritual growth would seem to involve an increased complexity of brain organization. Through successive modifications, spiritual growth progresses. As David Kahn points out (Forthcoming), a rigid reorganization may preclude future development, but complexification may also open the way for flexible and courageous growth in the future.

At each stage of faith, we see increased integration among abstract thinking, personal relationships, and responsibility. Unforeseeable personality developments emerge. Both knowledge and interrelationships widen and deepen, thereby increasing effectiveness. Here we see the qualities of convergence, emergence, and synergy that are key to complexification.

Finally, in persons who approach or enter stage 6, issues of faith and meaning making, and a passion for justice and equity, transcend conventional social categories. Such persons have concerns of great magnitude and links with others too numerous to count. Because they serve as centers of great complexification, their emergent abilities reach an unforeseeable magnitude. An exemplar who comes to mind is Nelson Mandela, who changed the world while imprisoned by a regime oppressive to his race, by working in concert with courageous allies.

The phenomena of spiritual transformation and spiritual growth, as presented here, mirror the constructive processes of the universe. They involve not only matters of personality change but also underlying neurological organization. They are most apt to occur during conditions that combine some predictability and some change—either neuronal development in the young or other changed conditions in the mature. They give rise to developments in personality that are indeed emergent. They promote synergy. And their manifestations do not end with the individual but extend beyond—in this case, to the larger society.

Issues and Explorations

Two important questions have been raised regarding this line of thinking, and I will address these questions here. One concern is that self-organization and emergence inevitably lead to hierarchy, and that hierarchy enables oppression. Indeed, emergence is a stepwise process, but it need not imply oppression, which occurs when a few ascend to a higher level and the many become subject to them. In regard to self-organization, consider the simple case of oxygen and hydrogen. When the two form water, the constituent gases are not left behind. They in fact *become* the water. Similarly, if a group of people organizes in a complex way, so that their energies converge, then synergies develop, new conditions emerge, and all the members of this society may benefit. The members of this society participate in its growth and need not be left behind.[4]

Some suggest that personal complexification may simply enable more powerful or effective evildoing, because some of the world's great evildoers had powerful personalities and led powerful organizations. I would argue, however, that these evildoers were complexified in an incomplete or distorted way. Increase of love is not only characteristic of spiritual growth, it is also evidence of ever-widening concerns and convergent linkages, as we saw in our discussion of stage 6 spiritual development. The concern with love that characterizes many religions could be interpreted as a call for action that promotes individual and societal growth of complexity, rightly understood. More questions will doubtless be raised. The application of complexity theory to spirituality opens fruitful paths for reflection that await exploration.

Conclusions from a Theistic Perspective

What has been presented here aims toward an understanding of human religious experience that integrates a scientific understanding of human beings as embodied selves; a view of religious experience as multileveled, involving persons as bodily, emotional, intellectual, and social beings; and a dynamic, multivariate understanding of the human spiritual journey. Though we live in a world influenced by lawfulness, openness also plays an important role and enables choice. Our choices are not simply chaotic or random, like the spin of a roulette wheel. *Choices result organically from the nature of our individuality, which we have each helped to build, and continue to construct. They also depend upon the nature of the culture we collectively devise.*

It seems to me that dynamic spiritual growth, not merely our assent to its precepts, is the heart of religion. Religion rests upon symbolic understandings, and it is expressed through the experiences and decisions of life—individual and cultural. As such, it is dynamic, involving thoughts, actions, interactions, feedback, and learning. Love that is applied has an effect in the world, and upon the person performing the actions. This circular pattern of action and growth promotes further complexification of the character—and the brain—of the individual, and unforeseeable emergences within the human project. The emergent phenomena yet to come are beyond prediction. They will depend to a considerable extent upon human creativity and choice.

We humans are truly part of the physical universe—composed of quarks and leptons, carbon and oxygen, limited by DNA-based information, and molded by experience. Any knowledge that we may have of God is necessarily mediated by our brain and shaped by the thought forms with which the brain operates. As a theist, I find appealing Fraser Watts's view that comprehension of divine purpose arises within the dance of living rather than in the abstract. Watts observes,

> It seems both more likely scientifically, and more theologically congenial, that God would want to relate to us as the integrated physical-mental spiritual creatures that we are. . . . When God acts in relation to people or reveals himself to them, we should expect this to be reflected in, and mediated through, all levels of our person. (2002, 105)

Thus, God's influence on people normally "arises from a kind of enactive knowing, in which understanding and action are held together" (110; for more on Watts's thought, see Albright 2003, 243).[5]

I have edited many books over the course of my career, and when I have finished with one, I have gained a deep sense of the character and thought processes of the writer, even if I have never met her or him and the work is not autobiographical. Could it be that the character of the universe also reflects, in a deep way, the character of its creator, of a ground of being? If so, can we conclude anything about the creator from the fact that some conditions are predictable and some are open, so that emergence may occur? Are not we, like the rest of the universe, both stuff and process, static and dynamic, dogged by entropy and lured by complexification? If so, are personal and spiritual growth, as emergents, goals of the human condition, but not guaranteed outcomes? Are wholeness and healing related to the level of integration and spiritual emergence that result? Is the world arranged so as to provide conditions for our growth— and if so, do these conditions point to love on the part of the creator? And, finally, is the creator also dynamic yet predictable, responsive and interactive—the most complex that can be imagined?

Notes

1. For a more extensive discussion, including contributions by William James (1997/1902), Abraham Maslow (1964), Erik Erikson (1994), Jean Piaget (2000), Carol Gilligan (1993), Lawrence Kohlberg (1981), and others, the reader is referred to my book *Growing in the Image of God* (2002).

2. For the sake of scientific clarity, it is important to note that complexification does not prevent the overall progression of entropy, mainly because increases in organization generate wastes that are less organized. For example, animals, which of course are complex life forms, exhale carbon dioxide, a smaller, less-organized molecule than the hydrocarbons they took in as food and used to maintain their complexity. Thus, even as some substances complexify, others decomplexify or are decomplexified as a result. In this way, increase of entropy continues.

3. For the metaphor of the fishnet and the spiderweb, I am indebted to Cary Neeper of Los Alamos, New Mexico.

4. Many examples of this sort of process come to mind. For example, several of the founders of modern physics—John von Neumann, Leo Szilard, Edward Teller, Eugene Wigner—were high-school friends in Budapest. Paul Dirac joined the group by marrying Wigner's sister.

5. It is interesting that the viewpoints expressed in this paper are in some consonance with feminist views, in which embodiment and ties of relationship have high standing. As we have seen, however, thinkers of both genders have expressed such views.

References

Albright, C. R. 2002. *Growing in the Image of God*. Toronto: Novalis.

———. 2003. Theology and psychology: An essay review on Fraser Watts. *Interdisciplinary Science Reviews* (December): 241–44.

Ashbrook, J., and C. R. Albright. 1997. *The Humanizing Brain: Where Religion and Neuroscience Meet*. Cleveland, Ohio: Pilgrim.

Brown, W. S. 1999. A neurocognitive perspective on free will. *CTNS Bulletin* 19 (1): 22–29.

Changeux, J.-P., and P. Ricœur. 2000. *What Makes Us think? A Neuroscientist and a Philosopher Argue about Ethics, Human Nature, and the Brain*, trans. M. B. DeBevoise. Princeton, N.J.: Princeton University Press.

Coveney, P., and R. Highfield. 1995. *Frontiers of Complexity*. New York: Fawcett Columbine.

Damasio, A. R. 1994. *Descartes' Error: Emotion, Reason, and the Human Brain*. New York: Putnam.

———. 1999. *The Feeling of What Happens: Body and Emotions in the Making of Consciousness*. New York: Harcourt Brace.

Diamond, M. C. 1998. *Enriching Heredity: The Impact of the Environment on the Heredity of the Brain*. New York: Free Press.

Donald, M. 2001. *A Mind So Rare: The Evolution of Human Consciousness*. New York: W.W. Norton.

Eliot, T. S. 1980. *The Hollow Men: The Complete Poems and Plays*. New York: Harcourt, Brace. (Orig. pub. 1925.)

Erikson, E. 1994. *Identity and the Life Cycle*. New York: W.W. Norton.

Fowler, J. 1995. *Stages of Faith*. San Francisco: Harper San Francisco. (Orig. pub. 1981.)

———. 2001. Stages of faith and the human brain. Paper presented at the Montreal CTNS Advanced Workshop in Neuroscience, Religious Experience, and the Self, Montreal, May 31–June 5.

Gell-Mann, M. 1994. *The Quark and the Jaguar: Adventures in the Simple and Complex*. New York: W.H. Freeman.

Gilligan, C. 1993. *In a Different Voice: Psychological Theory and Women's Development*. Cambridge: Harvard University Press.

Goodenough, U. 1998. *The Sacred Depths of Nature*. New York: Oxford University Press.

Gould, S. J. 2002. *The Structure of Evolutionary Theory*. Cambridge: Belknap Press of Harvard University Press.

James, W. 1997. *The Varieties of Religious Experience: A Study in Human Nature*. New York: Simon and Schuster. (Orig. pub. 1902.)

Jeeves, M. 1994. *Mind Fields: Reflections on the Science of Mind and Brain*. Grand Rapids, Mich.: Baker Books.

Kahn, D. Forthcoming. From chaos to self-organization: The brain, dreaming, and religious experience. In *Soul, Psyche, Brain: New Directions in the Study of Religion and Brain-Mind Science*, ed. K. Bulkeley. New York: Palgrave Macmillan.

Kaufman, S. 1995. *At Home in the Universe*. New York: Oxford University Press.

Kierkegaard, S. 2000. *The Essential Kierkegaard*, ed. H. V. Hong and E. H. Hong. Princeton: Princeton University Press.

Koenig, H. 2004. *The Healing Connection*. Radnor, Pa.: Templeton Foundation Press.

Kohlberg, L. 1981. *The Meaning and Measurement of Moral Development*. Worcester, Mass.: Clark University Press.

LeDoux, J. 2002. *Synaptic Self: How Our Brains Become Who We Are*. New York: Viking.

Levy, J. 2005. Ideas of nature: The brain and self. Lecture presented at the Advanced Seminar in Religion and Science, Lutheran School of Theology at Chicago, February 21. Quotes verified by Levy.

Maslow, A. H. 1964. *Religions, Values, and Peak Experiences*. Columbus: Ohio State University Press.

Piaget, J., and B. Inhelder. 2000. *The Psychology of the Child*, trans. H. Weaver. New York: Basic Books. (Orig. pub. 1969.)

Watts, F. 2002. *Theology and Psychology*. Aldershot, U.K.: Ashgate.

Wieman, H. N. 1946. *The Source of Human Good*. Carbondale: Southern Illinois University Press.

Wright, R. 2000. *Non-zero: The Logic of Human Destiny*. New York: Pantheon.

PART IV

NEUROSCIENTIFIC PERSPECTIVES ON SPIRITUAL TRANSFORMATION AND HEALING

12

The Neurobiology of Spiritual Transformation

Andrew Newberg

The study of spiritual transformation is ultimately the study of a complex mental process. The study of spiritual transformation is also potentially one of the most important areas of research that may be pursued by science in the next decade. This may be an understatement, since spiritual transformation offers a fascinating window into human consciousness, psychology, and experience; the relationship between mental states and body physiology; emotional and cognitive processing; and the biological correlates of religious and spiritual experiences. In the past thirty years, scientists have explored the biology of various components of spiritual transformational practices and processes in some detail. Many studies have focused on specific practices such as prayer or meditation rather than on the specific moment of transformation that might be associated with such practices. However, since these practices can lead to transformative experiences, there certainly is value in understanding them. Thus, initial studies of such spiritual practices have measured changes in autonomic activity, such as heart rate and blood pressure, as well as electroencephalographic changes. More recent studies have explored changes in hormonal and immunological function associated with meditation. Functional neuroimaging has opened a new window into the investigation of states associated with spiritual practices by exploring the neurological correlates of these experiences.

Neuroimaging techniques include positron emission tomography (PET; Herzog et al. 1990–1991; Lou et al. 1999), single photon emission computed tomography (SPECT; Newberg et al. 2001), and functional magnetic resonance imaging (fMRI; Lazar et al. 2000). Each of these techniques provides different advantages and disadvantages in the study of meditation. Although fMRI offers improved resolution over SPECT and the ability of immediate anatomic correlation, it would be very difficult to utilize for the study of meditation because of noise from the machine and the problem of requiring the subject to lie down, an atypical posture for many forms of meditation. While PET imaging also provides better resolution than SPECT, if one strives to make the environment relatively distraction-free to maximize the chances of having a strong meditative experience, it is sometimes beneficial to perform these studies during nonclinical times, which may make PET radiopharmaceuticals such as fluorodeoxyglucose difficult to obtain.

With regard to transformative experiences, brain-imaging studies may be more problematic since the actual moment of a spiritual transformation is almost impossible to predict, and if it were interrupted in order to obtain a scan or assess the exact mental state, the transformative experience would be severely altered. On the other hand, individuals who are striving to attain transformative states could be imaged before such an attempt and then after the transformation has occurred, to determine trait-related changes in the brain's function. Thus, functional brain imaging offers potentially important techniques for studying spiritual transformation and related practices, although the best approach may depend on a number of factors.

In this chapter, I review the existing data on neurophysiology and physiology with relation to spiritual transformation and the practices that may bring on such experiences. I will attempt to integrate here the existing data into a comprehensive neurochemical model of such practices (see fig. 12.1 below). This model is designed to provide a framework of the neurological and physiological correlates of transformative experiences and to create a springboard for future research.

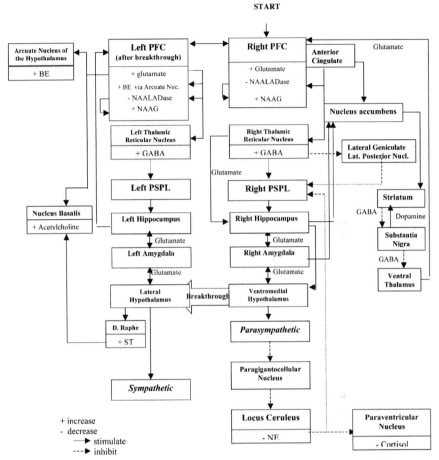

START

Figure 12.1. Schematic overview of the neurophysiological network possibly associated with meditative states. The circuits generally apply to both hemispheres; however, much of the initial activity is on the right.

Activation of the Prefrontal and Cingulate Cortex

Since some approaches to spiritual transformation involve practices in which the person on their own volition attempts to enter into such a state, I will begin with the parts of the brain that might be associated with the human will. Brain imaging studies suggest that willful acts and tasks that require sustained attention are initiated via activity in the prefrontal cortex (PFC), particularly in the right hemisphere (Frith et al. 1991; Ingvar 1994; Pardo, Fox, and Raichle

1991; Posner and Petersen 1990). The cingulate gyrus has also been shown to be involved in focusing attention, probably in conjunction with the PFC (Vogt, Finch, and Olson 1992). Since transformative types of practices such as meditation require intense focus of attention, it seems that there should be activation of the PFC as well as the cingulate gyrus. This notion is supported by the increased activity observed in these regions by several brain-imaging studies of volitional types of meditation, including those from our laboratory (Herzog et al. 1990–1991; Lazar et al. 2000; Newberg et al. 2001).

In our study of eight Tibetan Buddhist meditators, subjects had an intravenous line placed and were injected with a cerebral blood flow tracer while at rest in order to acquire a baseline image. They then meditated for approximately one hour, when they were again injected with the tracer while they continued to meditate. The tracer is fixed in the brain at the time of injection, so that when the images were acquired approximately twenty minutes later, they reflected the cerebral blood flow during the meditation state. These images demonstrated increased activity during meditation in the PFC bilaterally (greater on the right) and the cingulate gyrus. Therefore, meditation appears to start by activating the prefrontal and cingulate cortex associated with the will or the intent to clear the mind of thoughts or to focus on an object. Of course, meditation does not necessarily lead to transformation, so frontal-lobe activity alone does not seem to provide a complete understanding of these experiences. In fact, some transformative experiences are associated with feelings in which the self feels "overtaken" by the experience itself. The self feels as if it becomes absorbed into or lost in the experience. If the frontal lobe is involved in willful activity, then a transformative experience associated with a feeling of losing the self, or of the original self being overcome by something spiritual, might be associated with a lack of activity in the frontal lobes. However, this has not yet been studied.

Thalamic Activation

Several animal studies have shown that the PFC, when activated, innervates the reticular nucleus of the thalamus (Cornwall and

Phillipson 1988), particularly as part of a more global attentional network (Portas et al. 1998). Such activation may be accomplished by the PFC's production and distribution of an excitatory neurotransmitter glutamate, which the PFC neurons use to communicate among themselves and to innervate other brain structures (Cheramy, Romo, and Glowinski 1987). The thalamus itself governs the flow of sensory information to cortical processing areas via its interactions with the lateral geniculate and lateral posterior nuclei, and also likely uses the glutamate system in order to activate neurons in other structures (Armony and LeDoux 2000).

When excited, the reticular nucleus elaborates the inhibitory neurotransmitter gamma aminobutyric acid (GABA) onto the lateral posterior and geniculate nuclei, cutting off input to the posterior superior parietal lobe (PSPL) and visual centers in proportion to the reticular activation (Destexhe, Contreras, and Steriade 1998). During practices such as meditation, because of the increased activity in the PFC, particularly on the right, there should be a concomitant increase in activity in the reticular nucleus of the thalamus. While brain-imaging studies of meditation have not had the resolution to distinguish the reticular nuclei, our recent SPECT study did demonstrate a general increase in thalamic activity that was proportional to the activity levels in the PFC. This is consistent with, but does not confirm the specific interaction between the PFC and reticular nuclei. If the activation of the right PFC causes increased activity in the reticular nucleus during meditation, the result may be decreased sensory input entering the PSPL. Several studies have demonstrated an increase in serum GABA during meditation, possibly reflecting increased central GABA activity (Elias, Guich, and Wilson 2000). This functional deafferentation related to increased GABA would mean that fewer distracting outside stimuli would arrive at the visual cortex and PSPL, enhancing the sense of focus. During transformative experiences, similar mechanisms might be in place, although the interaction between the frontal lobe and the thalamus might be more complex, such that some states may be associated with mutual increases, some with mutual decreases, and some with one turned on and the other off. The mechanism of the latter is less clear at this time.

It should also be noted that the dopaminergic system, via the basal ganglia, is believed to participate in regulating the glutamatergic system and the interactions between the prefrontal cortex and subcortical structures. A recent PET study utilizing 11C-Raclopride to measure dopaminergic tone during Yoga Nidra meditation demonstrated a significant increase in dopamine levels during the meditation practice (Kjaer et al. 2002). The researchers hypothesized that this increase may be associated with the gating of cortical-subcortical interactions that leads to an overall decrease in readiness for action that is associated with this particular type of meditation. This decrease may effectively take the frontal lobes "off-line" and result in the sense of losing control. It is also well-known that the dopaminergic system is involved in euphoric states and thus may be associated with the transformative experiences of high emotional states. Future studies will be necessary to elaborate on the role of dopamine in spiritual transformation as well as on the interactions between dopamine and other neurotransmitter systems.

Posterior Superior Parietal Lobe Deafferentation

The PSPL is heavily involved in the analysis and integration of higher-order visual, auditory, and somaesthetic information (Adair et al. 1995). It is also involved in a complex attentional network that includes the PFC and thalamus (Fernandez-Duque and Posner 2001). Through the reception of auditory and visual input from the thalamus, the PSPL is able to help generate a three-dimensional image of the body in space, provide a sense of spatial coordinates in which the body is oriented, help distinguish between objects, and exert influences in regard to objects that may be directly grasped and manipulated (Lynch 1980). These functions of the PSPL might be critical for distinguishing between the self and the external world. It should be noted that a recent study has suggested that the superior temporal lobe may play a more important role in body spatial representation, although this has not been confirmed by other reports (Karnath, Ferber, and Himmelbach 2001). However, the actual relationship between the parietal and temporal lobes in terms of spatial representation remains to be seen.

Regardless, deafferentation of these orienting areas of the brain, I propose, is an important concept in the physiology of transformative practices and experiences. If, for example, there is deafferentation of the PSPL by the reticular nucleus's GABAergic effects, the person may begin to lose their usual ability to spatially define and orient the self. This is an experience frequently associated with meditative practices as well as with transformative types of experiences. Deafferentation of the PSPL has also been supported by two imaging studies demonstrating decreased activity in this region during intense meditation (Herzog et al. 1990–1991; Newberg et al. 2001). Further, our SPECT study showed a correlation between increasing activity in the thalamus and decreasing activity in the PSPL.

Hippocampal and Amygdalar Activation

In addition to complex cortical-thalamic activity, transformative processes might also be associated with altered activity in the limbic system, especially since stimulation of limbic structures is associated with profound emotional responses (Fish et al. 1993; Saver and Rabin 1997). The hippocampus acts to modulate and moderate cortical arousal and responsiveness, via rich and extensive interconnections with the prefrontal cortex, other neocortical areas, the amygdala, and the hypothalamus (Joseph 1996, 197). Hippocampal stimulation has been shown to diminish cortical responsiveness and arousal; however, if cortical arousal is initially at a low level, then hippocampal stimulation tends to augment cortical activity (Redding 1967). The ability of the hippocampus to stimulate or inhibit neuronal activity in other structures likely relies upon the glutamate and GABA systems respectively (Armony and LeDoux 2000).

My colleagues and I have previously suggested that the blocking of sensory information (i.e., deafferentation) of the PSPL might be associated with the loss of the sense of self or of the orientation of that self to other objects in the world. Since this loss of orientation of the self is often described in transformative experiences, the deafferentation of the PSPL might be an important mechanism underlying such experiences. If partial deafferentation of the right PSPL occurs during a transformative experience, the result may be stimulation of the right hippocampus because of the inverse modulation of the hippocampus in relation to cortical activity. If in addition there is simultaneous direct stimulation of the right hippocampus via the thalamus (as part of the known attentional network) and mediated by glutamate, then a powerful recruitment of stimulation of the right hippocampus could occur. Right hippocampal activity may ultimately enhance the stimulatory function of the PFC on the thalamus via the nucleus accumbens, which gates the neural input from the PFC to the thalamus via the neuromodulatory effects of dopamine (Chow and Cummings 1999; Newman and Grace 1999).

The hippocampus greatly influences the amygdala, such that they complement and interact in the generation of attention, emotion, and certain types of imagery (Joseph 1996). It seems that much of the prefrontal modulation of emotion is via the hippocampus and its connections with the amygdala (Poletti and Sujatanond 1980). Because of this reciprocal interaction between the amygdala and hippocampus, the activation of the right hippocampus likely stimulates the right lateral amygdala as well. The results of an fMRI study by Lazar et al. supports the notion of increased activity in the regions of the amygdala and hippocampus during practices such as meditation (2000). However, whether such functional changes are associated with spiritual transformation remains to be seen.

Hypothalamic and Autonomic Nervous System Changes

The hypothalamus is extensively interconnected with the limbic system. Stimulation of the right lateral amygdala has been shown to result in stimulation of the ventromedial portion of the hypothalamus with a subsequent stimulation of the peripheral parasympathetic system (Davis 1992). Increased parasympathetic activity should be associated with the subjective sensation first of relaxation, and eventually, of a more profound quiescence. Activation of the parasympathetic system would also cause a reduction in heart rate and respiratory rate. All of these physiological responses have been observed during meditation (Jevning, Wallace, and Beidebach 1992). Spiritual transformation can also cause a number of strong emotional responses ranging from bliss to ecstasy. Blissful elements of such experiences may be mediated in part by activity in the parasympathetic system.

Typically, when breathing and heart rate slow down, the paragigantocellular nucleus of the medulla ceases to innervate the locus ceruleus (LC) of the pons. The LC produces and distributes norepinephrine (NE) (Foote 1987), a neuromodulator that increases the susceptibility of brain regions to sensory input by amplifying strong stimuli, while simultaneously gating out weaker activations and cellular "noise" that fall below the activation threshold (Waterhouse, Moises, and Woodward 1998). Decreased stimulation of the LC results in a decrease in the level of NE (Van Bockstaele and Aston-Jones 1995). The breakdown products of catecholamines, such as NE and epinephrine, have generally been found to be reduced in the urine and plasma during meditation (Infante et al. 2001; Walton et al. 1995), which may simply reflect the systemic change in autonomic balance. However, it is not inconsistent with a cerebral decrease in NE levels as well. During a meditative practice, the reduced firing of the paragigantocellular nucleus probably cuts back its innervation of the locus ceruleus, which densely and specifically supplies the PSPL and the lateral posterior nucleus with NE (Foote 1987). Thus, a reduction in NE would decrease the impact of sensory input on the PSPL, contributing to its deafferentation. Thus, transformative experiences could be facilitated by such neuronal interactions.

The locus ceruleus would also deliver less NE to the hypothalamic paraventricular nucleus. The paraventricular nucleus of the hypothalamus typically secretes corticotropin-releasing hormone (CRH) in response to innervation by NE from the locus ceruleus (Ziegler, Cass, and Herman 1999). This CRH stimulates the anterior pituitary to release adrenocorticotropic hormone (ACTH; Livesey et al. 2000). ACTH, in turn, stimulates the adrenal cortex to produce cortisol, one of the body's stress hormones (Davies, Keyon, and Fraser 1985). Decreasing NE from the locus ceruleus during meditation would likely decrease the production of CRH by the paraventricular nucleus and ultimately decrease cortisol levels (Jevning, Wilson, and Davidson 1978; Sudsuang, Chentanez, and Veluvan 1991; Walton et al. 1995).

PFC Effects on Other Neurochemical Systems

As PFC activity increases, it produces increasing levels of free synaptic glutamate in the brain. Increased glutamate can stimulate the hypothalamic arcuate nucleus to release beta-endorphin (BE) (Kiss et al. 1997). BE is known to depress respiration, reduce fear, reduce pain, and produce sensations of joy and euphoria (Janal et al. 1984). That such effects have been described during meditation may implicate some degree of BE release related to the increased PFC activity. Further, the joy and euphoric feelings associated with spiritual transformation might similarly implicate the endogenous opioid system. Meditation has been found to disrupt diurnal rhythms of BE and ACTH, while not affecting diurnal cortisol rhythms (Infante et al. 1998). Thus, the relationship between opioid receptors and various spiritual experiences is not clear, especially in light of one very limited study demonstrating that blocking the opiate receptors with naloxone did not affect the experience or electroencephalogram (EEG) associated with meditation (Sim and Tsoi 1992).

Glutamate activates N-methyl d-Aspartate receptors (NMDAr), but excess glutamate can kill these neurons through excitotoxic processes (Albin and Greenamyre 1992). I propose that if glutamate levels approach excitotoxic concentrations during intense experiences, the brain might limit its production of N-acetylated-alpha-linked-acidic dipeptidase, which converts the endogenous NMDAr antagonist N-acetylaspartylglutamate (NAAG) into glutamate (Thomas et al. 2000). The resultant increase in NAAG would protect cells from excitotoxic damage. There is an important side effect, however, since the NMDAr inhibitor NAAG is functionally analogous to the disassociative hallucinogens ketamine, phencyclidine, and nitrous oxide (Jevtovic-Todorovic et al. 2001). These NMDAr antagonists produce a variety of states that may be characterized as either schizophrenomimetic or mystical, such as out-of-body and near-death experiences (Vollenweider et al. 1997). Whether such substances are elaborated within the brain during the short interval associated with a transformative experience is not yet clear.

Autonomic Cortical Activity

In the early 1970's, Gellhorn and Kiely (1972) developed a model of the physiological processes involved in meditation based almost exclusively on autonomic nervous system (ANS) activity, which, while somewhat limited, indicated the importance of the ANS during such experiences. These authors suggested that intense stimulation of either the sympathetic or parasympathetic system, if continued, could ultimately result in simultaneous discharge of both systems (what might be considered a "breakthrough" of the other system). My colleagues and I have suggested that this breakthrough is associated with the most intense, and potentially most transformative types of spiritual experiences (d'Aquili and Newberg 1993). Several studies have demonstrated predominant parasympathetic activity during meditation associated with decreased heart rate and blood pressure, decreased respiratory rate, and decreased oxygen metabolism (Jevning et al. 1992; Sudsuang et al. 1991; Travis 2001). However, a recent study of two separate meditative techniques suggested a mutual activation of parasympathetic and sympathetic systems by demonstrating an increase in the variability of heart rate during meditation (Peng et al. 1999). The increased variation in heart rate was hypothesized to reflect activation of both arms of the ANS. This notion also fits the characteristic description of meditative states in which there is a sense of overwhelming calmness as well as significant alertness. Also, the notion of mutual activation of both arms of the ANS is consistent with recent developments in the study of autonomic interactions (Hugdahl 1996).

Serotonergic Activity

Activation of the autonomic nervous system can result in intense stimulation of structures in the lateral hypothalamus and median forebrain bundle that are known to produce both ecstatic and blissful feelings when directly stimulated (Olds and Forbes 1981). Stimulation of the lateral hypothalamus can also result in changes in serotonergic activity. In fact, several studies have shown that, after meditation, the breakdown products of serotonin (ST) in urine are significantly increased, suggesting an overall elevation in ST during meditation (Walton et al. 1995). Moderately increased levels of ST appear to correlate with positive affect, while low ST often signifies depression (Van Praag and De Haan 1980). This relationship has clearly been demonstrated with regard to the effects of selective serotonin reuptake inhibitor medications (SSRIs), which are widely used for the treatment of depression. When cortical ST_2 receptors (especially in the temporal lobes) are activated, however, the stimulation can result in a hallucinogenic effect. Tryptamine-based psychedelic drugs, such as psylocybin and LSD, seem to take advantage of this mechanism to produce their extraordinary visual associations (Aghajanian and Marek 1999). The mechanism for this phenomenon is ST inhibition of the lateral geniculate nucleus, which greatly reduces the amount of visual information that can pass through (Funke and Eysel 1995; Yoshida, Sasa, and Takaori 1984).

Increased ST levels can affect several other neurochemical systems. An increase in serotonin has a modulatory effect on dopamine, suggesting a link between the serotonergic and dopaminergic system that may enhance feelings of euphoria (Vollenweider et al. 1999) frequently described during transformative states. Serotonin, in conjunction with the increased glutamate, has been shown to stimulate the nucleus basalis to release acetylcholine, which has important modulatory influences throughout the cortex (Manfridi, Brambilla, and Mancia 1999). Increased acetylcholine in the frontal lobes has also been shown to augment the attentional system and in the parietal lobes to enhance orienting without altering sensory input (Fernandez-Duque and Posner 2001).

Transformation, Plasticity, and Reductionism

While it is possible to offer several ideas about how transformative experiences might come about based on the existing research of spiritual practices, this does not necessarily explain the basis for the transformation itself. No matter how strong the experience, there is another crucial factor that is necessary for the dramatic altering of a person's physiology and psyche.

It is known that the brain has a characteristic called *plasticity* in which various connections can be rewired in order to learn or acquire some new memory, piece of information, or behavior. With transformative experiences, there is a fundamental problem with the more established notion of plasticity. The ability of neural connections to change does take some time and usually some degree of repetition. How then can we explain a momentary experience that results in a lifetime of change? The nerve cells could not break old connections and make new ones in such a short period of time. So there must be existing connections that are either not activated, are suppressed, or are excluded from the primary modes of consciousness that suddenly become activated and, in some sense, overpower the existing neural connections. If this is the case, then one might argue that we all harbor within us the potential for transformative experiences. At this time, no research has shown that this is the case, but at the moment it is difficult to find an alternative explanation.

Much work still needs to be done to better elucidate the intricate mechanisms underlying spiritual transformation. Most of the available studies have explored specific spiritual practices, such as meditation or prayer, upon which much of the hypothetical model presented in this chapter is based. In previous works, my colleagues and I have argued that these results can be extrapolated to intense mystical experiences, which can also be transformative. However, the lack of any significant data on spiritual transformation in particular places many of these theories on speculative grounds. Regardless, the neurophysiological effects that have been observed during meditative states seem to outline a consistent pattern of changes involving certain key cerebral structures in conjunction with autonomic and hormonal changes. These changes are also reflected in neurochemical changes involving the endogenous opioid, GABA, norepinephrine, and serotonergic receptor systems.

The model presented here, based on current literature about the interaction of these systems as well as brain imaging studies of meditative techniques, is an integrated hypothesis that may help elucidate the mechanism underlying the physical and psychological effects of such practices and experiences. It should also be mentioned that whatever neurophysiological bases of spiritual transformation are eventually discovered, they do not necessarily reduce such experiences to mere biology. The subjective state and the phenomenology of such experiences cannot be ignored or dismissed, especially considering that such experiences carry with them not only transformative properties, but that in a very strong sense they represent a more fundamental reality than that observed by science. Furthermore, the physiological means of entering into a spiritual state may simply reflect the brain's response to that experience rather than establish a true causal relationship. Regardless of the ultimate basis of such experiences, elucidating their physiological and psychological basis can only help in our overall understanding of how spiritual transformation comes about.

References

Adair, J. C., R. L. Gilmore, E. B. Fennell, M. Gold, and K. M. Heilman. 1995. Anosognosia during intracarotid barbiturate anaesthesia: Unawareness or amnesia for weakness. *Neurology* 45:241–43.

Aghajanian, G. K., and G. J. Marek. 1999. Serotonin and hallucinogens. *Neuropsychopharmacology* 21:16S–23S.

Albin, R., and J. Greenamyre. 1992. Alternative excitotoxic hypotheses. *Neurology* 42:733–38.

Armony, J. L., and J. E. LeDoux. 2000. How danger is encoded: Toward a systems, cellular, and computational understanding of cognitive-emotional interactions in fear. In *The New Cognitive Neurosciences*, ed. M.S. Gazzaniga, 1073–74. Cambridge, Mass.: MIT Press.

Cheramy, A., R. Romo, and J. Glowinski. 1987. Role of corticostriatal glutamatergic neurons in the presynaptic control of dopamine release. In *Neurotransmitter Interactions in the Basal Ganglia*, ed. M. Sandler, C. Feuerstein, and B. Scatton. New York: Raven.

Chow, T. W., and J. L. Cummings. 1999. Frontal-subcortical circuits. In *The Human Frontal Lobes: Functions and Disorders*, ed. B. L. Miller and J. L. Cummings, 3–26. New York: Guilford.

Cornwall, J., and O. T. Phillipson. 1988. Mediodorsal and reticular thalamic nuclei receive collateral axons from prefrontal cortex and laterodorsal tegmental nucleus in the rat. *Neuroscience Letters* 88:121–26.

d'Aquili, E. G., and A. B. Newberg. 1993. Religious and mystical states: A neuropsychological model. *Zygon* 28:177–99.

Davies, E., C. J. Keyon, and R. Fraser. 1985. The role of calcium ions in the mechanism of ACTH stimulation of cortisol synthesis. *Steroids* 45:557.

Davis, M. 1992. The role of the amygdala in fear and anxiety. *Annual Reviews in Neuroscience* 15:353–75.

Destexhe, A., D. Contreras, and M. Steriade. 1998. Mechanisms underlying the synchronizing action of corticothalamic feedback through inhibition of thalamic relay cells. *Journal of Neurophysiology* 79:999–1016.

Elias, A. N., S. Guich, and A. F. Wilson. 2000. Ketosis with enhanced GABAergic tone promotes physiological changes in transcendental meditation. *Medical Hypotheses* 54:660–62.

Fernandez-Duque, D., and M. I. Posner. 2001. Brain imaging of attentional networks in normal and pathological states. *Journal of Clinical and Experimental Neuropsychology* 23:74–93.

Fish, D. R., P. Gloor, F. L. Quesney, and A. Olivier. 1993. Clinical responses to electrical brain stimulation of the temporal and frontal lobes in patients with epilepsy. *Brain* 116:397–414.

Foote, S. 1987. Extrathalamic modulation of cortical function. *Annual Reviews in Neuroscience* 10:67–95.

Frith, C. D., K. Friston, P. F. Liddle, and R. S. Frackowiak. 1991. Willed action and the prefrontal cortex in man: A study with PET. *Proceedings of the Royal Society of London* 244:241–46.

Funke, K., and U. T. Eysel. 1995. Possible enhancement of GABAergic inputs to cat dorsal lateral geniculate relay cells by serotonin. *Neuroreport* 6:474–76.

Gellhorn, E., and W. F. Kiely. 1972. Mystical states of consciousness: Neurophysiological and clinical aspects. *Journal of Nervous and Mental Disease* 154:399–405.

Herzog, H., V. R. Lele, T. Kuwert, K. J. Langen, E. R. Kops, and L. E. Feinendegen. 1990–1991. Changed pattern of regional glucose metabolism during Yoga meditative relaxation. *Neuropsychobiology* 23:182–87.

Hugdahl, K. 1996. Cognitive influences on human autonomic nervous system function. *Current Opinion in Neurobiology* 6:252–58.

Infante, J. R., F. Peran, M. Martinez, A. Roldan, R. Poyatos, and C. Ruiz et al. 1998. ACTH and beta-endorphin in transcendental meditation. *Physiology and Behavior* 64:311–15.

Infante, J. R., M. Torres-Avisbal, P. Pinel, J. A. Vallejo, F. Peran, and F. Gonzalez et al. 2001. Catecholamine levels in practitioners of the transcendental meditation technique. *Physiology and Behavior* 72:141–46.

Ingvar, D. H. 1994. The will of the brain: Cerebral correlates of willful acts. *Journal of Theoretical Biology* 171:7–12.

Janal, M. N., E. W. Colt, W. C. Clark, and M. Glusman. 1984. Pain sensitivity, mood and plasma endocrine levels in man following long-distance running: Effects of naxalone. *Pain* 19:13–25.

Jevning, R., R. K. Wallace, and M. Beidebach. 1992. The physiology of meditation: A review. A wakeful hypometabolic integrated response. *Neuroscience and Biobehavioral Reviews* 16:415–24.

Jevning, R., A. F. Wilson, and J. M. Davidson. 1978. Adrenocortical activity during meditation. *Hormones and Behavior* 10:54–60.

Jevtovic-Todorovic, V., D. F. Wozniak, N. D. Benshoff, and J. W. Olney. 2001. A comparative evaluation of the neurotoxic properties of ketamine and nitrous oxide. *Brain Research* 895:264–67.

Joseph, R. 1996. *Neuropsychology, Neuropsychiatry, and Behavioral Neurology.* New York: Williams and Wilkins.

Karnath, H. O., S. Ferber, and M. Himmelbach. 2001. Spatial awareness is a function of the temporal not the posterior parietal lobe. *Nature* 411:950–53.

Kiss, J., K. Kocsis, A. Csaki, T. J. Gorcs, and B. Halasz. 1997. Metabotropic glutamate receptor in GHRH and beta-endorphin neurons of the hypothalamic arcuate nucleus. *Neuroreport* 8:3703–7.

Kjaer, T. W., C. Bertelsen, P. Piccini, D. Brooks, J. Alving, and H. C. Lou. 2002. Increased dopamine tone during meditation-induced change of consciousness. *Brain Research and Cognition* 13, no. 2 (April): 255–59.

Lazar, S. W., G. Bush, R. L. Gollub, G. L. Fricchione, G. Khalsa, and H. Benson. 2000. Functional brain mapping of the relaxation response and meditation. *Neuroreport* 11:1581–85.

Livesey, J. H., M. J. Evans, R. Mulligan, and R. A. Donald. 2000. Interactions of CRH, AVP and cortisol in the secretion of ACTH from perifused equine anterior pituitary cells: "Permissive" roles for cortisol and CRH. *Endocrinology Research* 26:445–63.

Lou, H. C., T. W. Kjaer, L. Friberg, G. Wildschiodtz, S. Holm, and M. Nowak. 1999. A 15O-H2O PET study of meditation and the resting state of normal consciousness. *Human Brain Mapping* 7:98–105.

Lynch, J. C. 1980. The functional organization of posterior parietal association cortex. *Behavioral Brain Science* 3:485–99.

Manfridi, A., D. Brambilla, and M. Mancia. 1999. Stimulation of NMDA and AMPA receptors in the rat nucleus basalis of Meynert affects sleep. *American Journal of Physiology* 277:R1488–92.

Newberg, A. B., A. Alavi, M. Baime, M. Pourdehnad, J. Santanna, and E. G. d'Aquili. 2001. The measurement of regional cerebral blood flow during the complex cognitive task of meditation: A preliminary SPECT study. *Psychiatry Research: Neuroimaging* 106:113–22.

Newman, J., and A. A. Grace. 1999. Binding across time: The selective gating of frontal and hippocampal systems modulating working memory and attentional states. *Consciousness and Cognition* 8:196–212.

Olds, M. E., and J. L. Forbes. 1981. The central basis of motivation, intracranial self-stimulation studies. *Annual Review of Psychology* 32:523–74.

Pardo, J. V., P. T. Fox, and M. E. Raichle. 1991. Localization of a human system for sustained attention by positron emission tomography. *Nature* 349:61–64.

Peng, C. K., J. E. Mietus, Y. Liu, G. Khalsa, P. S. Douglas, and H. Benson et al. 1999. Exaggerated heart rate oscillations during two meditation techniques. *International Journal of Cardiology* 70:101–7.

Poletti, C. E., and M. Sujatanond. 1980. Evidence for a second hippocampal efferent pathway to hypothalamus and basal forebrain comparable to fornix system: A unit study in the monkey. *Journal of Neurophysiology* 44:514–31.

Portas, C. M., G. Rees, A. M. Howseman, O. Josephs, R. Turner, and C. D. Frith. 1998. A specific role for the thalamus in mediating the interaction attention and arousal in humans. *Journal of Neuroscience* 18:8979–89.

Posner, M. I., and S. E. Petersen. 1990. The attention system of the human brain. *Annual Reviews in Neuroscience* 13:25–42.

Redding, F. K. 1967. Modification of sensory cortical evoked potentials by hippocampal stimulation. *Electroencephalography and Clinical Neurophysiology* 22:74–83.

Saver, J. L., and J. Rabin. 1997. The neural substrates of religious experience. *Journal of Neuropsychiatry and Clinical Neurosciences* 9:498–510.

Sim, M. K., and W. F. Tsoi. 1992. The effects of centrally acting drugs on the EEG correlates of meditation. *Biofeedback and Self Regulation* 17:215–20.

Sudsuang, R., V. Chentanez, and K. Veluvan. 1991. Effects of Buddhist meditation on serum cortisol and total protein levels, blood pressure, pulse rate, lung volume and reaction time. *Physiology and Behavior* 50:543–48.

Thomas, A. G., J. J. Vornov, J. L. Olkowski, A. T. Merion, and B. S. Slusher. 2000. N-Acetylated alpha-linked acidic dipeptidase converts N-acetylaspartylglutamate from a neuroprotectant to a neurotoxin. *Journal of Pharmacological and Experimental Therapeutics* 295:16–22.

Travis, F. 2001. Autonomic and EEG patterns distinguish transcending from other experiences during Transcendental Meditation practice. *International Journal of Psychophysiology* 42:1–9.

Van Bockstaele, E. J., and G. Aston-Jones. 1995. Integration in the ventral medulla and coordination of sympathetic, pain and arousal functions. *Clinical and Experimental Hypertension* 17:153–65.

Van Praag, H., and S. De Haan. 1980. Depression vulnerability and 5-Hydroxytryptophan prophylaxis. *Psychiatry Research* 3:75–83.

Vogt, B. A., D. M. Finch, and C. R. Olson. 1992. Functional heterogeneity in cingulate cortex: The anterior executive and posterior evaluative regions. *Cerebral Cortex* 2:435–43.

Vollenweider, F. X., K. L. Leenders, C. Scharfetter, A. Antonini, P. Maguire, and J. Missimer et al. 1997. Metabolic hyperfrontality and psychopathology in the ketamine model of psychosis using positron emission tomography (PET) and [18F]fluorodeoxyglucose (FDG). *European Journal of Neuropsychopharmacology* 7:9–24.

Vollenweider, F. X., P. Vontobel, D. Hell, and K. L. Leenders. 1999. 5-HT modulation of dopamine release in basal ganglia in psilocybin-induced psychosis in man—a PET study with [11C]raclopride. *Neuropsychopharmacology* 20:424–33.

Walton, K. G., N. D. Pugh, P. Gelderloos, and P. Macrae. 1995. Stress reduction and preventing hypertension: Preliminary support for a psychoneuroendocrine mechanism. *Journal of Alternative and Complementary Medicine* 1:263–83.

Waterhouse, B. D., H. C. Moises, and D. J. Woodward. 1998. Phasic activation of the locus coeruleus enhances responses of primary sensory cortical neurons to peripheral receptive field stimulation. *Brain Research* 790:33–44.

Yoshida, M., M. Sasa, and S. Takaori. 1984. Serotonin-mediated inhibition from dorsal raphe neurons nucleus of neurons in dorsal lateral geniculate and thalamic reticular nuclei. *Brain Research* 290:95–105.

Ziegler, D. R., W. A. Cass, and J. P. Herman. 1999. Excitatory influence of the locus coeruleus in hypothalamic-pituitary-adrenocortical axis responses to stress. *Journal of Neuroendocrinology* 11:361–69.

13

Narrative in Holistic Healing: Empathy, Sympathy, and Simulation Theory

Michael L. Spezio

The primary aim of this chapter is to establish that social neuroscience supports the notion that the practice of healing requires intersubjective exchange, and that this exchange allows spiritual transformation of both healers and those who seek their help. Social neuroscience seeks to understand the role and detailed function of neural systems in social cognition and behavior (Adolphs 2003). Social cognition is that area of thought and behavior having to do with understanding, responding to, and relating to others. Findings in social neuroscience strongly suggest that emotion is a much more important element in understanding others than is usually suspected, and that strict dichotomies or dualisms that wholly separate cognition from emotion are wrong. If this conclusion is correct, it has important implications for how healers can best do their work.

The argument in this chapter is straightforward. First, all systems of healing ethics *mind the other* in engaging in the practice of healing, where minding the other refers to the activity of imaginatively constructing the other's intentions, emotions, beliefs, and so forth. This is even true, at least implicitly, of those systems of healing ethics most explicitly dependent upon universal principles, for none of these principles can be applied in a given healing context without first minding the one who seeks healing. Second, all systems of healing ethics endorse an imperative regarding *how* the other should be minded: minding should be done for the purpose of genuine understanding, response, and relation. Third, accomplishing this authentic minding requires the active engagement of an other in a specific manner of empathic or sympathic relation, in order to avoid conceptualizing others in ways that negate their own self-understanding. Finally, since there is mounting evidence that authentic minding is impossible apart from embodied emotional processing, the practice of healing that requires authentic minding in turn requires ways of engaging embodied emotional processing within the healer-seeker relation. Intersubjective narrative is especially important in a healer-seeker relation facing transformative events, often necessitating deep loss and subsequent reconfiguration of the seeker's authentic self.

Within these transformative events, spiritual transformation of both seeker and healer is required for the authentic minding sought via intersubjective narrative. *Spiritual transformation* is taken here to mean a change in deeply held core values so as to include lasting changes in the conceptual, emotional, decision-action, and relational character of a person. This understanding of spiritual transformation overlaps with those of several other authors in this volume. Negative spiritual transformation, impeding the course of healing, is of course possible, especially in the wake of inauthentic mindings in healer-seeker relations. Yet the focus in this chapter will be on authentic minding and therefore on positive spiritual transformation.

Healing Ethics and the Imperative to Mind the Other

The first two claims I will make are that all healing ethics engage in minding the other, and that all specify that such minding be done in an authentic manner. Though it is not possible to fully establish these two claims within the scope of this chapter, we can accomplish a great deal by focusing on a system of healing ethics, often called *principlism*, widely applied within modern, Western healing contexts, such as hospitals and medical schools. Principlism holds that actions within all healing events should be strongly guided by a handful of universal principles: autonomy, nonmaleficence, beneficence, and justice (Beauchamp and Childress 1979).

The principles can be described in this way: *autonomy* requires that "rational persons be self-determining," *nonmaleficence* requires that the healer "above all, do no harm," *beneficence* requires that the healer "act in ways that benefit the welfare of others," and *justice* requires that the healer "treat like cases alike." On the face of it, principlism appears to leave out any serious consideration of minding the other. In truth, principlism as it is applied in medical schools and hospitals often proceeds without any explicit attention to authentic minding. Yet the above principles cannot be applied without at least an implicit minding of the other. For the healer to say a person is "rational" or "not rational" implies constructing a mind for that person—either imaginatively or by rote—and thus evaluating actions in light of that person's own reasons, desires, motivations, and so forth. For a healer to act while doing no harm to a person implies that the healer knows what the seeker's preferences are, and what, from the seeker's viewpoint, is harmful. For a healer to act for the benefit of another person implies the same: the seeker's intentions, preferences, and desires all must be apparent—unless they are merely assumed—by the healer. Finally, for a healer to treat like cases alike also assumes the healer's knowing of the seeker's mind. Consider two people who seek a healer's help because each suffers from the same excruciatingly painful, terminal disease. One seeker may want to undergo a painful and disfiguring procedure in order to have a chance to live longer. The other may want strong pain medication to help cope with the disease while preparing to face certain death. These two healer-seeker relations are anything but alike, and their distinguishing features are the seekers' minds and the healer's required response upon authentically minding in each case the person-in-relation. This interpretation of principlism in healing ethics shares aspects with critiques of principlism by "care ethics" (Gilligan 1982) and feminist healing ethics (Bair 1985). The emphasis here is on the fact that no healer-seeker relation can be free from minding the other.

To be clear, it is not that principlism denies minding the other, but principlism in practice often proceeds without sufficient attention to this necessary element, resulting in inauthentic mindings and negative spiritual transformations that may be associated with negative health outcomes. This fact about principlism in practice is regrettable, since the very principles defined above require that seekers be allowed to determine for themselves what is morally good, bad, or just regarding the healer's attentions. Some might object that authentic minding is not necessary for this outcome, since seekers can declare their emotions, preferences, or wishes by simple written instructions that the healer can follow. While this is a good first step, anyone familiar with e-mail will immediately see the extent to which simple written material can mislead or conceal emotions, intentions, motivations, and goals. Advocates of written instructions for healing, such as advance healthcare directives, recognize this and strongly recommend that all directives emerge from conversation—one might say shared narrative—between healers and seekers. Any attempt by healers to better understand seekers' written instructions in this way will require authentic minding.

So principlism does after all contain within it an imperative toward a certain type of minding: one that allows an authentic understanding of and response and relation to the other. This kind of intersubjective minding is described variously as *empathy* or *sympathy*, and *radical empathy* is the term used by several of the authors in this volume. Knowing what we mean by these terms is important if our goal is to guide healers and seekers by describing authentic minding, and it will helpful when comparing this discussion with the others in this volume. We will briefly turn to what is meant by empathy and sympathy in intersubjective relation before considering what social neuroscience has discovered about how humans might go about engaging in such relations.

Empathy, Sympathy, and the Intersubjective

Empathy is a term that is variously used and understood within Western culture, to say nothing of how it functions in non-Western cultural discourse. Derived from the work of Theodor Lipps (1903), who called it *einfühlung*, or "in-feeling," it originally meant a conscious projection of oneself into the experience of another person, to get as close as possible to what that person is experiencing from that person's point of view. Being an empathic person is often associated culturally with being caring, and empathy is often opposed in Western culture to sympathy, when the latter is thought to show less caring for a person.

Yet it must be kept in mind that *empathy* originally did and, in some prominent uses today, still does denote only the duplication of another person's experience within oneself, without any movement to care for that person. Indeed, in a recent film, *The Fog of War*, Robert McNamara, secretary of defense during the Vietnam War, listed as one of his greatest failures a "lack of empathy" with the enemy (Morris 2003). He did not mean that he failed to care for the Vietnamese; rather, he meant that he failed to understand their mindset, experiences, and goals so as to better vanquish them militarily. Note too the character Deanna Troy, who served aboard the Starship *Enterprise* in the television series *Star Trek: The Next Generation*. Troy, we are told, inherited her mother's ability to empathize with other people and to know what they were experiencing at any given time. While the character used this ability to better understand how to heal her own ship's crew when they were injured, she also was able to analyze enemies of the Starship *Enterprise* in order to understand their weaknesses. Once she knew the feelings and intentions of the ship's opponents, she could give this information to the spaceship's captain so he could use it for strategic purposes.

Caring, therefore, is not necessarily entailed by empathy, something recognized by Max Scheler in his work *The Nature of Sympathy* (1954). Here Scheler defines sympathy in a way that can be closely related to the kind of radical empathy considered elsewhere in this volume. For Scheler, sympathy (i.e., "fellow-feeling" or *mitgefühl*) is composed of two functions. One is the "vicariously visualized" feeling of the other—the sense we have of what another person is experiencing and feeling from their perspective—and the other is an intentional stance that these feelings belong to another *person* who faces us and whom we intentionally join so as to participate in their situation. But such participation is always as our own person, and identification is not the goal. Scheler's understanding of sympathy thus includes what is typically understood as empathy and an intentional stance of partnering in solidarity with the other. Doing the latter requires engaging in the former, but feeling empathy without an intentional stance with the other is possible and can be pathological. Scheler uses the example of a cruel person who torments others because, and not in spite of the fact that, he knows very well how much pain his torment causes them.

Since sympathic relation—including its authentic minding—always recognizes that there is an other who engages one and asks to be authentically understood, responded to, and related to, it remains an intersubjective relation. Sympathy never entails complete identification, and in fact discourages it. The threat posed by complete identification is that the one doing the minding may too easily substitute his or her own emotions, preferences, intentions, and goals for those of the person whose face is lifted up in relation. Sympathy is therefore always an ethical and moral relation, and can only take place in the context of an authentic minding of the other.

Yet the ethical nature of the sympathic healer-seeker relation is only an imperative, and true sympathy can never be merely a moral or ethical stance. Rather, the sympathic relation—when it occurs—is an event allowing the possibility of spiritual transformation. It does this for the very reason that authentic minding on the part of healers (and seekers also) allows seekers to act according to their deeply held values, and to explore actions that risk changing those values in a context that is accepting and affirming of the seekers' self-understanding. This takes place while healers partner with the seekers' efforts toward healing and transformation. Healers too cannot help but become exposed to the possibility of spiritual transformation themselves, since they radically reorient their perspective to that of the seekers, and shift their core values so as to be genuine participants in the healing and transformation of the seekers. Whether the possibility of spiritual transformation for the healer is actualized will depend on the specific characteristics of the healing event, but the chance is there within each sympathic healing encounter.

At this point, let us consider a brief summary of the argument thus far before turning to social neuroscience and what it tells us about how humans mind the other. We saw that healing ethics requires an authentic minding of the other, and we showed that authentic minding—one allowing authentic understanding, response, and relation with respect to the other—requires an intersubjective, sympathic relation. Otherwise, there is a danger that the healers will substitute their own minds for those of the seekers. Now we consider what social neuroscience can say about how humans mind the other. We will examine especially the relationship between neural systems of emotion and social cognition. Prior to doing this, however, we will turn briefly to how social neuroscience understands the key functions of cognition and emotion, without, however, implying that there is a strict distinction between them.

Cognition, Emotion, and the Brain

Cognition

The term *cognition* is used within most philosophical treatments of judgment and decision making as meaning thought-knowledge, and as thus referring to conscious, intentional processes (Lakoff and Johnson 1999, 11–12). Such usage is consistent with the origins of cognitive neuroscience within cognitive psychology. *Cognitive neuroscience*, as a term, emerged from a conversation in a taxicab between cognitive psychologist George A. Miller and neuroscientist Michael S. Gazzaniga, and it describes an aim to "study how the brain enables the mind" (Gazzaniga, Ivry, and Mangun 1998, 1). The aspects of mind to be investigated were perception, attention, memory, language, learning, reasoning, judgment, and higher order thought, all of which can come under conscious control. Given the emphasis on the role of brain processing in each of these cognitive activities, and the fact that most of these brain processes would be beyond conscious control, cognitive neuroscience did not restrict the term *cognitive* to mean conscious processing. Today, cognitive neuroscience generally follows cognitive psychology in referring to cognition as having to do with information processing, conscious or not, that contributes to any of the above-mentioned mental activities. However, it must be emphasized that using the term *cognition* to include nonconscious, automatic processing is a specialized usage developed within cognitive psychology and neuroscience, and one that does not easily mesh with the use of *cognition* in most other academic discourse.

Emotion

Gaining clarity in the meanings of key terms related to emotion is important if we are to understand how social neuroscience in its experiments and theoretical constructs treats emotion. Recent study in the field of emotion research has already yielded a case in which semantic differences over the meaning of *emotion* were mistakenly cast as deep disagreements over functional aspects of respective models (Scherer 2003). To begin with, one must recognize that some operational definitions of emotion are restricted to a few emotional categories (e.g., fear, anger, joy) while others attempt to explain emotion in terms of a few theoretical dimensions (e.g., valence [positive/negative], arousal [low/high] and motor plan [approach/avoid/neither]) that are taken to explain these categories (Heilman 1997).

Within social neuroscience, affect, mood, and emotion can occur independently of or concurrent with awareness. The term *feeling* is generally reserved for the *quale*, or first-person experience, associated with emotional processing (Damasio 1996), and thus feeling requires consciousness. Perhaps most importantly, the demonstration of affective response in social neuroscience requires a clear link to one or more accepted physiological signals and cannot be based solely on verbal responses or performance measures. Thus, *affect* retains its original connotation of developing in response to situations that palpably affect the body in some way.

For the purposes of this discussion of social neuroscience, we understand an information processing event to be emotional if (1) it evaluates the information present in an event in terms of a person's own normative or autonormative outcomes (i.e., goals), and (2) it results in affective responses in the body or in the activation of their representations in the brain. Categories of autonormative outcomes include subconscious or conscious goals, desires, values, and plans for action. Norms external to the person, such as social norms, are included in this understanding of emotion, as long as those social norms exert their action in an autonormative sense. Similarly, norms that are suggested by evolutionary history are included here, as long as there is a plausible internal mechanism for their action for a given individual within a given event. One example of such internalization of evolutionary norms is the drive toward *homeostasis*, defined as the relatively stable internal processes responsible for the maintenance of life.

With these specialized understandings of cognition and emotion in hand, we can now turn to an exploration of what social neuroscience is telling us about how humans understand, respond to, and relate to others.

Minding the Other: Simulation Theory and Social Neuroscience

Any discussion of neuroscience cannot help but refer to certain brain structures. To help readers who are nonspecialists, the following definitions of some anatomical terms may be useful for the discussion below: (1) *ventral*: toward the bottom of the brain, (2) *dorsal*: toward the top of the brain, (3) *anterior*: toward the front of the brain, and (4) *posterior*: toward the back of the brain.

Simulation Theory: A Proposal for How Humans Understand Others

Simulation theory advances the notion that the processing involved in the perception of one's own bodily states is also required for the accurate judgment of others' emotional states, via a partial simulation of those states within the person doing the judging (Goldman 1992). It is opposed to various "theory theories," which contend that properly understanding, responding to, and relating to others consists only in forming conceptual constructs about them and rationally applying those concepts to actions. Simulation theory has gained support from the discovery of *mirror neurons* in rhesus monkeys and putative homologous neural functions in humans (Gallese, Keysers, and Rizzolatti 2004). Mirror neurons were originally reported in recordings from single neurons in monkey motor area F5. The unifying principle in their identification was that they showed nearly identical neuronal firing both when a monkey performed an action and when that monkey observed the same or a similar action performed by a human experimenter or another monkey. These neurons constitute approximately 20 percent of the neurons in F5 (Gallese et al. 1996). Mirror neurons were classified as "strictly congruent" or "broadly congruent" based on the similarity between performed and observed action in generating neuronal firing, and approximately one-third of all mirror neurons in F5 were strictly congruent, with the remainder being broadly congruent.

While there is as yet no direct evidence of mirror neurons in the human brain, there is evidence of broadly overlapping neural tissue involved in both the sensation and in the judgment of emotion. This evidence comes from studies of the effects of lesions (i.e., damage to specific areas of the brain), from neuroimaging studies (fMRI and PET, for example), and from studies examining interference with emotional judgment due to transcranial magnetic stimulation. It is not possible to speak strictly of mirror neurons in these studies, for although the studies identify the large-scale similarity of brain areas involved in emotional sensation and judgment, in all these cases the degree of overlap is partial only. This observation may be important in elucidating a mechanism of emotional judgment that prevents confusion between one's own emotional states and the inferred emotional states of others, something that strict mirroring in all areas could not allow. It is useful to keep in mind that simulation theory does not require or postulate identity between the neural processing involved in sensing and judging emotion.

The clearest evidence in support of a simulation theory of emotional judgment comes from studies involving the somatosensory cortex and insula, two areas of the brain important for sensing one's own bodily state. An intensive study of the cortical areas involved in the judgment of emotions from faces included 108 people with focal brain lesions (Adolphs et al. 2000). All 108 lesioned brains were mapped onto a single healthy reference brain so that the lesions could be directly compared and lesion density overlap images could be constructed, showing those areas of the brain whose damage was associated most strongly with deficits in emotional judgment. Participants in the study were asked to look at pictures of faces and to report the emotions they saw in the faces, choosing from among six basic emotions: happiness, sadness, fear, anger, surprise, and disgust. When images of the brains of the participants who had the lowest performance scores on each emotion were examined, a consistent pattern emerged for all emotions: lesions in the right ventral parietal cortex and right frontal cortex were systematically and significantly associated with impaired recognition of emotion. The sites within which these lesions systematically resulted in impaired emotion recognition were concentrated in the somatosensory cortex, with involvement of the insula as well.

These areas are critical for our ability to sense our own bodily states, both in response to stimulation at the surface of the body and within the body. So areas of the brain that are required for feeling one's own body are also required for accurately judging emotion in the facial expressions of others.

The involvement of the somatosensory cortex in emotional judgment from faces alone has been confirmed by transcranial magnetic stimulation (TMS; Pourtois et al. 2004). TMS is a technique that induces a slight magnetic impulse in the focal brain area of interest. In a sense, TMS creates a temporary break in a brain circuit, allowing researchers to study how components of neural networks work. In the study by Pourtois et al., recognition of fear in fearful faces took longer when single pulse TMS was applied over the right somatosensory cortex. The application of the TMS pulse occurred between 100 msec and 200 msec following onset of the facial image, suggesting that the processing of facial emotion in the somatosensory cortex occurs very early on, perhaps in parallel with processing in the amygdala (see next section).

The most straightforward interpretation of these findings is one that invokes simulation theory: humans construct central images of the body state that would be associated with the visually observed emotion; that is, humans imagine how another person feels by simulating some of the neural network activation involved in the feeling that they perceive in that person. Just as the visual cortex is active during both visual perception and visual imagery (Ganis, Thompson, and Kosslyn 2004), the somatosensory cortex is active during both our perception of our own body state and our imagining how someone else feels.

The extensive study of lesioned patients described above also identified the right insula as important for emotional judgment from faces. The insula is known to be involved in sensations of disgust (Fitzgerald et al. 2004), and it strongly responds to images depicting bodily mutilation and contamination (Wright et al. 2004). A focused study of one patient, B, with extensive bilateral lesions involving the anterior insula, showed that the insula is required for the accurate judgment of disgust from faces. B was not only impaired in the ability to judge disgust from gustatory stimuli (e.g., high salinity solution) or visual stimuli (e.g., images of food covered with cockroaches), he was unable to judge disgust from dynamic facial stimuli, and he could not infer another person's disgust from events in a descriptive narrative (Adolphs, Tranel, and Damasio 2003). These results are consistent with neuroimaging studies that robustly and repeatedly show insula activation when viewing facial expressions of disgust (Wicker et al. 2003). In this case, the same participants were imaged either while smelling disgusting odors or during viewing of movies of facial disgust. An approximate 40 percent overlap in active brain areas in the left insula and inferior frontal gyrus was seen when comparing the two conditions (olfaction vs. viewing), again providing support for the mechanism described above in which simulation of emotional states is necessary for the judgment of the emotional states of others.

The primary conclusion from the findings reviewed here is that there is a great deal of evidence for a simulation theory applicable to judging others' emotions. Although the precise neural mechanism for simulation, as opposed to identification, is not known, a vigorous, ongoing research program within the cognitive neuroscience of social behavior is trying to determine just such a mechanism.

The findings discussed thus far with respect to simulation theory are also supported by evidence showing that brain areas important for emotional processing are crucial for understanding the other and are therefore critical for healthy social cognition. A crucial area of research providing this evidence suggests that neural systems implicated in emotional processing are required for understanding the emotions and intentions expressed by an other.

Emotion and Sympathy/Empathy

Is emotional processing required for making healthy judgments about the emotions, preferences, intentions, and beliefs of other people? Here again, emotional processing can include but does not exclusively refer to conscious feelings, and emotional judgments can include both those available to conscious reflection and those that are only subconscious associations influencing thought and behavior. The answer to this question then appears to be yes, according to proposals that use evidence from brain areas implicated both in healthy emotional experiences and in healthy social judgment to argue that both emotion and social judgment use shared neural systems.

Abundant evidence has revealed that several key brain areas that either are required for healthy emotional experience or are differentially activated by emotional conditions are also required for healthy social judgment or are differentially activated in social judgment tasks (Adolphs 2003). The areas that most consistently show this association are the ventromedial prefrontal cortex, the right insula and somatosensory cortices (Adolphs et al. 2000), and the amygdala.

Bar-On et al. (2003) tested six people with bilateral focal lesions of anterior and posterior ventromedial prefrontal cortex, three people with unilateral lesions of the right insular and somatosensory cortices, and three people with unilateral lesions of the amygdala on emotional intelligence (Bar-On 1997) and social functioning (Tranel, Bechara, and Denburg 2002). They compared performance of these groups with a group of controls who had lesions that did not involve the ventromedial prefrontal cortex, the right insula and somatosensory cortices, or the amygdala. The study found no difference between any of the experimental groups and control group in full IQ, executive function, perception, or memory, nor any indication of psychopathology. But each experimental group was significantly impaired on emotional intelligence compared to the control group. Combining all three experimental groups yielded significant deficits in social functioning compared to the control group.

Further, Shamay-Tsoory and colleagues (2003) tested on empathy and the recognition of social faux pas twelve people with focal lesions to the ventromedial prefrontal cortex. They found that these people, as a group, provided significantly lower empathy scores and were significantly more impaired at recognizing social faux pas than age-matched (but not IQ-matched) controls and people with unilateral lesions to the posterior cortex of the brain.

It has also been found that bilateral amygdala lesions impair attributions of trustworthiness (Adolphs, Tranel, and Damasio 1998). Stone and colleagues (2003) tested two people who had sustained bilateral amygdala damage after the age of fifty, using several tasks designed to assess whether these people could form beliefs about another person's state of mind (i.e., a "theory of mind"). The tasks included the recognition of social faux pas and the attribution of feelings and thoughts to a person based only on seeing that person's eyes. Compared to age-matched controls lacking any lesion, the people with a bilateral amygdala lesion performed significantly worse at detecting social faux pas, while one of the lesioned people performed significantly worse at making social attributions from the eyes alone.

We may conclude from the studies reviewed thus far that the neural networks implicated in our own ability to respond emotionally are also required to understand the mind of another person.

Healing and Spiritual Transformation: The Central Role of Narrative

If the growing consensus emerging from social neuroscience is right, it is nearly impossible to engage in the authentic minding of the other in a healer-seeker relation without engaging embodied, emotional processes. Such systems seem to be required for effectively understanding, responding to, and relating to other people. Moreover, we saw that such an authentic minding within the sympathic healer-seeker relation allows for the possibility of spiritual transformation for both persons-in-relation, but especially for the seeker if that minding accompanies and generates healing. This suggests that healers should engage seekers in ways that facilitate the activation of embodied emotional processes both in themselves and in seekers.

Cultural approaches to accomplish this engagement will vary, and several are discussed by other authors in this volume. They may include meaningful spiritual practices shared by the healer and seeker, shared music making, shared expressions in the visual arts, or therapeutic touch. One approach that is beginning to gain notice within modern Western healing practice and healing ethics is *narrative*.

Bioethicists such as Rita Charon and Laurie Zoloth have recently championed the centrality of narrative in an ethics of holistic healing (Charon and Montello 2002). Charon and Montello contend that narrative serves to identify and reveal the nuances of the person who appears before a physician or ethics committee, humanizing that person and at the same time disabusing physicians and nurses of many false assumptions they might have regarding that person's attitudes toward sickness, health, and treatment. Though in their discussion Charon and Montello do not suggest why this would be so, the discussion here implies that narrative may engage aspects of embodied, emotional processes involved in minding the other.

It is not difficult to find support for such a central role for narrative. Narrative, or story, may be defined as "a structured, coherent retelling of an experience. . . . A satisfying story will include the following elements: themes, goals, plans, expectations, expectation failures (or obstacles), and perhaps, explanations or solutions" (Schank and Berman 2002, 288). In this brief definition, it is already possible to see that narrative explicitly communicates key aspects of minding the other, that is, the goals, plans, and expectations of the person doing the telling. Coherent or not, narratives that include these elements cannot but convey, to an attentive and responsive listener, something about the person telling the story. Some might object, as we noted earlier, that a simple list of such personal characteristics would provide the same information. But this objection ignores all that we have learned from social neuroscience about the requirement for embodied, emotional systems when using such information to mind the other. Listening to a narrative as an other tells it is an active, embodied process, one that benefits from and can contribute to a sympathic healer-seeker relation. Perusing a decontextualized list of personal characteristics is a poor substitute. As emphasized by A. E. Denham, "the detail of the narrative is often all-important to a grasp of its interest; like paraphrases of good metaphors, summaries of good [narratives] can fail to convey the very considerations which we take to constitute their distinctive content" (2000, 351).

Holistic healing, then, welcomes the complex narratives of seekers after health because these narratives facilitate authentic minding of the other and so contribute to a sympathic healer-seeker relation that opens both seeker and healer to the possibility of spiritual transformation. Under current models of modern Western medicine, healers use only or primarily hyper-materialized patient histories to "understand" their patients, or depersonalized case studies to explore ethical decision making in transformative healing events. It is clear, however, that even under the ethical systems currently in use by modern Western (i.e., nonholistic) healthcare, there are, given the findings of social neuroscience, strong imperatives to grant a central role to extended narrative engagement with seekers after health. Acting in accordance with these imperatives can only serve to open healthcare systems to the benefits of positive spiritual transformation, for both seeker and healer.

References

Adolphs, R. 2003. Cognitive neuroscience of human social behavior. *Nature Reviews Neuroscience* 4:165–78.

Adolphs, R., H. Damasio, D. Tranel, G. Cooper, and A. R. Damasio. 2000. A role for somatosensory cortices in the visual recognition of emotions as revealed by three-dimensional lesion mapping. *The Journal of Neuroscience* 20:2683–90.

Adolphs, R., D. Tranel, and A. R. Damasio. 1998. The human amygdala in social judgment. *Nature* 393:470–74.

———. 2003. Dissociable neural systems for recognizing emotions. *Brain and Cognition* 52 (1): 61–69.

Bair, A. 1985. *Postures of the Mind*. Minneapolis: University of Minnesota Press.

Bar-On, R. 1997. *The Bar-On Emotional Quotient Inventory (EQ-i): A Test of Emotional Intelligence*. Toronto: Multi-Health Systems.

Bar-On, R., D. Tranel, N. Denburg, and A. Bechara. 2003. Exploring the neurological substrate of emotional and social intelligence. *Brain* 126:1790–1800.

Beauchamp, T. L., and J. F. Childress. 1979. *Principles of Biomedical Ethics*. New York: Oxford University Press.

Charon, R., and M. Montello, eds. 2002. *Stories Matter: The Role of Narrative in Medical Ethics*. New York: Routledge.

Damasio, A. R. 1996. The somatic marker hypothesis and the possible functions of the prefrontal cortex. *Philosophical Transactions of the Royal Society of London B Biological Sciences* 351:1413–20.

Denham, A. E. 2000. *Metaphor and Moral Experience*. Oxford: Clarendon Press.

Fitzgerald, D. A., S. Posse, G. J. Moore, M. E. Tancer, P. J. Nathan, and K. L. Phan. 2004. Neural correlates of internally-generated disgust via autobiographical recall: A functional magnetic resonance imaging investigation. *Neuroscience Letters* 370 (2–3): 91–6.

Gallese, V., L. Fadiga, L. Fogassi, and G. Rizzolatti. 1996. Action recognition in the premotor cortex. *Brain* 119:593–609.

Gallese, V., C. Keysers, and G. Rizzolatti. 2004. A unifying view of the basis of social cognition. *Trends in Cognitive Sciences* 8 (9): 396–403.

Ganis, G., W. L. Thompson, and S. M. Kosslyn. 2004. Brain areas underlying visual mental imagery and visual perception: An fMRI study. *Cognitive Brain Research* 20 (2): 226–41.

Gazzaniga, M. S., R. B. Ivry, and G. R. Mangun. 1998. *Cognitive Neuroscience: The Biology of the Mind*. New York: W.W. Norton.

Gilligan, C. 1982. *In a Different Voice*. Cambridge, Mass.: Harvard University Press.

Goldman, A. 1992. In defense of the simulation theory. *Mind and Language* 7:104–19.

Heilman, K. M. 1997. The neurobiology of emotional experience. *Journal of Neuropsychiatry and Clinical Neurosciences* 9 (3): 439–48.

Lakoff, G., and M. Johnson. 1999. *Philosophy in the Flesh: The Embodied Mind and Its Challenge to Western Thought*. New York: Basic Books.

Lipps, T. 1903. Einfühlung, innere nachahmung und organempfindug. *Archiv für die Gesamte Psychologie* 1:465–519.

Morris, E. 2003. *The Fog of War*. Sony Pictures Classics.

Pourtois, G., D. Sander, M. Andres, D. Grandjean, L. Reveret, E. Olivier, and P. Vuilleumier. 2004. Dissociable roles of the human somatosensory and superior temporal cortices for processing social face signals. *European Journal of Neuroscience* 20 (12): 3507–15.

Schank, R. C., and T. R. Berman. 2002. The pervasive role of stories in knowledge and action. In *Narrative Impact: Social and Cognitive Foundations*, ed. M. C. Green, J. Strange, and T. C. Brock, 287–313. Mahwah, N.J.: Lawrence Erlbaum Associates.

Scheler, M. 1954. *The Nature of Sympathy*, trans. P. Heath. London: Routledge and Kegan Paul.

Scherer, K. R. 2003. Introduction: Cognitive components of emotion. In *Handbook of the Affective Sciences*, ed. R. J. Davidson, H. Goldsmith, and K. R. Scherer, 563–71. New York: Oxford University Press.

Shamay-Tsoory, S. G., R. Tomer, B. D. Berger, and J. Aharon-Peretz. 2003. Characterization of empathy deficits following prefrontal brain damage: The role of the right ventromedial prefrontal cortex. *Journal of Cognitive Neuroscience* 15 (3): 324–37.

Stone, V. E., S. Baron-Cohen, A. Calder, J. Keane, and A. Young. 2003. Acquired theory of mind impairments in individuals with bilateral amygdala lesions. *Neuropsychologia* 41:209–20.

Tranel, D., A. Bechara, and N. L. Denburg. 2002. Asymmetric functional roles of right and left ventromedial prefrontal cortices in social conduct, decision-making, and emotional processing. *Cortex* 38:589–612.

Wicker, B., C. Keysers, J. Plailly, J. P. Royet, V. Gallese, and G. Rizzolatti. 2003. Both of us disgusted in my insula: The common neural basis of seeing and feeling disgust. *Neuron* 40 (3): 655–64.

Wright, P., G. He, N. A. Shapira, W. K. Goodman, and Y. Liu. 2004. Disgust and the insula: fMRI responses to pictures of mutilation and contamination. *Neuroreport* 15 (15): 2347–51.

14

Healing of the Self-in-Context: Memory, Plasticity, and Spiritual Practice

David Allen Hogue

Not long ago spirituality and religion were nearly synonymous. More recently it has become common to make distinctions between spirituality and religion, between our personal experiences of the transcendent and the social institutions and corporate practices that constitute religion. Such distinctions generally value spirituality over religion, reacting to the frequently restrictive activities of some religious institutions that seem more intent on maintaining themselves than on the spiritual transformation of their members. A recent NBC poll, for instance, reported that 51 percent of respondents consider themselves "spiritual," while 21 percent describe themselves as "religious" (Peter D. Hart Research 2005).

In this chapter we will consider the relationship between spirituality and religion, drawing specifically on resources from the neurosciences, to argue that spirit and faith communities, like soul and body, require rather than compete with each other. We will first offer a brief working definition of spirit and consider its relationship to the self. The embodied nature of spirit will then draw our attention to research on memory, narrative, and ritual. We will suggest that neural plasticity offers a promising key to understanding transformations of spirit. Finally, we will argue that established religious communities provide unique support for spiritual transformation, including corporate (worship, small groups) and individual ritual practices (pastoral counseling, spiritual direction) that

offer liminal experiences in which memories can be encoded, retrieved, and reinterpreted in ways that lead to both spiritual formation and transformation. Established religious communities also
offer meta-narratives that provide a context for the reinterpretation
of personal stories. In short, we will argue for the critical role of religion in support of spiritual development and transformation.

Spirit and the Self

Spirit (or soul) indicates that dimension of personhood that embodies and expresses a relationship with the transcendent, with the
divine. We want to avoid viewing spirituality as a distinct or unusual human ability, however, for spiritual relatedness grows out
of capacities for relationship to others and to the self. Spirituality,
then, is a particular expression of basic human capacities, including
language, theory of mind, episodic memory, conscious top-down
agency, future orientation, and emotional modulation (Brown,
Murphy, and Malony 1998, 103–4). Sharp distinctions between
spirit and self are difficult to maintain.

Notions of personal identity range widely, of course, involving
biological, psychological, cultural, and theological factors. Christian theology has varied substantially in the ways it has articulated
the relationship between body, mind, and soul or spirit. Theologian
Nancey Murphy has outlined a history of this conversation, arguing that the Hebraic roots of Christian theology stand in contrast to
the dualism of mind or soul and body that were introduced from
Hellenistic sources, particularly in the writings of Saint Paul
(Brown, Murphy, and Malony 1998, 1–25). Rather than accepting a
sharp dualism that posits an immaterial spirit distinct from a physical body and which is capable of surviving bodily death, Murphy
suggests that Jewish and Christian core beliefs in the resurrection
of the body are more congruent with contemporary neuroscientific
understandings of the basic inseparability of mind or spirit and
brain. Murphy concludes that recent developments in the neurosciences make at least a hard dualism untenable, while at the same
time arguing that personhood and spirituality are not ultimately
reducible to the physical, chemical, and biological systems they require. Soul and body constitute a unity.

Spirit and Memory

Since spirit is a dimension of personhood, spirit relies on the same neural capacities as the self. The cognitive neurosciences have provided important avenues for understanding the processes necessary for developing and maintaining a sense of self, including the central role of memory. Memory researchers distinguish between *implicit* (or unconscious) and *explicit* memories (which are conscious or are available to consciousness). Implicit memory includes skill development (procedural memory), but also includes dimensions of semantic memory (Schacter 1996, 171–72). Implicit memories also appear to include the brain's ongoing monitoring of the body's condition and orientation as part of its representations of objects in the environment. Neurologist Antonio Damasio, for example, suggests that the brain's representations of objects in the environment simultaneously include the body's awareness of its own status and relationship to the perceived objects. Therefore the brain "thinks" and "remembers" in terms of the self's relationship to the environment (1994, 226–35). This deep connection between self and the environment will be crucial in our discussion below of spiritual transformation.

But explicit memories play an equally central role in conceptions of the self. Neuropsychologist Michael Gazzaniga has described the brain's drive to organize experience as a function of a left hemisphere system that he dubs the "interpreter." This system constructs stories to make sense of current perceptions and experiences, even when conflicting data is received from each hemisphere, as in the case of split-brain patients (2000, 1293–1326). The neural networks underlying the interpreter, Gazzaniga argues, are responsible for the coherent and continuous sense of self and agency we generally experience in our own thoughts and actions. Biogenetic structuralists have credited similar functions to a set of *cognitive operators*, apparently supported by discrete neural systems, and most specifically to a *causal operator* (d'Aquili and Newberg 1999, 150–54). The causal operator, they speculate, makes meaning by constructing explanatory narratives to organize internal cognitive maps of the environment and to locate the self within the world. Left hemispheric support for language, then, is the primary neurological substrate for stories, though human narrative construction requires the contextual framework of the right hemisphere as fully as it does the language centers of the left (Gazzaniga 2000, 1293–1326).

Damasio has suggested a multi-tiered concept of the self that includes both implicit and explicit memories and representations. He sketches a nonconscious *proto-self* consisting of the brain's multiple representations of the organism itself, a conscious but transient *core self* that represents the organism's nonverbal awareness of its own agency and capacity for "knowing," and finally an *autobiographical* (or *extended*) *self* that depends on working memory and its capacity to access both episodic and declarative long-term memories to construct a coherent sense of both self and the environment (1999, 199–200; Cozolino 2002, 156.) Damasio believes that the core self is generally impervious to change (other than through neurological damage due to injury or disease), but that conscious autobiographical memories are capable of some malleability.

Scholars in other disciplines, of course, have also noted the central role of narrative in the formation of personal identity. Psychologist Dan McAdams (1993) has argued for the identity of self with personal stories. Psychologist Louis Cozolino notes the role of autobiographical memories in defining the core self and suggests correlations between narrative and neural structures (2002, 34). Pastoral theologian James Ashbrook (Ashbrook and Albright 1997, 173) argues that memories are the basis of the soul, and with the loss of memories comes loss of the soul. Few of us would underestimate the central role of memories in understandings of the self.

Personal identities are not constructed ex nihilo, nor do they represent idiosyncratic interpretations of unique historical experiences. The raw materials for personal stories are received from the larger culture, particularly as caregivers transmit cultural and religious stories to children in the early years of life. Not only are models learned from cultural heroes; the very structures for personal stories are adapted from cultural narratives (McAdams 1993, 60–65). One of the dilemmas of a pluralistic and postmodern cultural setting such as twenty-first-century North America is the lack of a unifying meta-narrative that provides shared and accepted qualities of effective participation in the culture. We will return to this dilemma later. First we consider memory's structures.

Memory's Forms

When considering long-term memory, researchers distinguish at least three different modes of memory, each likely supported by distinct neural networks (Levine et al. 2004; cf. Schacter 1996, 17). *Episodic* or *autobiographical* memory includes those memories of discrete events that we recall with some sense of personal involvement. *Semantic* memory involves the subject's sense of the world, the facts of the universe within which the subject lives. *Procedural* memory includes particularly those physical actions performed over time, the how-to of any practice from riding a bicycle to playing the piano or reciting the Lord's Prayer.

While it appears that personal identity consists substantially in the remembered narratives held by persons, semantic and procedural memories are critical to a cohesive sense of self, even though they may not be immediately available to conscious recall. Spiritual practices designed to form and transform persons will attend to the different consequences offered by procedural, semantic, and episodic memory. We will consider the role of religious communities in transforming spiritual practices later, but first we consider how memories are formed.

Vivid Memories

An impressive body of research suggests that memories encoded under particular circumstances may be recorded with greater reliability and ease of recall. In settings in which emotional arousal is increased, some evidence suggests those events are recorded more reliably and with greater vividness than events experienced under neutral emotional conditions. Such encoding has been called *flashbulb memory*, in light of the fact that brief bursts of attention are focused on the event. More recent research suggests that even flashbulb memories are subject to distortion, though the gist of a story in flashbulb memory is generally more reliable than memories of day-to-day events (Schacter 1996, 195–201). Flashbulb memories occur when subjects experience a deep sense of personal involvement (including personal risk). Such memories can be either pleasant or unpleasant, and appear to involve the amygdala-hippocampus-medial temporal lobe system of fear response (LeDoux 1996, 206–8; Dolcos, LaBar, and

Cabeza 2005). Emotionally charged memories are more accurately retrieved up to a year later, and such recall involves the amygdala, entorhinal cortex, and hippocampus (Dolcos, LaBar, and Cabeza 2005; McGaugh 2004).

These findings suggest a continuum of memorability, with emotional arousal constituting a central variable. They also suggest that specific properties of the central nervous system underlie both the formation of memories and their transformation. One critical capacity is the brain's ability to learn from experience—what neuroscientists refer to as *neural plasticity*.

Changing Brain, Changing Spirit

Neural plasticity, the brain's capacity to "rewire" itself in response to new information, represents a promising avenue for understanding spiritual transformation. An accumulating body of data suggests that memory recall is a reconstructive process; that is to say, each recollection of an event is a new creation (Schacter 1996, 69–71). Discrete dimensions of individual memories are stored throughout the brain in areas that receive and process those sensory inputs; for example, visual images are stored in the occipital visual cortex, and auditory memories in the temporal lobes, while medial temporal lobe structures appear to coordinate their encoding and recall (Greenberg and Rubin 2003). At the moment of recall, the brain draws together these discrete dimensions to create the subjective experience of a seamless memory. Whether an event is recalled intentionally or spontaneously, it appears to be constructed anew each time it is retrieved. A significant literature has also developed around notions of false memory. This literature demonstrates the ways in which different details, or even memories of an entire event, can be inserted and still produce high levels of subjective credibility for the experiencer (compare for example, de Rivera and Sarbin 1998; and Schacter 1995).

The work of neurosurgeon Wilder Penfield in the 1960s suggested that human memories are stored in perpetuity in the recesses of the brain and, under the right circumstances, can be recalled. More recent research has called this conviction into question (Schacter 1996, 77–81). Forgetting is an adaptive response, particularly as years of lived experience accumulate. Intentional recall and repetition of memories appear to be critical to their being maintained.

One possible mechanism for memory change proposes a state of lability during memory recall (Walker et al. 2003). This research suggests a three-stage process in the formation of procedural memories. Following initial learning, a period of stabilization occurs that requires up to six hours. However, learning another skill within less than six hours may interfere with consolidation of the first learning. Sleep plays a critical role in consolidation of those memories in ways that an equivalent passage of time without sleep does not. Even more relevant to our current discussion, this research also suggests that recalling a memory might reintroduce a state of lability during which that memory must be reconsolidated, otherwise it may be lost. Such a process may underlie the acknowledged degradation of memory to which we referred above. Ironically, recall might lead then to memory loss or modification rather than to consolidation, as is more commonly the result of rehearsal (Schacter 1996, 112). Though these findings may not be generalized to other domains, similar mechanisms could underlie consolidation for autobiographical or semantic memory as well (Walker et al. 2003, 619).

For the purposes of healing and care, such a claim proposes neurological mechanisms by which problematic memories might be addressed and changes in personal identity understood. Minor changes in specific memories might produce significant changes in the network of meanings with which those memories are associated, and in a fortuitous set of circumstances might lead to healing. Cozolino argues that language organizes the brain, and that the recall of stories can serve to help reorganize the brain in psychotherapy (2002, 113, 154). Pastoral theologian Christy Neuger describes a feminist narrative approach to pastoral counseling that calls for careful listening to women's stories (particularly the stories of victims of domestic violence and abuse) for both a dominant theme and also for the small variations in that theme that provide exceptions. By raising awareness of those variations and then amplifying them, client and therapist alike have an opportunity to subvert the control of oppressive personal stories (2001, 90–92). Neuger labels this process "deconstructive listening." These opportunities for transformations of brain, mind, and spirit are intriguing, and they prompt questions about the optimal conditions for memory transformation.

Narrative is a central activity of all religious communities. Undoubtedly such practices serve multiple purposes, but stories appear especially to engage neural mechanisms that are essentially untouched by abstract conceptual thinking (Ornstein 1997, 73). However, narratives by themselves constitute only part of the equation in spiritual formation and transformation. Story and ritual require each other (Anderson and Foley 1998, 20–35).

Ritual

Narrative accounts of the self and of the community are most easily remembered and reinterpreted when they are embodied in ritual activities that produce affective engagement. While ritual has defied precise definition (Bell 1997, xi, 253), anthropological sources suggest that ritual contributes to both the continuity and the transformation of personal and community identities.

Elsewhere I have described six dimensions of ritual structure relevant to the practices of religious communities: prescription, symbol, performance, repetition, ritual's public nature, and ritual's effectiveness (Hogue 2003, 122–44). While not all six dimensions will be present in all rituals or will carry equal importance, they provide a framework for distinguishing ritual experience from daily living. *Prescription* refers to an awareness that common rituals are received from others, such as ancestors, God, or founders of religious traditions. *Symbol* acknowledges that rituals point beyond themselves to a transcendent reality. *Performance* observes that rituals must be enacted; they are not texts or descriptions, but lived, meaningful activities. *Ritual's public nature* derives from the fact that rituals are repeated, if not by individuals as primary "patients" of the ritual, then by communities as other members participate (McCauley and Lawson 2002, 48–56). Paradigmatically, rituals are performed in the presence of witnesses, whether those observers are understood to be gods, ancestors, or an internalized, imagined community. This dimension distinguishes religious rituals from private ritual practices. Finally, a *ritual's effectiveness* suggests that rituals accomplish something; they bring about a state different from the one that preceded them, or they maintain a status that would be lost without ritual enactment.

Ritual structures and participation set time and space apart from the ordinary and everyday, and anthropologists call these experiences *liminal*, from the Latin word for "threshold" (van Gennep 1960, 21; Turner 1969, 95–112). Such participation is believed to engage the body's autonomic nervous system, frequently alternating between the sympathetic and parasympathetic subsystems. These processes then arouse or quiet subcortical neural processing and hormonal involvement, resulting in emotional engagement (d'Aquili and Newberg 1999, 112–16). Corporate worship and some small group and counseling settings represent liminal conditions that involve ritual or ritual-like activities (Hogue 2003).

D'Aquili and Newberg (1999) have proposed a model of neural mechanisms that undergird ritual practice, contending that deafferentation of the left association area of the brain is the physiological substrate for a loosened sense of personal boundary and sense of connection with others. Likewise, they propose a deafferentation of the right association area, which leads to loss of a sense of bodily location in space, producing an out-of-body experience. For our purposes, such explanations support our contention that ritual experiences provide a significant "container" in which emotional memories can be rehearsed, encoded, retrieved, and potentially reencoded. Such practices then are promising mechanisms for spiritual formation and transformation.

Cognitive anthropologists McCauley and Lawson argue that the maintenance of communal memory is a central function of ritual. Although such functions are likely more critical in nonliterate cultures, McCauley and Lawson believe that understanding the ways ritual functions in those cultures can provide insight into the functions of ritual in literate societies as well (2002, 38). Drawing heavily on research supporting the relative reliability of flashbulb memory, McCauley and Lawson observe that less-frequently performed rituals require higher levels of pageantry in order adequately to encode both the details and significance of the given ritual. Noting that emotional arousal alone provides an inadequate explanation of variable reliabilities in flashbulb memory, they outline two key dimensions of such memories that are relevant to our discussion here. First, they note that a sense of participation in the episodes being encoded strengthens their reliability; second, they note the role of a narrative construction that unfolds in the days and weeks following an event in establishing the meaning and ongoing impact of personally encountered events. McCauley and Lawson outline a "cognitive alarm hypothesis," which holds that

> when current circumstances are the cause of our emotional arousal, we will increase the attention and cognitive resources we devote to them, which, in turn, will increase the probability of their subsequent recollection. But that sort of memory consolidation may only arise if that initial, heightened alertness receives ongoing vindication in subsequent experience concerning our sense of the event's significance. (2002, 78)

Michael Gazzaniga describes research conducted by Schacter and Singer in 1962 in which subjects were injected with epinephrine, resulting in activations of the sympathetic nervous system with increased heart rate, hand tremors, and facial flushing (cited in Gazzaniga 2000, 1316). Subjects were then placed with confederates who expressed either euphoria or anger. Those subjects who were with a euphoric confederate described their feelings as euphoric, and those with the angry confederate described themselves as angry. Gazzaniga suggests that the left-brain interpreter is at work interpreting otherwise ambiguous data about the self. Such a proposition suggests that in both counseling and worship experiences, participants who experience emotional arousal might tend to interpret those experiences in a way similar to those around them or in ways "explained" by a story they recall or hear. Such a possibility introduces yet one more way in which psychotherapy and worship might contribute to the reconstruction of self-narratives.

Since both emotional arousal and narrative consolidation underlie effective memory processes, we can both support and critique the traditional worship and nurture practices of communities of faith. The self-conscious attention that is focused on both narrative and ritual performance in corporate worship settings undoubtedly creates a constellation of circumstances in which memories may be recalled and re-encoded.

Serving Communities, Serving Persons

The complex phenomenon of ritual, of course, is not homogeneous, since a variety of ritual structures are available within religious communities. At least three primary forms of ritual experience are practiced in religious communities: public worship, small group activities, and individual counseling or spiritual direction. Professional leaders conduct some of these practices, while non-clergy specialists or the participants themselves facilitate others. What these practices have in common is the central role in them that both story and ritual play. What distinguishes them from each other is a relative emphasis on the individual's personal story (as in counseling or spiritual direction) as opposed to communal stories in larger settings.

It is important to distinguish between the function of rituals for groups and their function for individuals. While the continuation of communal memories and traditions is important for group continuity, individual participants also require continuity and opportunities for change in the memories that underlie their identity. Some functions bridge the two as they help establish or maintain a member's position with a resulting personal sense of status and belonging. Such experiences can be supported in smaller group settings as well as larger gatherings. But corporate rituals must also permit some personal accommodation so that communal and personal stories may intersect and shape each other. Anthropologist Roy Rappaport (1999) thus distinguishes between the canonical and self-referential meanings of ritual, describing the mechanism by which rituals engage individuals. "By participating in a ritual the performer reaches out of his *private* self, so to speak, into a *public* canonical order to grasp the category that he then imposes on his private processes" (105–106).

Community rituals provide a framework for the shaping and reshaping of spirit. We turn, then, to consider spiritual transformation.

Spiritual Transformation and Spiritual Care

Spiritual *transformation* assumes practices of spiritual *formation*, since transformation implies a shift from one formed state to another, or from an unformed state to a formed state. Spiritual practices include both personal and corporate activities. Prayer, meditation, and other activities can often be undertaken privately, and some forms of contemporary spiritual practice rely primarily, or entirely, on such solitary activities. Most active Christian traditions, however, emphasize communal religious activities that call together persons with shared faith commitments, worldviews, and history. In addition, such communities often provide counseling, spiritual direction, and other forms of direct care to members. Drawing sharp distinctions between personal and corporate spiritual practices is therefore not feasible, since many private spiritual practices are embedded in corporate worship, and many private religious activities utilize practices and literatures provided by larger religious communities.

Acts of focused care, such as pastoral counseling or psychotherapy and spiritual direction, frequently are offered not only to members of congregations but also to persons outside any religious community (American Association of Pastoral Counselors, www.aapc.org). Such mental and spiritual care services are offered with respect for the client's own faith tradition, but acknowledge the search for spiritual meaning that often motivates persons to seek help. Healing practices like pastoral counseling utilize methods found in contemporary psychotherapeutic strategies, but they are shaped by the understandings of personhood and the cosmos that constitute the legacy of religious traditions. Spiritual transformation in such settings is deepened by centuries of accumulated wisdom.

Some Speculations about the Role of Community

In addition to rituals and relationships of care to support spiritual transformation, faith communities offer extended relationships within which religious activities are practiced. Religious fellowships at their best serve as extended family-like networks for support and accountability. In fact, without such communities, religious practice has been perceived as problematic. This is the point at which religion and spirituality find each other. As Sandra Schneiders says,

> *Institutionalization* as an organized religion is what makes *spirituality* as a daily experience of participation in a *religious tradition*

> possible for the majority of people. . . . Institutionalized religion
> initiates people into an authentic tradition of spirituality, gives
> them companions on the journey and tested wisdom by which to
> live, and supports them in times of suffering and personal insta-
> bility. (Schneiders 2003, 171, 172)

Recent neuroscientific research also underscores the critical role that relationships with others play in shaping and reshaping the human brain. From the very beginning of life the quality of caretaker-infant interactions influences the development of the orbitofrontal cortex, which then enables the maturing infant to regulate its own emotional responsiveness (Schore 1994; Siegel 1999). Empathic responsiveness to the infant's changing emotional experiences is therefore a key to healthy development. These early developmental processes provide a solid foundation for later interpersonal relationships, and underscore the ways in which social relationships shape the brain.

We noted above the suggestion that neural changes occur in the brains of experienced meditators and produce a self-reported lack of self-boundaries (d'Aquili and Newberg 1999). D'Aquili and Newberg go on to suggest that similar processes occur during group ritual experience as well. Such neurobiological substrates for connectedness with others would, at least in theory, be applicable to persons who have had little or no personal contact with each other before a given ritual experience. Yet communities of faith generally exhibit an extended familiarity among fellow worshipers, and it is likely that the rich (and emotionally multivalent) store of memories of both individuals and the group as a whole further heightens effects on the autonomic nervous system responses of individual participants. Not only is increased social familiarity present, but there is also generally some degree of consensus in the values and narratives that shape the individual's experience of corporate worship. Repeated reading and hearing of sacred stories and texts elicit empathic responses from participants, further contributing to the sense of self-transcendence that would appear to provide the participating individuals with opportunities for deep spiritual transformation.

We suggested above that the brain is constantly evaluating the environment in relation to the self, monitoring its own internal milieu. So posture, movement, and gesture, as well as state of arousal, will have a "bottom-up" effect on participants' experience in corporate worship. Effective religious worship then will engage participants in movement and gesture, thus making use of the somatic, subcortical experiences that deepen experiences of the self. Ritual practices that do not include physical awareness and movement may miss critical opportunities for formation and transformation. Ritual practices in enduring religious communities that balance contemplation and physical activity, in the context of shared stories, both express and shape the brain's cognitive and affective structures and processes in profound ways that contribute to spiritual transformation.

Conclusion

Spirituality is frequently considered an individual and private matter. Indeed, spiritual transformation involves deeply personal experiences and can produce profound changes in the individual. Yet we have argued here that research in the cognitive sciences, particularly regarding neurological development and memory, implies that even our most personal experiences of transcendence and change are grounded in our relatedness to those around us. The stories that we construct to make sense of our lives rely on the broader cultural stories within which we are first formed. Our very brains develop within a web of relationships to others, including the divine.

Religious communities that share stories and ritual practices of care and worship offer meta-narratives within which individuals can reimagine their own personal narratives and experience the bimodal forces of belonging and differentiating. One of the many characteristics of pastoral counseling that distinguishes it from other forms of psychotherapeutic endeavor is the implicit frame of meaning within which the counseling takes place—not as an unexamined, tightly disciplined network of moral imperatives, but rather as an interlocking series of narratives that provide rich meaning contexts within which both counselor and client can find themselves and locate their own personal stories within stories of ultimate meaning. Pastoral counseling and worship at their best are mutually enriching dimensions of Christian communities, engaging both the stories and rituals of the community with the narratives and embodied practices of human beings.

References

American Association of Pastoral Counselors. www.aapc.org (last accessed December 13, 2005).

Anderson, H., and E. Foley. 1998. *Mighty Stories, Dangerous Rituals: Weaving Together the Human and the Divine*. San Francisco: Jossey-Bass.

Ashbrook, J. B. and C. R. Albright. 1997. *The Humanizing Brain: Where Religion and Neuroscience Meet*. Cleveland, Ohio: Pilgrim.

Bell, C. 1997. *Ritual: Perspectives and Dimensions*. Oxford: Oxford University Press.

Brown, W. S., N. Murphy, and H. N. Malony. 1998. *Whatever Happened to the Soul? Scientific and Theological Portraits of Human Nature*. Minneapolis, Minn.: Fortress.

Cozolino, L. 2002. *The Neuroscience of Psychotherapy: Building and Rebuilding the Brain*. New York: W.W. Norton.

Damasio, A. 1994. *Descartes' Error: Emotion, Reason, and the Human Brain*. New York: G. P. Putnam's Sons.

———. 1999. *The Feeling of What Happens: Body and Emotion in the Making of Consciousness*. New York: Harcourt Brace.

d'Aquili, E. G., and A. B. Newberg. 1999. *The Mystical Mind: Probing the Biology of Religious Experience*. Minneapolis, Minn.: Fortress.

de Rivera, J., and T. Sarbin. 1998. *Believed-In Imaginings: The Narrative Construction of Reality*. Washington, D.C.: American Psychological Association.

Dolcos, F., K. LaBar, and R. Cabeza. 2005. Remembering one year later: Role of the amygdala and the medial temporal lobe memory system in retrieving emotional memories. *Proceedings of the National Academy of Sciences* 102 no. 7 (February 15): 2626–31.

Gazzaniga, M. A. 2000. Cerebral specialization and interhemispheric communication: Does the corpus callosum enable the human condition? *Brain* 123:1293–1326.

Greenberg, D. L., and D. C. Rubin. 2003. The neuropsychology of autobiographical memory. *Cortex* 39 (Sep–Dec): 687–728.

Hogue, D. A. 2003. *Remembering the Future, Imagining the Past: Story, Ritual, and the Human Brain*. Cleveland, Ohio: Pilgrim.

LeDoux, J. 1996. *The Emotional Brain: The Mysterious Underpinnings of Emotional Life*. New York: Touchstone.

Levine, B., G. R. Turner, D. Tisserand, S. J. Hevenor, S. J. Graham, and A. R. McIntosh. 2004. The functional neuroanatomy of episodic and semantic autobiographical remembering: A prospective functional MRI study. *Journal of Cognitive Neuroscience* 16 no. 9 (November): 1633–46.

McAdams, D. P. 1993. *Stories We Live By: Personal Myths and the Making of the Self*. New York: William Morrow.

McCauley, R. N., and E. T. Lawson. 2002. *Bringing Ritual to Mind: Psychological Foundations of Cultural Forms*. Cambridge: Cambridge University Press.

McGaugh, J. L. 2004. The amygdala modulates the consolidation of memories of emotionally arousing experiences. *Annual Review of Neuroscience* 27:1–28.

Neuger, C. C. 2001. *Counseling Women: A Narrative, Pastoral Approach*. Minneapolis, Minn.: Fortress.

Ornstein, R. 1997. *The Right Mind: Making Sense of the Hemispheres*. New York: Harcourt Brace.

Peter D. Hart Research. 2005. *Faith in America: Results of NBC Survey on Religion and American Life*, (March 8–10). Retrieved June 6, 2005 from www.msnbc.com/id/7231603

Rappaport, R. 1999. *Ritual and Religion in the Making of Humanity*. Cambridge: Cambridge University Press.

Schacter, D. L., ed. 1995. *Memory Distortion: How Minds, Brains, and Societies Reconstruct the Past*. Cambridge, Mass.: Harvard University Press.

———. 1996. *Searching for Memory: The Brain, the Mind, and the Past*. New York: Basic Books.

Schneiders, S. M. 2003. Religion vs. spirituality: A contemporary conundrum. *Spiritus* 3 no. 2 (Fall): 163–85.

Schore, A. 1994. *Affect Regulation and the Origin of the Self: The Neurobiology of Emotional Development*. Hillsdale, N.J.: Lawrence Erlbaum Associates.

Siegel, D. J. 1999. *The Developing Mind: How Relationships and the Brain Interact to Shape Who We Are*. New York: Guildford.

Turner, V. 1969. *The Ritual Process: Structure and Anti-structure*. New York: Aldine de Gruyter.

van Gennep, A. 1960. *The Rites of Passage*. Chicago: University of Chicago Press.

Walker, M. P., T. J. Brakefield, J. A. Hobson, and R. Stickgold. 2003. Dissociable stages of human memory consolidation and reconsolidation. *Nature* 425 (October 9): 616–19.

PART V

CLINICAL PERSPECTIVES ON SPIRITUAL TRANSFORMATION AND HEALING

15

Spirituality, Spiritual Experiences, and Spiritual Transformations in the Face of HIV

Gail Ironson, Heidemarie Kremer,
and Dale S. Ironson

Being diagnosed with HIV or AIDS is often an event that initiates a reexamination of spiritual and religious issues and one's connection to the sacred. This chapter explores how people who have been diagnosed with a life-threatening illness, such as HIV, respond to this challenge and the role that religion, spirituality, and spiritual transformation play in their lives. Subjects in our study described how HIV transformed their lives, the impact of spirituality on their coping with HIV, as well as other issues in their lives (e.g., getting off drugs). In addition, participants shared whether they felt there was a reason, in the larger scheme of things, why they got HIV.

This chapter is divided into three sections. The first section covers the role spirituality and religion play when one is facing a diagnosis of HIV; the second section looks at what kinds of spiritual transformations people report, including their antecedents and consequences; and the third section looks at the forms spiritual experiences take and how people are changed by them.

Methods

In-depth interviews of ninety-five people with HIV form the basis for this study.[1] Two groups of HIV-positive people were recruited from AIDS organizations, physicians' offices, and community events.

The first group included seventy-six participants from a longitudinal study of the psychology of health and long-term survival with HIV/AIDS. Participants of this study, which examined stress and coping and assessed numerous psychological factors, have been seen for between four and eight years (see Ironson et al. 2005). These participants were therefore not coming for a study on spirituality. The interview was carefully designed not to "prime" people about our interest in spirituality. First we asked about "important experiences" in the subjects' lives. Then we probed to determine whether spirituality was involved in these experiences and how HIV might be involved.

A preliminary classification of these seventy-six participants (based on one rater) shows that 28 percent described a spiritual transformation and 21 percent a possible spiritual transformation, whereas 51 percent described turning points in their lives in which spirituality was little or not at all involved.[2] This classification was based on Pargament (see chap. 2) and Schwartz (2000), who defines a spiritual transformation as "a radical reorganization of one's identity, meaning and purpose in life" (5), which is accompanied by "dramatic changes in religious beliefs, attitudes, and behavior" (4), as well as in world- and self-views that are often linked to discrete experiences that can occur gradually or "over relatively short periods of time" (4).

A second group of seventy-four people was recruited specifically for a study on spirituality and HIV. Entry criteria required that participants consider themselves spiritual and have had spiritual experiences that changed their views of life. As this is a study in progress, we have to date transcribed nineteen interviews with participants who described a spiritual transformation.

Of these ninety-five participants (seventy-six from the first sample and nineteen from the second sample), 89 percent reported being raised with a religious affiliation (25 percent Protestant, 21 percent Catholic, 6 percent Baptist, 28 percent other Christian religions, 5 percent Jewish, 1 percent Muslim, 1 percent Buddhist, 1 percent Hindu, and 1 percent Rastafarian), and 11 percent reported being raised nonreligious. Their mean age was 40.2 years (standard-deviation (SD) = 9.2). Most participants were African American (52 percent), followed by Latino (21 percent), Caucasian (20 percent), and other (7 percent). The proportion of women (43 percent) was high.[3] Fifty-seven percent were heterosexual and 43 percent gay or bisexual. Sixty-eight percent had an annual income below ten thousand dollars. Forty-seven percent had more than a high-school education. AIDS-defining symptoms were experienced by 37 percent. Blood draws at the interviews indicated that 20 percent of the participants had serious immune damage (CD4-cells below $200/\mu l$), and 46 percent had an immune-depletion with CD4-cells between $200–500$ cells/μl, whereas 34 percent had CD4-cells in the normal range (above 500 cells/μl). Viral-load was undetectable in 49 percent. A low viral-load (below 10,000 copies/ml) was detected in 19 percent, whereas a viral-load above 10,000 copies/ml was measured in 32 percent. Seventy-five percent were taking HIV medication.[4]

The Role Spirituality and Religion Play in the Lives of People with HIV

This section begins with a discussion of the distinction between being religious and being spiritual because it is an issue that many people with HIV consider important. Next, several themes will be addressed that emerged from the interviews: being diagnosed with HIV as a catalyst for spiritual change; attributions related to why people felt they got HIV; the usefulness of spirituality or religiousness in coping with HIV; redefining one's relationship to the sacred in light of the stigmatizing views of some religious denominations; and afterlife beliefs and fear of death.

The distinction between being religious or spiritual is important to most but not all of the people interviewed in this study. Some people struggle to differentiate between the concepts, while others feel that "there is no difference between religiousness and spirituality" and that the "truth is going to be revealed to us, whatever path we take." Very few participants consider themselves as solely religious. Most participants consider themselves more spiritual than religious. In fact, people in the longitudinal sample report being significantly more spiritual (mean of 6.97 on a scale of 1 to 10; SD = 2.44) than religious (mean of 4.30; SD = 3.18). Statements such as "Organized religion is not my thing" and "To be a good person, you don't have to have a religion" reflect these feelings. Consistent with this, many studies have observed that much of the religious experience among people with HIV is expressed in terms of a God or a higher power rather than in terms of belonging to a religious denomination or of attendance at religious services (Pargament et al. 2004). Pargament and colleagues note that this may be due to the stigma that many religious institutions attach to HIV and its related modes of transmission.

The religious construct refers to belonging to a religious denomination, whereas our sample described spirituality as involving one's relationship to the soul and the inner or higher self, as reflected in statements such as "God is inside of us" and "My spirituality is getting in touch with my inner self." Some participants felt that "not being judgmental is becoming spiritual."

Zinnbauer and Pargament (Forthcoming) note that both religiousness and spirituality involve a search for the sacred, but that religiousness involves the search within a traditional sacred context. Religiousness tends to involve a group context, whereas spirituality is more often associated with a personal search, but not necessarily so. One can view either religiousness or spirituality as the broader construct.

Those identifying themselves as religious tended to link their beliefs to institutional, traditional, ritualized, and social expressions of faith. In contrast, those who identified themselves as spiritual presented their beliefs and practices as mechanisms for transcendence and connectedness (Woods and Ironson 1999). Similarly, Miller and Thoresen (2003) contrast "institutional, organized, social aspects of religion" to "personal, transcendent, and relatedness aspects" (30) of spirituality. Hill et al. (2000) propose that the sacred lies at the core of both constructs, but that religion provides "the means and the methods of this search that receive validation and support from an identifiable group of people" (66). A scale developed by Ironson et al. (2002) to span both religious and spiritual aspects of the search for the sacred has four major dimensions: *sense of peace, faith in God, religious behavior,* and *compassion for others.* In this study, Ironson et al. showed that all four of these dimensions were positively related to both long-term survival with

HIV and the experiencing of less distress. In addition, *being judgmental* (a fifth factor) was negatively related to long-term survival. The major dimension of this scale that distinguishes it from traditional measures of religiousness is sense of peace. Having a sense of peace was also significantly correlated with lower cortisol, providing a physiological basis for an association with long-term survival.

The Impact of HIV on Spirituality: Being Diagnosed with HIV as a Catalyst for Spiritual Change

For some people, becoming HIV-positive is just one small event in the middle of the turmoil of life and has no impact at all on their spirituality. For others, the HIV diagnosis triggers a spiritual transformation in their search to find new meaning while living with HIV. In our longitudinal sample, 54 percent of the participants believed that getting HIV made them more spiritual. Sarah is one example.

Sarah, a good-looking Caucasian woman, learned at age thirty that she was HIV-positive, during an exam at a clinic where she had asked for birth-control pills. Unable to find a support group that she felt fit her needs, she founded a nonprofit grassroots organization. The stated mission of her group is to inform, educate, guide, and empower individuals to heal the body, mind, and spirit of those living with HIV/AIDS. Sarah recently received a community appreciation award for epitomizing the ideals of holistic healing and unconditional love. She reports:

> I got HIV because it is my purpose of being. I had to understand what it is like so I can help the community on a different level and help create social change. I didn't know that I had these powers inside of me, that I can be a dynamic leader and be an inspiration to others. I was just the shy girl being a workaholic and not knowing, just waiting for a paycheck and not being emotionally connected to people other than having friends.

Eleven years after her HIV diagnosis, she has not had any symptoms of the disease, and her immune parameters (300 CD4-cells/μl, 38,000 viral-load copies/ml) are still in a range where there is no need to start HIV medication. She is extremely energetic, working nonstop as the executive director of her support organization, jetting around the globe, and planning to extend her work on an international basis and write a book about her life.

In contrast with Sarah, who found a purpose in life after an HIV diagnosis, *Carlos*, a Latino man, floundered and lost his purpose in life. Carlos remembers,

> I was planning to finish my BA, moving to New York. I found out that my ex partner had been doing drugs and cheating with other relationships. I was very scared, and I didn't deal with it. For six months I didn't get tested. When I did find out, I had no friends in New York so I had to deal with it on my own. I turned to cocaine, my life changed dramatically; I was sort of spiraling downhill, near the lowest point in my life. It changed everything, it changed my behavior, it changed my ambition, I didn't have the same drive that I had going in after school to pursue my career. Things were so bad that any belief that I had in a higher being or in a spiritual presence was completely extinguished. I was on a course downhill. I just didn't care.

Carlos was diagnosed with HIV nine years ago, but his infection progressed rapidly to AIDS. He suffered from serious opportunistic infections and has very low CD4-cells ($24/\mu l$) and a detectable viral-load (30,000 copies/ml) despite taking HIV medication.

Why Me?

There are many answers, both positive and negative, to the "Why me?" question. While one person states, "I think I was just in the wrong place at the wrong time," others feel they got HIV due to a larger reason that goes far beyond risky behavior. These larger reasons range from positive appraisals such as "I was selected [to get HIV] to get me enlightened" or "I got HIV to get closer to God," to negative appraisals such as "God said if you have sex before marriage you will be cursed with disease."

Some of the participants who interpret their having HIV as part of a divine plan often find a new meaning in life through their disease, such as Sarah above, saying that "Volunteering in the HIV arena gave me a sense God was using me," "God has a plan. I was destined to do great things," or "God gave me HIV to stop [me doing] drugs."

There is an association between a positive perception of the HIV infection and an attitude of gratitude. One person reports, "In a way I'm glad I got HIV. It made me search for the reason why. I started appreciating a lot. It made me love myself and love my life." Another describes "HIV and hepatitis C as a blessing."

In contrast, *Yvonne*, an African-American woman in her forties, had a negative experience:

> I thought I had been cursed. I used to say, "Why, God?! Why me?! How could you allow this to happen?!" I was angry with what I choose to call my God. I was angry with everybody. I wouldn't tell nobody. I was still having unprotected sex. I was risking other people's lives and not telling them, because I said, "I want to take more out just like me . . . I won't die on my own by myself."

Are Spirituality and Religiousness Helpful in Coping with HIV?

In the face of HIV, people often tap into their spiritual and religious resources. Meditation, prayer, and belief in a higher power are common and powerful spiritual and religious coping methods (Pargament et al. 2004). Our interviews underscore this. For example, participants state that "Believing in God allows me to cope with the virus" and "I think without religion I would not be able to be alive and coping with disease." Spirituality can also help with more concrete issues, such as taking medication. For example, "Every day God gives me is a gift, so I take my medicines because I need to honor life." It is worth mentioning that a religious or spiritual frame of reference can function as a negative as well as a positive method of cognitive coping. It changes the way people look at events, and therefore changes the way they react to events. The transition from a view of a judgmental God to a loving one is an example of reframing that has an enormously positive impact on coping. The spiritual frame of reference varies from expressing anger at God and feeling punished by God (as Yvonne above) to seeking a loving God from whom one can seek forgiveness and help (as Carlos below).

Coming to Terms with HIV, Sexuality, and the Church: From Being Judged to Being Loved

Reviewing the literature, Pargament et al. (2004) describe the fear of judgment that people with HIV face, since some religious institutions condemn homosexuality, view promiscuity as a sin, and regard HIV as a punishment. In our interviews, some women report beliefs such as "God said if you have sex before marriage you will be cursed with disease." In addition, some men describe difficulties in coming to terms with their gay or bisexual orientation. They struggle, noting that "Homosexuality is a sin in a conservative church," or pointing out that "There are no homosexuals in the Kingdom of God." Some start "looking for a church that validated my homosexual orientation." Others even state, "I would pray for God to make me straight."

Rick, a Caucasian military man, has belonged to a conservative Christian church since he was a teenager. He explains,

> After HIV, I was too sick to go to church. All of a sudden, I felt out of place in a place I felt a part of for a good number of years. I would see men and women together in church with their kids. All of a sudden, that wasn't me anymore. I felt as if at a certain point, the protection of the Holy Spirit left me. So I need to try to find ways to regain it. I started searching myself. . . . Where was my new place to be? If I'm this way, who am I supposed to be now? It was so set in concrete when I was fifteen; the type of person I was supposed to be. All of a sudden, I'm not this person because of the understanding that my sexuality is different. So I had to go through a whole process of discovering myself. One thing was for sure, I wanted to believe that the way that I was was not sinful, or criminal, or against God.

While some of the individuals in our sample feel rejected by religious institutions, others are able to find accepting churches or ministers. Two years after being diagnosed with HIV, Carlos notes:

> I was at my worst. I went to a church that I used to go to. It was Easter Sunday. I didn't know about any programs for addiction, like Alcoholics Anonymous. I was trying to do it on my own. I was completely looking for answers and also looking for hope. And the minister basically said, as an individual you can change

your belief system whenever you want to. You don't have to believe in any God that doesn't love you or any God that isn't here
to help you. Because I had a Catholic background, during my addiction I felt like I was being judged, that I was being punished. I
thought I was going to die for my sins. So when I went to this service and I heard that, [it] changed my God to one that was loving
and helpful. It was revolutionary.

Shortly thereafter, Carlos went to Alcoholics Anonymous and became sober.

The Fear of Death: What Do You Think
Happens to Your Soul When You Die?

Fear of death and beliefs about what happens after death are
important concerns for many living with HIV. Most people with
HIV believe that the soul lives on in some form. Statements such as
"When you are dead, you're done" are rare. Two afterlife beliefs are
common: belief in heaven and hell, and belief in reincarnation. It
appears as if a belief in heaven and hell is most common in the female African-American and Latino populations, regardless of
whether they consider themselves spiritual or religious. For some,
what happens is quite simple: "If you're right with God, then
you're going to heaven. But if you ain't right with God, then I believe you're going to hell." A significant proportion of participants
who consider themselves spiritual report a belief in reincarnation.
This belief contrasts with the belief that there is punishment in hell
for bad behavior. The belief that "HIV is a karmic lesson" is constructive for many of those in our sample, such as the person who
said, "My belief in reincarnation prepared me for the moment I was
HIV-positive."

Spiritual Transformations of People with HIV

In our study, we defined a *turning point* as an experience that
changed an individual's life or that profoundly impacted his or her
life. A *spiritual transformation* (defined above), as opposed to a turning point, involves a religious or spiritual framework (Hood et al.

1996, 276). In addition, Hood et al. distinguished the process of a spiritual transformation from a spiritual experience by noting that a spiritual transformation results in a more profound change in the sense of the self, with radical consequences (because new ideas, behaviors, and changed habits of life follow). A spiritual experience, typically a discrete event, can but does not always trigger a spiritual transformation.

Miller (2004) introduced the term *quantum change* for a "vivid, surprising, benevolent and enduring personal transformation" and distinguished two types of change: the "mystical type," which is similar to an enduring spiritual transformation (Mahoney and Pargament 2004), and the "insightful type," which is a turnaround experience lacking a connection to the sacred (Miller 2004). While most spiritual transformations are reported to be positive, long-lasting, and life-changing, sometimes people report that the transformation can wear off over time. Factors that make transformations more lasting include a supportive context (e.g., drug recovery programs, HIV support groups, religious organizations, or loving relatives and friends), supportive activities (e.g., meditation, prayer, spiritual exercises, writing, or painting), and helping others. For example, Alcoholics Anonymous has been mentioned by several of our participants as particularly helpful. One person stated, "Alcoholics Anonymous has been a very good influence for me to improve my state of being and coming to a God of my own understanding. And definitely spirituality has always been a part of it."

Conversion Experiences among People with HIV

Confronting the challenges of HIV sometimes has the impact of a spiritual transformation, transforming a life of substance abuse, disrupted relationships, or imprisonment to a life with new meaning and purpose. The term *spiritual transformation* is sometimes equated with that of *conversion experience* (Schwartz 2000). Among our participants we find two types of reported spiritual transformations: conversion experiences, and intensification of devotion to a religion or a spiritual practice. One-third of the participants reporting spiritual transformations in our interviews describe a conversion. Within conversion, three types are described: (1) conversion from a religious tradition to spirituality or atheism, (2) conversion from one religious tradition to another, and (3) conversion from spirituality or atheism to religion. The spiritual conversion of Vanessa and the religious conversion of Dominique reported below reveal that hitting rock bottom in a life characterized by substance use, imprisonment, and disrupted personal relationships set the stage for the transformation that was about to happen.

Vanessa, a single, African-American woman, describes the first type of conversion, from traditional Christianity to spirituality:

> That moment, that last drug I used back in 1992 was my transformation. I was so deep in the ground until, I use to always think this was my last hit, I am going to die. I had found out I was pregnant. I walked and walked all the twenty-five blocks to the detox. I felt that this was going to be my only hope because I did not want to bring a crack baby [into the world] that run a risk of having the virus because I knew I had the virus. I started praying: "God help me, God I need you, God I am tired of being out here, I know this is not what you created me for. I am still alive." God was paving the way for me, and he gave me the strength and he gave me the courage just to keep walking and don't look back, and that's what I did. I am so grateful to God. God did that. That made me more spiritual. I just think we put too much into religion and God just wants us to love him with all our heart and all our soul and our strength. From that moment on I believe in God in everything I do and say.

Vanessa's life on crack and prostitution had started after her teenage pregnancy. Now, twelve years after this call for God's help, she is a responsible mother of four and grandmother of four. She was diagnosed with HIV fifteen years ago and is still asymptomatic. Her lowest CD4 count was 100 cells/μl. On HIV medication, she now has good immune parameters (675 CD4-cells/μl and 661 viral-load copies/ml).

Dominique, an African-American woman in her forties, describes the third type of conversion (to Christianity). Because she felt blamed by her family for the death of a relative from cancer, she says,

> I got onto drugs and I got so disturbed that I used to pray to God to let me see some kind of sign. I was nineteen. I had kids then, I

just left home. I was so drawn into the drug world that I didn't know what to do. One time I got high on a Sunday and I saw God. I saw a hand out there that just grabbed me. I swore I saw a hand. I just said something had to give so I just went on to Christ. I got my life together. I walked into the jailhouse because it's the only place I felt safe. I sat in the prison for about a year and a half and I read the whole Bible straight through. Once I came out, I didn't want no more drugs. My family didn't accept me when I got out, they didn't even know who I was. I had to find friends. I go to church all the time. I rely on God for everything. I think that if it weren't for him, I wouldn't be where I am today. I asked him to take me off crack and alcohol.

Dominique was diagnosed with HIV eight years ago and still does not need HIV medication because her CD4-cells are high (483 cells/μl), and her viral-load is very low (2630 copies/ml).

Antecedents of Spiritual Transformations in People with HIV

Being diagnosed with HIV is one of the life crises that can set the conditions for a spiritual transformation. But we should note that although getting HIV is often associated with an increase in spirituality (see prior section), the HIV diagnosis is not the most frequent antecedent of spiritual transformation in our sample. Hitting rock bottom with drugs or alcohol is the most frequent context in which spiritual transformations are reported in this study. Precursors of the spiritual transformations reported in our sample include openness to being helped, a genuine desire to get better and to be healed, or feelings of shame, contrition, or repentance. Asking for help is a frequent antecedent associated with a spiritual transformation, as Vanessa, Dominique, and Grace (below) point out.

Grace, an African-American woman, recalls going out the back of a bar after thirty years of addiction to drugs and alcohol:

They had this big dumpster. When I looked in it, I saw a Mecca. It was like more aluminum cans than I had ever seen in my life. So I went into the dumpster and once I got in, I couldn't get out. Well, being an addict at that time, I couldn't call anybody to help me get out of there. But that night I really talked to God. I said, "Look, this is it, I have had enough, I am trying to stop, and I have stopped but couldn't stay stopped. You got to do something. I have asked you before and it worked for a little while but I kept going back, but now I need to do something." That night I had to stay there all night, but that morning, that Sunday morning when the garbage man came to empty the garbage and to help me out. That next morning they [the people at church] put me in a recovery facility and they didn't ask me to pay them.

That night in the dumpster, Grace surrendered her life to God, and she has remained sober since and helped other people recover from drug addiction. She is doing remarkably well ten years past her diagnosis, with high CD4-cells ($624/\mu$l) and an undetectable viral-load on HIV medication. Grace describes a sequence of hitting rock bottom, admitting loss of control, calling for help, and surrendering control to God or a higher power, which is similar to the mechanisms of change described and advocated by Alcoholics Anonymous and Narcotics Anonymous (Forcehimes 2004).

Another common pathway to spiritual transformation is having a spiritual experience. *John*, a gay African-American man in his forties with a college education, describes an out-of-body experience that overcame him shortly after he had helped a drunk, homeless white man in distress:

I felt like I was floating over my body, and I'll never forget this, as I was floating over my body, I looked down, it was like this shriveled-up prune, nothing but a prune, like an old dried skin. And my soul, my spirit was over my body. Everything was so separated. I was just feeling like I was in different dimensions, I felt it in my body like a gush of wind blows. I remember saying to God, "God! I can't die now, because I haven't fulfilled my purpose," and, just as I said that, the spirit and the body, became one, it all collided, and I could feel this gush of wind and I was a whole person again.

John remembers this transformational experience, which was ten years ago, as if it happened yesterday. He continues,

That was really a groundbreaking experience. Before becoming HIV-positive my faith was so fear based. I always wanted to feel I belonged somewhere, that I fit in, or that I was loved. What helped me to overcome the fear of God and the fear of change was that I realized that no one had a monopoly on God. I was able to begin to replace a lot of destructive behavior with a sort of spiritual desire. I think also what changed, my desire to get close to God, to love myself, and to really embrace unconditional love.

The death of a loved one is a fourth, very intense transformational experience described by this sample. Losing a loved one, particularly if he or she dies of AIDS, often reminds people with HIV of the potential fatality of their own diagnosis. For example, one participant recalls, "When a friend of mine died, she had HIV also; I thought about my two little boys and said, 'Lord, I don't want nobody else to raise my children.' That really opened up my eyes because I had children and that's what really changed me."

Other key antecedents of spiritual transformations are childbirth or parenting, marriage, or wanting to give up or escape criminal activities, homelessness, or a promiscuous lifestyle. Readings are also mentioned as being helpful (e.g., the Bible, *A Course in Miracles*, *Conversations with God*, *You Can Heal Your Life*). For example, one participant talks about the helpfulness of "reading books like Louise Hay's *You Can Heal Your Life*. She wrote about accepting yourself and loving yourself and realizing that the way we look at other people has such a dramatic influence on our own health."

What Changes Are Associated with a Spiritual Transformation?

After being asked, "What changed?" a participant's frequent response is "Everything." Changes often involve new beliefs, behaviors, attitudes, cognition, self-view, and worldview. Changes in belief include changes in religiousness or spirituality, as well as the change from belief in a judgmental God to belief in a loving God or higher power. The most common change in behavior is a drastic change in lifestyle, from excessive use of drugs or alcohol, engaging in criminal activities, living on the streets, or engaging in prostitution or promiscuity to a new way of living, which includes taking care of one's own health, striving for and engaging in supportive relationships, and helping and caring for other people. As a result of such spiritual transformations, negative emotions are often replaced with feelings of love, acceptance, and inner peace. Dramatic changes in attitudes are reported, and participants may go from being reckless, careless, hostile, and aggressive to feeling peace, joy, compassion, honesty, forgiveness, gratitude, and a sense of being blessed. Spiritual transformations also involve a relief from fear, anxiety, tension, anger, and depression.

Changes in cognition also occur and can dramatically effect one's reaction to stress. For example, when we are faced with an irritable person who is insulting, changing our cognition from fear and anger to the realization that there is something greater than ourselves may help soften our reaction and may lead to more compassionate behavior. Self-views among our participants often switch from reflecting low self-esteem, self-centeredness, and a feeling of being out of place and empty to reflecting higher self-esteem and self-knowledge and a feeling of being other-centered. This new self-view is often accompanied by finding a new place in the world, finding a new meaning and purpose in life, and setting new priorities and values in life. Examples of this are giving up prostitution or drug addiction for responsible parenthood, becoming a minister at a church, founding an HIV support organization, taking care of the dying, or volunteering in the field of HIV/AIDS or substance use. Similar to what John reports above, these changes often go along with an acceptance of the HIV diagnosis and a positive change in the participant's relationship with family and friends.

The findings in our interviews are consistent with the literature. Franks, Templer, and Cappelletty (1991) found that gay men with HIV who experienced a conversion reported a significant reduction in anxiety associated with the fear of death. In an analysis of narratives of drug users, being diagnosed with HIV was often perceived as a chance to move from chaos and addiction to a healthier life (Mosack et al. 2005). Miller (2004) found that common effects of spiritual transformation were a release from chronic negative affect, the forming of more meaningful and peaceful intimate relationships, an abrupt but enduring shift in most central values, a reduction in materialism, and the adoption of spirituality as a more central part of life.

Spiritual Experiences of People with HIV

The spiritual experiences described in our interviews include near-death experiences; out-of-body experiences; contacts with deceased loved ones; visitations with or hearing the voices of God, angels, or other transcendent beings; and experiencing the power of prayer. Some of our participants even describe the HIV diagnosis as a spiritual experience, as does Grace, who testifies, "HIV is calling because I need a purpose in my life." Other spiritual experiences reported are transcendent mediation, voodoo ceremonies, and experiences with clairvoyance, visualization, and channeling. Sometimes these experiences seem to occur out of the blue—as a warning or a wake-up call, or as an opportunity for the person to make another choice in life.

Near-Death Experiences

Elements of the near-death experiences reported in our study are similar to what is described in the literature (Greyson 1993; Moody 1975) and include feelings of peace and contentment; out-of-body experiences; the sense of moving through a tunnel into a bright light; the meeting of deceased loved ones or transcendent others (who often tell the experiencer that it is not yet their time to die); the sense of seeing one's life pass before one's eyes; and the finding of an out-of-body experience so wonderful that one doesn't want to return to one's body.

Miranda, an African-American woman in her fifties who almost died in a car accident, "started going through this tunnel full of light." Miranda continues, "It was beautiful. White light. But all of a sudden it stopped and somebody said, 'I am not ready for you yet.' The voice was deep and calm and it made me feel relaxed and I started coming back from this tunnel and it started getting darker and darker." Miranda's life changed after this experience.

> It made me put more value on life and more value on family. It made me appreciate the birds and the trees. It made me determined to make that journey out of the light. It made me more of a survivor. God presented himself and he let me know that I was here for a purpose. Until he is ready for me, I am not going anywhere.

Miranda's testimony is consistent with the findings of an eight-year prospective study of 344 survivors of cardiac arrest (Van Lommel et al. 2001), in which 18 percent reported a near-death experience. Those who had had a near-death experience during cardiac arrest showed a significant increase in belief in an afterlife and a decrease in fear of death, received higher scores of interest in the meaning of life, and demonstrated more love for and acceptance of others, in comparison with those who had not had a near-death experience. Many retrospective studies describe comparable spiritual transformations following near-death experiences (Groth-Marnat and Summer 1998).

Out-of-Body Experiences

An out-of-body experience is a dramatic experience that makes people feel that they are more than just their physical body, that is, that they are spiritual beings and that their consciousness can operate beyond the limitations of their physical body (see John's description above). Such an experience feels profound and liberating to the person experiencing it, helps to greatly reduce their fear of death and mortality, and gives them an expanded perspective on life and living (Ironson 1975). Out-of-body experiences can occur spontaneously but seem more likely to occur when the experiencer is physically relaxed and mentally calm, such as during dream states or meditation, and they may also occur when the experiencer is under extreme emotional stress or is unusually fatigued. Such experiences often seem to be triggered by near-death situations such as accidents (Ironson 1975; Monroe 1985; Twenlow, Gabbard, and Jones 1982).

Communication with Deceased Loved Ones

Following the loss of a loved one, a common spiritual experience described in our study is after-death communication. *Pedro*, a Latino man in his forties, describes such an event.

> This lady [a close relative who had died] appeared to me in a dream. And she said, "Pedro, you not dead yet?" I was surprised. Why would she say that? She said, "When are you going to

change?" It was a shock to me. I didn't want to die in prison. She came across to me that it was time for me to change because I was not dead. She told me that only God can change you and why don't you go back to church. I had got to that point where I was totally against all religions and everything. I was an atheist. After that dream I started going to church in the prison, to all different services, Muslim, Christian, Native American. Everything changed. God must really love me. Look how many good things I've done while I'm in this prison. I've gotten my GED. I'm helping to tutor. The inmates say, "Pedro you're not so irritable anymore. Are you taking your medication?" One of the main things that changed was that I stopped being judgmental.

Encounters with Angels

Carlos describes an encounter with his guardian angel that was triggered by a severe motorcycle accident:

The motorcycle was completely totaled and there was this little man there the whole time, this little Mexican man. He comes up to me and he says, "I want you to do me a favor," and I was thinking, How can somebody ask me for a favor at this point in time? And he says, "I want you to look across the street." So I looked and there was a synagogue. To the right of that was a Presbyterian church and behind me was a Catholic church. And he said, "This is why you're here." And he walked away. And seriously there was no way that I could have walked away from that accident unscathed. It was a miracle. From that moment on I had felt like somebody is watching over me and there is a reason why I'm here. That was my guardian angel. My vision grew, I got myself into a great school, I ended up going to Europe, and I studied abroad after all this.

As in the cases of Carlos and Pedro, most encounters with angels, deceased loved ones, God, or other transcendent beings are perceived as catalyzing the process of spiritual transformation.

From Being High on Drugs to Being High on Spirituality?

Spiritual experiences often occur under the influence of drugs or alcohol. Testimonies such as "getting high on drugs" and "getting high on the Bible" suggest that spirituality may substitute for the euphoria that people report from drugs. There might even be a neurobiological explanation for this. Imaging studies show that the reinforcing effects of drugs often abused are associated with increases in dopamine, that brain dopamine function is markedly decreased after chronic drug abuse and during withdrawal (Volkow, Fowler, and Wang 2003), and that meditation-induced changes in consciousness are able to increase endogenous dopamine release (Kjaer et al. 2002).

Conclusion

Spirituality and religion help empower people to deal with HIV and other challenges, such as getting off drugs, taking better care of themselves, and finding new meaning and purpose in life. People with HIV often identify themselves as more spiritual than religious. They may struggle to redefine their relationship to religion in the face of being judged for being HIV-positive or gay. HIV can catalyze a positive spiritual transformation and can as well trigger a negative spiral of hopelessness, depression, fear, and despair. Spiritual beliefs described in our study as helpful include the belief in a loving God, the belief that one's soul lives on, the belief that one will be forgiven, and the belief that there is a divine purpose.

Potential preconditions of spiritual transformations include but are not limited to hitting rock bottom; getting tired of a life of drugs, prostitution, or homelessness; and asking God or a higher power for help. A variety of spiritual experiences, such as near-death experiences, out-of-body experiences, perceived visitations with deceased relatives, and perceived encounters with the divine, are often pathways to spiritual transformation as well. Consistent with the working definitions of Pargament (see chap. 2) and Schwartz (2000), spiritual transformations in our sample include changes in view of self, view of others, worldview, belief and cognition, attitude, behavior, and values. This seems to enable HIV-positive people to transform the challenge of living with HIV to a higher quality of life with a greater sense of peace, love, and connectedness to life and others.

One day in the not-too-distant future, we may recognize spirituality as an important factor in helping people deal with their illnesses and in aiding in the process of recovery. By adding the dimension of spirituality to treatment, the authors of this study feel, and research suggests, that levels of wellness, coping, and quality of life can be significantly improved.

Acknowledgments

We are grateful to Dr. Solomon Katz, the Metanexus Institute, and the Templeton Foundation for funding this study. We also express our appreciation to Annie George for conducting excellent interviews, and to Joan Koss-Chioino and Margaret Stivers for their helpful comments on drafts of the manuscript.

Notes

1. This study was approved by the Institutional Review Board (IRB). All participants gave informed consent. Names used in this chapter are not the real names of the participants.

2. One should not generalize from these data on the incidence of spiritual transformations in the HIV-positive population, as the longitudinal study is not a randomly selected sample (participants have been in the study a long time, and the entry criteria excluded people who were drug-dependent at baseline).

3. In the United States, women comprise only 25 percent of the HIV-positive population.

4. Selected HIV medications may have central nervous side effects (e.g., 53 percent of patients receiving efavirenz [Sustiva] perceive central nervous-system side-effects such as insomnia, confusion, abnormal dreaming or thinking, hallucinations, or depersonalization). Only a small number of participants in our sample received these medications.

References

Forcehimes, A. A. 2004. De profundis: Spiritual transformations in Alcoholics Anonymous. *Journal of Clinical Psychology* 60 (5): 503–17.

Franks, K., D. I. Templer, and G. G. Cappelletty. 1991. Exploration of health anxiety as a function of religious variables in gay men with and without AIDS. *Omega* 22:43–50.

Greyson, B. 1993. Varieties of near-death experience. *Psychiatry* 56:390–99.

Groth-Marnat, G., and R. Summer. 1998. Altered beliefs, attitudes, and behaviors following near-death experiences. *Journal of Humanistic Psychology* 38:110–25.

Hill, C., K. I. Pargament, R. W. Hood, M. C. McCullough, J. P. Swyers, and D. B. Larson et al. 2000. Conceptualizing religion and spirituality: Points of commonality, points of departure. *Journal for the Theory of Social Behavior* 30:51–77.

Hood, R., B. Spilka, B. Hunsberger, and R. Gorsuch. 1996. *The Psychology of Religion: An Empirical Approach.* New York: Guilford.

Ironson, D. S. 1975. An investigation into the preconditions, characteristics, and beliefs associated with the out-of-the-body experience. PhD diss. San Francisco: Saybrook Institute.

Ironson, G., S. Solomon, E. Balbin, C. O'Cleirigh, A. George, and M. Kumar et al. 2002. The Ironson-Woods Spirituality/Religiousness Index is associated with long survival, health behaviors, less distress, and low cortisol in people with HIV/AIDS. *Annals of Behavioral Medicine* 24 (1): 34–48.

Ironson, G., E. Balbin, R. Stuetzle, M. A. Fletcher, C. O'Cleirigh, and J. P. Laurenceau et al. 2005. Dispositional optimism and the mechanisms by which it predicts slower disease progression in HIV, proactive behavior, avoidant coping, and depression. *International Journal of Behavioral Medicine* 12 (2): 86–97.

Kjaer, T. W., C. Bertelsen, P. Piccini, D. Brooks, J. Alving, and H. C. Lou. 2002. Increased dopamine tone during meditation-induced change of consciousness. *Brain Research: Cognitive Brain Research* 3 (2): 255–59.

Mahoney, A., and K. I. Pargament. 2004. Sacred changes: Spiritual conversion and transformation. *Journal of Clinical Psychology* 60 (5): 481–92.

Miller, W. R. 2004. The phenomenon of quantum change. *Journal of Clinical Psychology* 60 (5): 453–60.

Miller, W. R., and C. E. Thoresen. 2003. Spirituality, religion, and health: An emerging research field. *American Psychologist* 58:24–35.

Monroe, R. A. 1985. *Far Journeys.* New York: Doubleday.

Moody, R. 1975. *Life after Life: The Investigation of a Phenomenon, Survival of Bodily Death.* New York: HarperCollins.

Mosack, K. E., M. Abbott, M. Singer, M. R. Weeks, and L. Rohena. 2005. If I didn't have HIV, I'd be dead now. *Qualitative Health Research* 15 (5): 586–605.

Pargament, K. I., S. McCarthy, P. Shah, G. Ano, N. Tarakeshwar, and A. Wachholtz et al. 2004. Religion and HIV: A review of the literature and clinical implications. *Southern Medical Journal* 97 no. 12 (December): 1201–9.

Schwartz, A. J. 2000. The nature of spiritual transformation: A review of the literature. Retrieved June 29, 2005 from www.metanexus.net/spiritual_transformation/research/literature_review.html

Twenlow, S. W., G. O. Gabbard, and F. C. Jones. 1982. The out-of-body experience: A phenomenological typology based on questionnaire responses. *American Journal of Psychiatry* 139 no. 4 (April): 450–55.

Van Lommel, P., R. van Wees, V. Meyers, and I. Elfferich. 2001. Near-death experience in survivors of cardiac arrest: A prospective study in the Netherlands. *Lancet* 358:2039–45.

Volkow, N. D., J. S. Fowler, and G. J. Wang. 2003. The addicted human brain: Insights from imaging studies. *Journal of Clinical Investigation* 111 (10): 1444–51.

Woods, T. E., and G. H. Ironson. 1999. Religion and spirituality in the face of illness: How cancer, cardiac, and HIV patients describe their spirituality/religiosity. *Journal of Health Psychology* 4 (3): 393–412.

Zinnbauer, B., and K. I. Pargament. Forthcoming. Religiousness and spirituality. In *Handbook of Psychology and Religion*, ed. R. Paloutzian and C. Parks. New York: Guilford.

16

Spiritual Engagement and Transformation in Cancer Patients: The Experience of the Patient, the Role of the Physician

Jean L. Kristeller and Leonard M. Hummel

Spiritual engagement and transformation often follow from times of personal crisis. A serious illness, such as cancer, brings with it feelings of vulnerability and often raises issues of existential identity and mortality. As many as 80–90 percent of cancer patients in a number of studies report drawing on spiritual and religious resources in coping with cancer (Ford, Fallowfield, and Lewis 1996; Miller, Pittman, and Strong 2003; Roberts et al. 1997; Steinhauser et al. 2000), and approximately half of a cohort of women diagnosed with gynecologic cancer indicated they had drawn more on their religious resources than they expected to (Roberts et al. 1997). A substantial portion of patients want their physician to be aware of their spiritual or religious beliefs and concerns, and they express interest in this aspect of life being addressed within the context of their medical care (Ford, Fallowfield, and Lewis 1996; McCord et al. 2004; Miller, Pittman, and Strong 2003). Whether this is a viable undertaking on the part of the physician, how such an inquiry would play a role in the experience of the patient, and the potential impact of this on the course of adjustment to cancer are all central questions.

The Traditional Context of Spiritual and Religious Engagement in Illness

The religious and theological literature, both contemporary and classical, often focuses on the value of religious and spiritual experience, both in coping with serious illness, and in facilitating recovery. "Life-threatening disease" was among the tribulations in which New England Puritans perceived the hand of God and out of which, therefore, conversion might issue (Minkema 2001, 276). Many prominent religious individuals appear to have come to radical insights via their illness; and whatever the intrapsychic struggles involved in his conversion, it seems clear that the physical suffering of Saint Ignatius of Loyola was that conversion's major precipitant (Meissner 1991). Medical anthropologists have identified experiences such as *transformation* among the ill (Becker 1997). Patients may also seek out transformative experience. For example, in order to receive an extension of the reportedly conversion-wrought cancer-healing grace experienced by Saint Peregrine Laziosi (1260–1345), millions have made novenas to that saint in order that "the very fiber of [their] being" might also be restored. Further, a hospital chaplain who has cared for cancer patients over the years characterizes some of the narratives of these patients as "reminiscent of religious conversion" (Aldridge-Clanton 1998, 19). Traditionally, care of illness by the healing profession has also been embedded within the religious traditions of the culture, from the healing rituals of shamanism (Balzer 1996) and the work of Catholic nursing orders to, in a more contemporary context, medical centers operated by religious organizations. Yet the presumption that religious engagement actually contributes to healing has been and remains controversial (Sloan and Bagiella 2002). Regardless of whether engaging spiritual resources contributes to physical healing, engaging such resources within the context of medical care may be of value to the patient who looks to the physician for empathic support and for whom these issues form an important aspect of coping with a major life trauma.

The Debate: Addressing Religious and Spiritual Concerns within Contemporary Medicine

How the religious or spiritual concerns of patients with serious illness should be addressed within contemporary medicine is controversial and is under active debate. This is a debate that has produced much heat, though it appears to us, less corresponding light. On the one hand, Walter Larimore, an affiliate of Focus on the Family, a conservative evangelical group, has called for clinicians to incorporate positive spirituality into their practices. He expresses displeasure with the nonreligious direction that he judges most current medical practice has taken, with the result that "naturalism, empiricism, secular humanism, and libertarian morality are the primary sources of ethics and values" (Larimore, Parker, and Crowther 2002, 69). Elsewhere, Larimore has argued the extreme position that the failure of physicians to provide spiritual counsel is tantamount to medical malpractice (Larimore 2001).

Harold Koenig, a physician who has compiled the most extensive review of the literature on religion and health to date (Koenig, McCullough, and Larson 2001), is not as dismissive of contemporary medical practice as Larimore, yet he also calls for stronger physician attention to spiritual matters. "Physicians," Koenig writes, "should be aware of the role that religion plays in how patients cope with illness" (Koenig 2001).

The call of Koenig and others for physicians to involve themselves in their patients' spiritual concerns has generated strong negative responses from some. They contend that the evidence is limited regarding religion and health because the research is either flawed or not applicable to clinical practice (Sloan and Bagiella 2002). More substantially, Sloan and others, including pastoral practitioners (Sloan et al. 2000), express broader and deeper concerns about the competence and appropriateness of medical personnel engaging in such practices. "It is pure fantasy," Lawrence (2002) suggests, "to think that physicians will undertake the major new time-consuming task of examining patients' spirituality with no way to bill for time involved. If they do undertake this task, what important aspects of clinical practice will they exclude to make time for it?" (74).

It may be that the intensity of heat and lack of light of the debate reviewed above is related to its being part and parcel of larger disputes about the role of religion in private practice and the public square, disputes that have born little fruit. It may also be that some presumptions regarding the nature of spiritual engagement for patients are extreme—either that this is not a particularly meaningful issue for most people, or conversely, that it is so profound and personal that it is inappropriate for exploration. Yet there may be a middle way. Physicians are regularly called upon to address a wide range of issues that are not purely biomedical in nature, including emotional adjustment, nutrition, family support issues, and other aspects of psychosocial adjustment. Therefore, the fervor of the debate may have more to do with believing that such issues are outside normal discourse or are particular, rather than universal, in nature. Our interest has been to explore the possibilities of re-embedding the value of spiritual and religious engagement as an important and legitimate aspect of cancer care; redefining the role of the physician as viably addressing such areas; understanding the breadth of spiritual and religious experience for the patient; and indicating how these experiences relate to adjustment to a serious medical illness like cancer.

Spiritual Engagement in Adjustment to Cancer

Evidence suggests that religious and spiritual practices are associated with less discomfort, hostility, anxiety, and social isolation in cancer patients (Chibnall et al. 2002; McClain, Rosenfeld, and Breitbart 2003; McIllmurray et al. 2003). Religious or spiritual beliefs, however, may also be sources of stress in the face of the threat of cancer, stress that may or may not be resolved in the course of treatment (Carpenter, Brockopp, and Andrykowski 1999). More strikingly, evidence suggests that positive engagement may contribute to decreased mortality (McCullough et al. 2000), and that spiritual or religious struggle may adversely affect the course of medical illness (Pargament et al. 2001). Early work investigating the role of spirituality as an aspect of overall quality of life found that cancer patients who reported high levels of spiritual well-being were far more likely to report being able to "enjoy life," even with high levels of cancer pain and fatigue, than if they were low in their sense of inner meaning and peace (Peterman et al. 2002). Spiritual well-being, more than religious observance, may in particular relate to positive emotional adjustment (Kristeller et al., 2006). Yet this important aspect of a patient's well-being is not generally taken into account when a physician assesses a patient's quality of life (Fisch et al. 2003) or judges a patient's overall adjustment.

Attitudes of Physicians toward Addressing Spiritual Concerns

Our initial exploration of these issues attempted to place the question of addressing spiritual concerns within the context of a broad range of issues pertinent to psychosocial aspects of a serious medical diagnosis. Previous research had focused only on whether physicians should address spiritual concerns, and we wanted to place the issue in the more realistic context of a busy medical practice. We wanted to be sensitive to the issue of time constraints in particular, but also to the saliency of different psychosocial issues, and we wanted to assess how physicians perceive their role in addressing spiritual concerns in relation to other sensitive issues, such as alcohol intake, family distress, or stopping smoking. Oncologists in our study were presented with a list of eighteen possible issues to explore with patients. The issues were related to care but not to medical outcome, and included "spiritual concerns" along with such concerns as financial problems, functional status, family issues, prognosis, diet, pain, and fatigue. The oncologists were provided with patient vignettes that depicted varying prognoses, from excellent to poor, and were told to identify the top three and lowest three issues to address if they had only ten minutes left in an office visit, a scenario judged to be realistic by our physician consultants. They were also asked a series of questions related to making referrals, other resources available, and whether they saw themselves as appropriate to address the cited concerns.

What we found was somewhat surprising. While few oncologists (3.2 percent) ranked spiritual concerns in their top three for patients with a good prognosis, this went up to 12 percent in regard to patients with a poor prognosis, a fourfold increase. While these figures represent the relatively low saliency of this issue for these physicians, over a third (37.5 percent) nevertheless felt that it was entirely appropriate for themselves to address such concerns. At the same time, 85 percent felt that ideally a chaplain should be involved. When we interviewed patients from several of the same practices, we found, however, that few had ever had such concerns addressed and only 3 percent had ever been referred to a chaplain (Turns and Kristeller 2001). Furthermore, when we asked patients to rank the importance of each of the eighteen issues, the gap between their ratings and the physicians' ratings was the largest for "spiritual concerns." In addition to underestimating the importance of this area for patients, physicians in our study also expressed concerns about lack of time, their lack of skills, and the appropriateness of such discussions within the context of the medical encounter (Chibnall and Brooks 2001; Kristeller et al. 2002; Kristeller, Zumbrun, and Schilling 1999). This ambivalence and avoidance might best have been captured by the physician who told us that he would be glad to talk about spiritual concerns "if the patient brought it up first," and the patient who noted that she would only talk about it "if the doctor mentioned it first."

The OASIS Study: A Model for How Physicians Can Address Spiritual Issues with Patients

The Oncologist Assisted Spirituality Intervention Study (OASIS; Kristeller et al., 2006) is designed to offer some light on the debate, and perhaps remove some heat, by proposing a relatively modest hypothesis. That hypothesis, based on the findings of our survey study and the debate in the literature, is that physician inquiry into patient spirituality is appreciated by most patients, is feasible in terms of time, and has a generally positive impact on patients.

OASIS evaluates a brief (five-to-seven-minute) patient-centered approach to addressing spiritual concerns, using a structure that has been shown to be effective with other sensitive issues, such as smoking and alcohol use (Ockene et al. 1991; Ockene et al. 1999). It utilizes basic Rogerian patient-centered counseling and communication

---

Box 16.1

I.   Introduce Issue in Neutral Inquiring Manner
     "When dealing with a serious illness, many people draw on religious or spiritual beliefs to help cope. It would be helpful to me to know how you feel about this."

II. Inquire Further, Adjusting Inquiry to Patient's Initial Response
     a. Positive-Active Faith Response: "What have you found most helpful about your beliefs since your illness?"
     b. Neutral-Receptive Response: "How might you draw on your faith or spiritual beliefs to help you?"
     c. Spiritually Distressed Response (e.g., anger or guilt): "Many people feel that way . . . what might help you come to terms with this?"
     d. Defensive/Rejecting Response: "It sounds like you're uncomfortable I brought this up. What I'm really interested in is how you are coping. Can you tell me about that?"

III. Continue to Explore Further as Indicated
     "I see. Can you tell me more (about . . .)?"

IV. Inquire about Ways of Finding Meaning and a Sense of Peace
     "Is there some way in which you are able to find a sense of meaning or peace in the midst of this?"

V.   Inquire about Resources
     "Whom do you have to talk to about this/these concerns?"

VI. Offer Assistance as Appropriate and Available
     "Perhaps we can arrange for you to talk to someone . . ."; "There's a support group . . . "

VII. Bring Inquiry to a Close
     "I appreciate you discussing these issues with me. May I ask about it again?"

---

skills designed to empower the patient toward self-exploration and awareness, while establishing the provider as a source of empathic support. Box 16.1 outlines the OASIS inquiry.

Several aspects of the inquiry are notable. It is framed very broadly to cover virtually any type of religious or spiritual belief experience; it is designed to encourage patients in their own words to identify ways in which they engage spiritual or religious resources; and it does not require any specific knowledge on the part of the physician. Such an approach communicates the physician's interest in the patient's experience, and also encourages individuals to consider these issues more deeply themselves (Bertakis, Roter, and Putnam 1991). The oncologist introduces the topic by acknowledging spirituality or religious belief as a potential resource for coping, then explores how the patient utilizes spiritual or religious beliefs in coping with their cancer. Further exploration follows, depending on how the patient first responds (see box 16.1, II: a–d). While the majority of patients are, in fact, highly responsive and open to the physician's raising the topic, we had to prepare the physician for the person who might be defensive or even hostile. In this regard, note that the "scripts" in box 16.1 are actually abbreviated examples of the actual intervention material. The physician determines when within the visit the inquiry should be initiated and is encouraged to use his or her own words in following the steps of the inquiry and in providing reassurance, support, and referral to other resources such as a chaplain, as appropriate.

This research addressed three key questions: (1) whether the OASIS approach to exploring spiritual or religious concerns is feasible for physicians; (2) whether it is acceptable for patients; and (3) whether there is benefit to patients' well-being, adjustment to cancer, and their perception of their physician. We believed that patients who were offered the opportunity to explore spiritual or religious concerns with their oncologist would respond positively, experience their physician as more caring, and report positive changes on indicators of quality of life and mood, compared to patients who did not receive this opportunity.

We were interested in approximating the clinical environment as much as possible. Therefore, we recruited study participants from patients in the waiting rooms of four oncologists just before the patients were to see their physician. Almost 95 percent of the patients we approached agreed to participate (a total of 118) in what they understood to be a study focused on "physician communication." They had a wide range of cancer diagnoses and had been seeing the same oncologist, on average, for about two years but for at least two months. Fifty-five percent were female, 80 percent identified themselves as Christian, and the average age was sixty (the range being twenty-three to eighty-two years old). Half the patients were in remission. Approximately half the participants were assigned to receive their usual care, and the other half to receive their usual care and the OASIS intervention. Before the intervention, immediately after, and three weeks later, all patients completed measures of emotional adjustment (Brief Symptom Inventory-Depression Scale; Derogatis 1975) and of cancer-related quality of life (FACT-G; Cella et al. 1993); a measure of spiritual well-being (Functional Assessment of Chronic Illness—Spiritual Well-Being Scale [FACIT-Sp]; Brady et al. 1999; Peterman et al. 2002); and the Primary Care Assessment Survey (PCAS; Safran et al. 1998), which is a measure of patient feelings about their relationship and communication with their physician. Both patients and physicians also answered questions regarding their degree of comfort with the inquiry and the inquiry's expected value.

The oncologists represented a range of practices and backgrounds. They were from two community practices and a university-based hematology clinic; two were Christian, one was Hindu, and one a Sikh. Each physician participated in a two-to-three-hour training program that provided an overview of the study and training in the OASIS approach.

Our results were encouraging. Patients who received the OASIS intervention generally responded positively to the experience both immediately and three weeks later. Over 75 percent of them said they were quite comfortable with the intervention, and over half said it would influence how they would cope with their cancer. They also rated their physician significantly higher than did patients not receiving this intervention on such characteristics as patience, warmth, respect, concern, and improved communication. More religiously observant patients reported more satisfaction with the intervention at both the immediate and the three-week follow-up, but no one expressed overt distress. Physicians also rated themselves as quite comfortable with over 80 percent of the patients. While doing the inquiry extended the length of the visit somewhat, as might be expected, physicians felt they could be effective by taking as little as five to six more minutes.

But this six minutes made a difference. Far from being distressed by the inquiry, patients whose physicians explored these issues with them reported significantly less depression both immediately after the inquiry and three weeks later. They also reported improved quality of life in day-to-day activities, even after controlling for other variables. As might be expected, these improvements were most evident for patients who had lower levels of spiritual well-being prior to the intervention.

Understanding Spirituality, Religion, and Cancer

We increasingly understand that spirituality and religiousness are multidimensional aspects of human experience. But while having a physician open up questions about spiritual well-being was well-accepted, and even seen as beneficial in patients' overall adjustment, we didn't really understand how this very brief inquiry might function in the context of a patient's entire life. While we didn't expect such a brief contact to be transformational, the next step in our work was to gain a better understanding of how the breadth of patient experience related to their spiritual lives and, more specifically, both how patients viewed this brief contact, and how it might play a role in the larger fabric of their being. We took two approaches: first, we expanded our evaluation of change in spiritual and religious well-being by asking patients in our next study (about one hundred to date) to complete a broader set of questionnaires about these aspects of their life, both prior to and after the OASIS inquiry from their physician, including such measures as the RCOPE (Pargament, Koenig, and Perez 2000) and Benefit Finding (Carver and Antoni 2004). Second, we sat down with the patients after they had met with their oncologist and had these issues raised, and asked them about both their memory of the experience and of how they were drawing on their spiritual and religious resources in coping with cancer.

Almost without exception, patients were appreciative of their oncologists' opening up discussion and exploration of these issues. They praised their physicians for doing so, and expressed more of a sense of connectedness with them. The exceptions were few and somewhat particular to the person; for example, one woman noted that raising the question of how she drew on religious resources during her medical visit made her uncomfortable, not because she wasn't doing so—or because she was offended—but because the inquiry somehow cracked the facade of denial about her cancer, maintained even in the midst of a visit to her oncologist.

More compelling was the virtual universality of the importance of these individuals' spiritual and religious lives in dealing with their cancer. Although there were exceptions (consistent with our first study, about 10 percent told us that this was really not an important part of their life), the overwhelming majority recounted ways in which their faith, their church community, or their relationship to God was the key to managing the fear and anxiety of cancer diagnosis, treatment, and the extended uncertainty of remission. There was also the expression of tremendous appreciation for the support received from others and, strikingly, a desire to return that sense of support via expressions of compassion for others—an opening of the heart. A small number of people also recounted experiences best described as physical signs of their contact with God: the touch of an unseen hand, a Bible falling open to a healing paragraph, the call of a friend at the "right" moment.

Transformation: Uncommon but Compelling

Using Pargament's definition of *spiritual transformation*, "the individual experiences a dramatic change of the self, a change in which the self becomes identified with the sacred" (Pargament 1997), we found that instances of spiritual transformation were extremely unusual. Out of the first one hundred individuals interviewed, only one reported such an experience, either by our definition or from the individual's own perspective. However, this account stands out as particularly compelling and even extraordinary. Mrs. P had been experiencing increasing abdominal discomfort, and one evening, in the midst of a family gathering, she collapsed in pain and was taken to the emergency room. She shared with us how she realized that something was terribly wrong and that she began praying intensely. The pain was such that she was floating in and out of consciousness, yet she continued to pray. Over several days of tests, it became apparent that a tumor had infiltrated her abdominal cavity, and emergency surgery was scheduled. Her family was prepared for the possibility that she would not survive the surgery, and she recounted that she was also aware of this. She said she simply continued praying, and found herself utterly caught up in a prayerful state. She noted that the pain was such that even with sedation, she sensed she slept little, but remained in a prayerful state. Shortly before the surgery, she noted that she felt "something come over me, a warmth coming in through my head and moving down through my body," and that, with this, she felt somehow changed.

The surgery in fact revealed several large tumors that had metastasized, and the surgeon, although doing the best he could, expressed concerns to the family that the prognosis was very poor. Mrs. P recounted to us that she woke after surgery almost pain free, and somehow with a sense of freedom and inner peace. She felt that she had received a gift of grace. This was approximately six months before our interview. Although she was still under care for her cancer, she was optimistic, as was her oncologist. More striking was the pervasive sense of joy and well-being that she communicated to us in her voice and her presence. She noted that her life had not changed in substantive ways. She had returned to the work she found fulfilling, as a cafeteria worker in a local school. However, her entire sense of connectedness with others, with opening up her heart to her life, had shifted in ways that were enduring and that she had never previously experienced.

A Deepening Spirituality, A Deepening Bond

This chapter has addressed the general question of the quality of the spiritual experience of the patient and the related question of how such issues might be appropriately explored within the medical setting by the physician. It has also addressed the question of whether there is an appropriate and effective way for oncologists to explore the issue of spiritual or religious concerns with their patients, and it has explored how patients may experience both that type of inquiry and their own experiences in drawing on spiritual or religious resources. Our research suggests that not only does a brief, patient-centered inquiry, such as the OASIS approach, appear to be acceptable to most patients and relatively comfortable for physicians, but there is an increase in patients' satisfaction with care and at least preliminary evidence of improved quality of life for some patients. Whether it is appropriate for physicians to explore the spiritual or religious concerns of their patients remains a matter of legitimate debate (Anandarajah and Hight 2001; McCord et al. 2004; Post, Puchalski, and Larson 2000; Sloan et al. 2000), and we support the importance of avoiding pitfalls, such as physicians going beyond their expertise, imposing their beliefs on the patient, or trying to provide inappropriate reassurance or answers to questions of faith (Post et al. 2000). Yet we have also found that the overwhelming majority of patients engage these issues in a manner that, while deepening their faith and spiritual experience, should not raise excessively challenging or problematic questions for the oncologist.

We believe the OASIS model addresses most, if not all the concerns raised by Sloan and others: time constraints, need for training, the inappropriateness of imposing personal beliefs on the patient, and lack of impact. Physicians trained for as little as two hours were able to smoothly integrate this five-minute exploration into their usual contact with the patient, initiate a patient-centered empathic inquiry, and positively impact both the patient's sense of closeness to the physician and their emotional well-being. Whether an individual physician chooses to engage in such an exploration with a particular patient would, of course, be a personal and professional decision. However, far from being distressed by such an inquiry, patients appeared to appreciate the exploration into their use of spiritual or religious resources, even if this exploration remained only one aspect of their larger spiritual or religious experience. Patients told us in our more in-depth inquiry how important that aspect of their life was in dealing with cancer, yet few recounted experiences that would have stretched the scope of the patient-physician relationship. Rather, they spoke to a meaningful deepening of faith and of strength in the face of the challenge of dealing with a serious illness. Listening to such experiences might well help physicians better understand and appreciate the value they can contribute to their patients, not only with their medical knowledge but by their presence. By raising the question of spiritual and religious resources in the face of cancer, the oncologist enters, in an empathic, sensitive way, into an arena that is highly valued by a substantial proportion of patients.

Therefore, we conclude that the argument that explorations of religious or spiritual issues by the physician will engender discomfort or hostility, decrease a patient's satisfaction with medical care, raise issues inappropriate to the examining room, or consume an inordinate amount of time cannot be supported based upon this research. Again, we note that it is not prayer with patients, nor altering their treatment, nor even referral for spiritual counseling that may bring strength and further healing to patients, but simply asking them a series of questions about their spiritual and religious resources. At the same time, expectations for positive impact need to be kept realistic. Regardless of whether they received such an inquiry, most patients in our sample were already drawing substantially on their religious faith and spiritual resources in coping with their illness, a phenomenon that is being documented in research on "post-traumatic growth" (Tedeschi and Calhoun 2004) and "benefit finding" (Carver and Antoni 2004; Tomich and Helgeson 2004) as a response to serious illness. For most patients, this inquiry will entail a process of deepening or further engaging such resources, rather than a dramatic transformative engagement. The physician can choose to become part of that process and, as our evidence suggests, is likely to be welcomed.

As noted earlier, we believe that this series of studies supports a middle way between the seemingly entrenched positions of those advocating for physicians' involvement in nearly all matters spiritual and those admonishing physicians to steer clear of such matters. This middle way proposes that physician inquiry into patient spirituality is appreciated by most patients and may be positively related to improvements in patients' quality of life. In contrast to the perspective of Sloan and his associates, such an inquiry does not involve healthcare personnel usurping the provision of spiritual care. Indeed, this research demonstrates that it is not expertise in spiritual matters that is valued but the expression of caring and an acknowledgment of what the patient finds important. On the other hand, in contrast to Larimore's concern, such an inquiry does not need to entail the extensive involvement of healthcare personnel in religious or spiritual matters.

These findings seem congruent with the theoretical musings of Rita Charon (2004) about the importance of narrative and empathy in the practice of medicine. Our results also seem consistent with studies showing that, of all physician interventions into spirituality, patients rate empathic inquiry most highly, and that exploring such questions with patients communicates understanding and compassion. Furthermore, in the sense that the spiritual changes most patients report are neither dramatic nor transformative, an exploration of spiritual engagement feels even more like a natural part of the medical encounter.

We believe that it is open exploration with the physician that is of particular value to the patient. And it is the process of exploration and inquiry that provides value, not the specific answers given. How might inquiry itself facilitate change? We turn to the thought of the American philosopher Charles Sanders Peirce to offer a possible explanation. Peirce (1991) proposed that human inquiry was itself a way of advancing divine purposes in and for the world. Those asking and those being asked constitute what Peirce calls "a community of inquirers" striving to transform the world—and by striving to do so, *do* do so (Peirce 1991). While we never obtain certainty in understanding ourselves, the world, or God, we may participate in a community of inquirers who can help us achieve a better understanding of these things. Knowing that, and knowing that there are only provisional answers to life's larger questions—or, in some cases, no apparent answers, and only the process of our careful asking—perhaps that is, for now, the answer to these questions. From this Peircean perspective, asking is itself healing, and may be more important than answering. Or to say this differently, asking may be a part of the answer.

Note

The research cited in this chapter was made possible by grants from the Walther Cancer Institute, Indianapolis, Indiana, and the Metanexus Institute, Philadelphia, Pennsylvania. We also express appreciation to the oncologists who assisted us with this research, including Dr. Larry Cripe of the Indiana University Cancer Center, Indianapolis, Indiana; Dr. Chandra Reddy of the Hope Center, Terre Haute, Indiana, and to the Hoosier Oncology Group for assistance in early project development; to Dr. Virgil Sheets, Indiana State University, for assistance with data analysis, and to Dr. Mark Rhodes and Dr. Martine Turns, who provided insight, effort, and persistence in the course of completing their doctoral dissertations.

References

Aldridge-Clanton, J. 1998. *Counseling People with Cancer*. Louisville, Ky.: Westminster John Knox.

Anandarajah, G., and E. Hight. 2001. Spirituality and medical practice: Using the HOPE questions as a practical tool for spiritual assessment. *American Family Physician* 63:81–88.

Balzer, M. M. 1996. Shamanism. In *Encyclopedia of Cultural Anthropology*, ed. D. Levinson and M. Ember. New York: Henry Holt.

Becker, G. 1997. *Disrupted Lives: How People Create Meaning in a Chaotic World*. Berkeley: University of California Press.

Bertakis, K., D. Roter, and S. Putnam. 1991. The relationship of physician medical interview style to patient satisfaction. *Journal of Family Practice* 32:175–81.

Brady, M., A. Peterman, G. Fitchett, M. Mo, and D. Cella. 1999. A case for including spirituality in quality of life measurement in oncology. *Psycho-Oncology* 8:417–28.

Carpenter, J. S., D. Y. Brockopp, and M. A. Andrykowski. 1999. Self-transformation as a factor in the self-esteem and well-being of breast cancer survivors. *Journal of Advanced Nursing* 29 (6): 1402–11.

Carver, C. S., and M. H. Antoni. 2004. Finding benefit in breast cancer during the year after diagnosis predicts better adjustment 5 to 8 years after diagnosis. *Health Psychology* 23:595–98.

Cella, D., D. Tulsky, G. Gray, B. Sarafian, E. Linn, and A. Bonomi et al. 1993. The functional assessment of Cancer Therapy Scale: Development and validation of the general measure. *Journal of Clinical Oncology* 11:570–79.

Charon, R. 2004. Narrative and empathy. *New England Journal of Medicine* 350:862–65.

Chibnall, J. T., and C. A. Brooks. 2001. Religion in the clinic: The role of physician beliefs. *South Medical Journal* 94:374–79.

Chibnall, J. T., S. D. Videen, N. Duckro, and D. K. Miller. 2002. Psychosocial spiritual correlates of death distress in patients with life-threatening medical conditions. *Palliative Medicine* 16:331–38.

Derogatis, L. 1975. *Brief Symptom Inventory*. Baltimore, Md.: Clinical Psychometric Research.

Fisch, M. J., M. L. Titzer, J. L. Kristeller, J. Shen, J. Loehrer, and S. J. Jung et al. 2003. Assessment of quality of life in outpatients with advanced cancer: The accuracy of clinician estimations and relevance of spiritual well-being—a Hoosier Oncology Group study. *Journal of Clinical Oncology* 21:2754–59.

Ford, S., L. Fallowfield, and S. Lewis. 1996. Doctor-patient interactions in oncology. *Social Science and Medicine* 42:1511–19.

Koenig, H. G. 2001. Spiritual assessment in medical practice. *American Family Physician* 63: 30.

Koenig, H. G., E. McCullough, and D. B. Larson. 2001. *Handbook of Religion and Health*. Oxford: Oxford University Press.

Kristeller, J., S. Johns, L. Cripe, and V. Sheets. 2002. The PIAS (Provider Issues with Addressing Spirituality): Initial validity of scale to assess barriers to addressing spiritual issues. Poster presented at Spiritual and Healing Medicine, Salt Lake City, Utah.

Kristeller, J., M. Rhodes, L. Cripe, and V. Sheets. 2006. Exploring spiritual and religious concerns with cancer patients improves quality of life and relationship with physician. *International Journal of Psychiatry in Medicine* 35:329–47.

Kristeller, J., C. Zumbrun, and R. Schilling. 1999. "I would if I could": How oncologists and oncology nurses address spiritual distress in cancer patients. *Psycho-Oncology* 8:451–58.

Larimore, W. L. 2001. Providing basic spiritual care for patients: Should it be the exclusive domain of pastoral professionals? *American Family Physician* 63:36–40.

Larimore, W. L., M. Parker, and M. Crowther. 2002. Should clinicians incorporate positive spirituality into their practices? What does the evidence say? *Annals of Behavioral Medicine* 24:69–73.

Lawrence, R. 2002. The witches' brew of spirituality and medicine. *Annals of Behavioral Medicine* 24:74–76.

McCord, G., V. J. Gilchrist, S. D. Grossman, B. D. King, K. F. McCormick, and A. M. Oprandi et al. 2004. Discussing spirituality with patients: A rational and ethical approach. *Annals of Family Medicine* 2:356–61.

McClain C. S., B. Rosenfeld, and W. Breitbart. 2003. Effect of spiritual well-being on end of life despair in terminally-ill cancer patients. *Lancet* 361:1603–7.

McCullough, M., W. Hoyt, D. Larson, H. Koenig, and C. Thoresen. 2000. Religious involvement and mortality: A meta-analytic review. *Health Psychology* 19:11–222.

McIllmurray, M. B., B. Francis, J. C. Harman, S. M. Morris, K. Soothill, and C. Thomas. 2003. Psychosocial needs in cancer patients related to religious beliefs. *Palliative Medicine* 17:49–54.

Meissner, W. W. 1991. Psychoanalytic hagiography: The case of Ignatius of Loyola. *Theological Studies* 52:3–33.

Miller, B. E., B. Pittman, and C. Strong. 2003. Gynecologic cancer patients' psychosocial needs and their views on the physicians' role in meeting those needs. *International Journal of Gynecological Cancer* 13:111–19.

Minkema, K. P. 2001. The spiritual meaning of illness in eighteenth-century New England. In *Religion of the United States in Practice*, Vol. 1, ed. C. McDannel, 269–98. Princeton, N.J.: Princeton University Press.

Ockene, J. K., A. Adams, T. G. Hurley, E. V. Wheeler, and J. R. Herbert. 1999. Brief physician- and nurse practitioner-delivered counseling for high-risk drinking: Does it work? *Archives of Internal Medicine* 159:2198–2205.

Ockene, J., J. Kristeller, R. Goldberg, T. Amick, P. Pekow, and D. Hosmer et al. 1991. Increasing the efficacy of physician-delivered smoking intervention: A randomized clinical trial. *Journal of General Internal Medicine* 6:1–8.

Pargament, K. I. 1997. *The Psychology of Religion and Coping: Theory, Research, Practice*. New York: Guilford.

Pargament, K. I., H. G. Koenig, and L. M. Perez. 2000. The many methods of religious coping: Development and initial validation of the RCOPE. *Journal of Clinical Psychology* 66:519–43.

Pargament, K., H. G. Koenig, N. Tarakeshwar, and J. Hahn. 2001. Religious struggle as a predictor of mortality among medically ill elderly patients. *Archives of Internal Medicine* 161:1881–85.

Peirce, C. S. 1991. Some consequences of four incapacities. In *Peirce on Signs: Writings on Semiotic by Charles Sanders Peirce*, ed. J. Hoopes, 54–84. Chapel Hill: University of North Carolina Press.

Peterman, A. H., G. Fitchett, M. J. Brady, L. Hernandez, and D. Cella. 2002. Measuring spiritual well-being in people with cancer: The functional assessment of chronic illness therapy-spiritual well-being scale (FACIT-SP). *Annals of Behavior Medicine* 24:49–58.

Post, S. G., C. M. Puchalski, and D. B. Larson. 2000. Physicians and patient spirituality: Professional boundaries, competency, and ethics. *Annals of Internal Medicine* 132:578–83.

Roberts, J. A., D. Brown, T. Elkins, and D. B. Larson. 1997. Factors influencing views of patients with gynecologic cancer about end-of-life decisions. *American Journal of Obstetrics and Gynecology* 176 (1): 166–72.

Safran, D., M. Kosinski, A. Tarlov, W. Rogers, D. Taira, and N. Lieberman et al. 1998. The primary care assessment inventory: Test of data and quality and measurement performance. *Medical Care* 36:711–23.

Sloan, R. P., and E. Bagiella. 2002. Claims about religious involvement and health outcomes. *Annals of Behavioral Medicine* 24:14–21.

Sloan, R. P., E. Bagiella, L. Vandercreek, M. Hover, C. Casalone, and H. T. Jinpu et al. 2000. Should physicians prescribe religious activities? *New England Journal of Medicine* 342:1913–16.

Steinhauser, K. E., N. A. Christakis, E. C. Clipp, M. McNeilly, C. McIntyre, and J. A. Tulsky. 2000. Factors considered important at the end of life by patients, family, physicians, and other care providers. *Journal of the American Medical Association* 284 (19): 2467–82.

Tedeschi, R. G., and L. G. Calhoun. 2004. Post-traumatic growth: Conceptual foundations and empirical evidence. *Psychological Inquiry* 15:1–18.

Tomich, and V. Helgeson. 2004. Is finding something good in the bad always good? Benefit finding among women with breast cancer. *Health Psychology* 3:16–23.

Turns, M., and J. Kristeller. 2001. Psychosocial concerns in cancer care: Patient-physician perspectives. Paper presented at the Society of Behavior Medicine, Seattle, Washington.

Index

acceptance: changes in self-view with, 255; of suffering for healing, 63, 68–69, 73; of "what is" in spiritual connection, 71–73

Adams, Noah, 29

affective response in social neuroscience, 213

afterlife beliefs of HIV patients, 249, 257

alcohol addiction, curing, 85

Alekseev, Ivan, 92

All Things Considered (NPR), 29

Anderson, S., 72

angels, encounters with, 258

animating principle, 28, 139

anthropology, spiritual belief in, 35–36

Arctic hysteria (*ménérik*), 78, 87

Ashbrook, James, 226

attributional frameworks, 160–62

Augustine, Saint, 136

autobiographical self, 142, 143–44, 148, 226

Barnes, A. M., 37

Bar-On, R., 218

Being Changed by Cross-Cultural Encounters (Young and Goulet), 36

Berger, Peter, 27, 32, 35

Bhirendra of Nepal, 107–9, 113

Birth of the Living God, The (Rizzuto), 19

Borysenko, J., 72

Bourne, E. J., 52

Bowlby, J., 15

the brain: and cognition, 212; complexity of with stages of faith development, 181; and emotion, 212–13, 217–19; and mind, 174–76; as a mirror to personality, 174, 181; organization of, 171–74, 181; plasticity characteristic, xvi–xvii, 172, 200–202, 228–30; relationships in shaping, 235; and spiritual transformation, 171–73

the brain, locating areas of: emotional sensation and judgment, 215–17; empathy, 218; meditative states, *191*, 191–96; memory encoding, 227–28; relationships, 235; ritual, 231; social judgment, 217–19; terminology, 214; transformative experiences, 194–95

brain-imaging: measuring emotional judgment, 216; of meditative states,

source of existence, 136; spiritual communion with, 49; theistic/nontheistic perspectives, 13–14

sacred, search for the: after spiritual transformation, 21–22; in childhood, 14–15; critical processes in, 14–16, 21–22; overcoming barriers in, 20–21; spirituality defined by, 14, 30, 126

Sacred and the Profane, The (Eliade), 126

sacred interaction, Darwinian model of, 140–41

sainthood, 171

Sakha (Yakut): hero-shamans of the, 78–79, 93; Russian patients compared, 88; term for shamans, 93. *See also* shamans, Sakha (Yakut)

Sakha sickness (*Sakha yald'ar*), 82

Samuels, A., 56, 57

Santa Fe Institute, 176

Schacter, D. L., 232

Scheler, M., 55, 210

Schleiermacher, Friederich, 32

Schneiders, Sandra, 234–35

Schwartz, Richard, 148, 242

séances, use by Sakha shamans, 80–82, 84, 85, 92–93, 95, 98n15

secularization versus disenchantment, 34

the self: in evolutionary theology, 141–43; faith stage of development, 171; feelings of loss in transformative experiences, 192; multi-tiered concept, 142, 226; organization of the, 176–77, 182; spirit and, 175, 224

self-awareness of bodily states, 194–95, 216–17, 225

self-consciousness in humanness, 158–59

self-determination, 175

self-identity: confrontations with death and, 143–44; continuity of the transformed personality, 165–66, 250; dimensions of, 143–44; disease

as a challenge to, 143–44; memory in creating, 142, 225–26, 228–29; narrative in forming, 226–27; narrative in reconstructing, 229–30, 232; narrative in transforming, 229–30. *See also* personality

self-other relationship: awareness in the moment, 142, 148; in empathy, 210; simulation theory of emotional judgment, 214–19; in sympathy, 210–11

self-transcendence, 235

serve (*therapeuo*), 120–21

shaman ethic, 106

shamanic call, 91, 101–3, 107–10

shamanic illness (*éttéénii*), 82, 86–87, 91

shamanic initiation: empathy learned during, 82–84; fugue state in, 102, 104; glossolalia during, 105; by life-threatening illness, 47–49, 109; physical experiences of, 107, 110; processes critical to, 102–3, 106, 108; spiritual transformation role in, 47

shamanic initiation, Sakha: processes critical to, 80, 94; "ritual of tearing apart," 83–84; spirit-torture in, 80, 82, 86–87

shamanic initiation, stories of: Bhirendra of Nepal, 107–9; Claire, the Inuit healer, 104–7; Kehuq, the Inuit hunter, 103–4, 108; Muchona of Zambia, 109–13; similarities in, 108, 112

shamanic state of consciousness, 109

shamans: dead, power of, 113; inherited ability, 113; power of, 104, 113; Sakha term for, 94. *See also* healers

shamans, Sakha (Yakut): development process, 94; female (*udagan*), 87; gender differences, 87, 97n5; generational differences, 79, 86; helper spirits of, 90, 92; inherited ability, 80–84, 86–88, 90–91; intuition in, 87, 88, 94; misuse of spirit power, 97n7; psychological

About the Contributors

Carol Rausch Albright was for nine years executive of *Zygon: Journal of Religion and Science*, and for six years she was a regional codirector of the John Templeton Foundation Religion and Science Course Program. She also spent ten years as author of a large-circulation medical newsletter. Albright is coauthor of *The Humanizing Brain: Where Religion and Neuroscience Meet* (with James B. Ashbrook; 1997), and author, coauthor, or editor of four other books on religion and science.

Marjorie Mandelstam Balzer is a research professor at Georgetown University in the Sociology and Anthropology Department and the Center for Eurasian, Russian, and East European Studies (CERES). She is editor of the journal *Anthropology and Archeology of Eurasia*, and editor of the books *Shamanic Worlds: Rituals and Lore of Siberia and Central Asia* (1997), *Culture Incarnate: Native Anthropology from Russia* (1995), and *Russian Traditional Culture* (1992). She is also author of *The Tenacity of Ethnicity: A Siberian Saga in Global Perspective* (1999). Her fieldwork since 1986 has focused primarily on the Turkic-speaking Sakha (Yakut) of the Russian Federation, and in the 1990s she helped organize exchanges of Native American and Native Siberian leaders.

Dr. Balzer has taught at Grinnell College, the University of Illinois, and the University of Pennsylvania, and has held postdoctoral research appointments at Harvard University, Columbia University, and the Woodrow Wilson Center's Kennan Institute.

Mary Ann Bucklin is a professional artist who studies spiritual experience using ethnographic methods. She has done fieldwork with the Shaker community at Sabbathday Lake in Maine, and in Ireland and Pennsylvania. She has used this research in her art, which includes the creation of brief essays drawn from interviews to accompany her graphic work. She has a special interest in the tension between the spiritual experiences of ordinary people and contemporary academic theory.

Bonnie Glass-Coffin is an associate professor of anthropology at Utah State University. She has been conducting research on Peruvian shamanism since 1987, and she published *The Gift of Life: Female Spirituality and Healing in Northern Peru* (1998). She was recently named Utah Professor of the Year by the Carnegie Foundation for the Advancement of Teaching and the Council for Advancement and Support of Education (CASE).

Philip Hefner is professor emeritus of systematic theology at the Lutheran School of Theology at Chicago. He is also editor-in-chief of *Zygon: Journal of Religion and Science*. Among his publications are *The Human Factor: Evolution, Culture, Religion* (1993) and *Technology and Human Becoming* (2003). His publications have dealt with classical Christian theological themes, religion and science, and the arts. Hefner serves on the advisory board of the Science and Spiritual Transformation project of the Metanexus Institute (of which he is also a senior fellow). He is an ordained minister of the Evangelical Lutheran Church in America.

Dr. David Allen Hogue is ordained in the Presbyterian Church (USA) and has served congregations in Illinois and Indiana. He has also served as chaplain and pastoral counselor at Methodist Hospital in Indianapolis. He is the author of *Remembering the Future, Imagining the Past: Story, Ritual, and the Human Brain* (2003) and is coauthor of *Promising Again* (with Herbert Anderson and Marie McCarthy; 1995).

Ralph W. Hood Jr. holds a joint doctorate in sociology and psychology from the University of Nevada at Reno. He is past president of the Division of Psychology of Religion of the American Psychological Association and has been a recipient of its William James Award for research in the psychology of religion. He is a cofounder of the *International Journal for the Psychology of Religion*, and he is a past book-review editor and coeditor of that journal. He has been an editor of the *Journal for the Scientific Study of Religion*, and he is currently a coeditor of the *Archive for the Psychology of Religion* (*Archiv für Religionspsychologie*). He has published over 150 papers on the psychology of religion and has authored, coauthored, or edited nine books on this topic.

David J. Hufford, PhD, is university professor and chair of humanities, professor of family and community medicine, and professor of neural and behavioral sciences at Penn State College of Medicine, Hershey, Pennsylvania. He is also adjunct professor of religious studies at the University of Pennsylvania. He has taught, studied, and published on folk belief, spirituality, and health for over thirty years. In 1992 he received the Manuel de la Cruz Award from the Mexican Academy of Traditional Medicine for his research in folk medicine. Dr. Hufford's research focuses on the role of experience and reason in the development of spiritual belief and in traditional approaches to healing. He has used this research in *The Terror That Comes in the Night: An Experience-Centered Study of Supernatural Assault Traditions* (1982), a crosscultural study of sleep paralysis as a transcendent experience, in which he develops an experience-centered theory of spiritual experience.

Leonard M. Hummel is associate professor of pastoral theology and care at the Lutheran Theological Seminary, Gettysburg, Pennsylvania. His previous appointments have been to the Divinity School and Graduate Department of Religion of Vanderbilt University. He received his AB in philosophy from Haverford College, his MDiv and STM from Yale Divinity School, and his PhD in religious and theological studies from Boston University. He recently completed *Clothed in Nothingness: Consolation for Suffering* (2003), and is currently working on two books: *The Very Fiber of Our Being: A Practical Theology of Cancer* (forthcoming), and *By Its Fruits: Pragmatics of Religious Coping* (forthcoming). He also is preparing a coedited volume, *Practical Bearings: Lived Religion in Pastoral Theology* (forthcoming).

Dr. Dale S. Ironson has been involved in the psychology of consciousness and in phenomenology as a researcher, instructor, and corporate consultant throughout his career. He was an associate professor of psychology at Franklin Pierce College in New Hampshire and adjunct faculty at the Antioch Graduate School in Keene, New Hampshire. Dr. Ironson has also served as academic director of external degree programs for the Institute of Transpersonal Psychology, a leading graduate school in the field of transpersonal psychology, which focuses on studying the spiritual dimension of human experience and the evolution of consciousness.

Dr. Ironson's current work seeks to integrate a spiritual dimension into the needs and realities of work in modern business organizations. He writes and speaks on topics in these areas, and also consults with leading corporations.

Gail Ironson, MD, PhD, is professor of psychology and psychiatry at the University of Miami, and is board certified in psychiatry. Dr. Ironson specializes in behavioral medicine and served as president of the Academy of Behavioral Medicine Research in 2002. She has received grants from the National Institutes of Health (NIH) and the Metanexus Institute Spiritual Transformation Scientific Research Program to study spiritual transformation in AIDS patients. She has served on the editorial boards of five journals and has published over 125 articles and chapters on numerous topics.

Solomon H. Katz is director of the Krogman Center for Research in Child Growth and Development, professor of physical anthropology at the University of Pennsylvania, and principle investigator of the Spiritual Transformation Scientific Research Program at the Metanexus Institute on Religion and Science. His work in science and religion spans thirty years, including leadership of the Institute on Religion in an Age of Science (IRAS), where he served as president between 1977 and 1984. He has also served as president of the Center for Advanced Studies in Religion and Science (1989–2002), of the Metanexus Institute on Religion and Science (2001–2004), and was a founding member (1994–2001) of Dialogue on Science, Ethics, and Religion (DoSER) of the American Association for the Advancement of Science (AAAS). Dr. Katz is also a founding fellow member of the International Society for Science and Religion. He has served as cochair of the publication board for *Zygon: Journal of Religion and Science*, and as an associate editor of the journal since 1979. He has published numerous books and papers and recently served as editor-in-chief of the Dartmouth Medal–recipient *Encyclopedia of Food and Culture* (2003).

Joan D. Koss-Chioino, member of the advisory board for the Spiritual Transformation Scientific Research Program, is professor emerita in anthropology at Arizona State University. She was formerly professor of psychiatry at the School of Medicine, University of New Mexico, and is currently research professor at George Washington University and adjunct professor in the Department of Psychiatry and Neurology, Tulane Medical Center. Koss-Chioino focuses her topical interests on medical anthropology, cultural psychiatry, psychological anthropology, tropical medicine, and art and ritual. She has done research in Puerto Rico, Mexico, and New Mexico; among Puerto Ricans, Mexican Americans, and African Americans in the United States; and in Bali, Indonesia. She is the author of numerous articles and chapters and five books.

Dr. Heidemarie Kremer is a German specialist in HIV Medicine and she works in the Behavioral Medicine Research Program at the University of Miami. In addition to her publications in the field of HIV research, she has published psychosocial and medical guidebooks for people living with HIV. Her current research is on spiritual transformation in people living with HIV.

Dr. Jean L. Kristeller received her doctorate in clinical and health psychology from Yale University in 1983, and her MS in psychophysiology and clinical psychology from the University of Wisconsin in 1978. She is currently professor of psychology at Indiana State University and adjunct associate professor at the Indiana University School of Medicine. She is also director of the Center for the Study of Health, Religion, and Spirituality at Indiana State University. Dr. Kristeller's previous appointments have been to the University of Massachusetts Medical School and Harvard University Medical School. Her recent research in the area of spirituality includes funding from the Metanexus Institute on Religion and Science under the Spiritual Transformation Scientific Research Program for a study of spiritual resources in cancer patients. Another focus of Dr. Kristeller's research has been the use of meditation as a therapeutic modality. She currently has funding through the National Institutes of Health (NIH) Center for Complementary and Alternative Medicine for a study of the use of mindfulness meditation in treating obesity. She has taught courses and led workshops on the psychology of meditation and spirituality, and she has received a teaching fellowship in these areas from the Center for Contemplative Study and the Fetzer Institute.

Andrew Newberg is assistant professor of radiology and psychiatry in the University of Pennsylvania Health System. He has actively pursued a number of neuroimaging research projects, including the study of aging and dementia, epilepsy, and other neurological and psychiatric disorders. His research has focused not only on specific disorders, but also on various activation studies designed to explore how brain function is associated with various mental states. He has published numerous articles and chapters on the topics of brain function and neuroimaging and has presented his research at both national and international meetings. In both the clinical and research aspects of his career, Dr. Newberg has been particularly involved in the study of mystical and religious experiences as well as in the study of more general mind and body relationships. Much of his research has focused on the relationship between brain function and various mystical and religious experiences. He has coauthored two books that explore the relationship between neuroscience and spiritual experience: *Why God Won't Go Away: Brain Science and the Biology of Belief* (with Eugene G. d'Aquili and Vince Rause; 2001), and *The Mystical Mind: Probing the Biology of Religious Experience* (with Eugene G. d'Aquili; 1999), the latter receiving the Outstanding Books in Theology and the Natural Sciences award presented by the Center for Theology and the Natural Sciences in 2000.

Kenneth I. Pargament is currently professor of psychology in the Clinical Psychology Doctoral Program at Bowling Green State University, Bowling Green, Ohio. He has published extensively in the psychology of religion, stress, and coping. A fellow of the American Psychological Association and the American Psychological Society, Dr. Pargament is author of the book *The Psychology of Religion and Coping: Theory, Research, Practice* (1997) and coeditor of the book *Forgiveness: Theory, Research, and Practice* (with Michael E. McCullough and Carl E. Thoresen; 2000). He is past president of Division 36 (Psychology of Religion) of the American Psychological Association. Dr. Pargament consults with national and international health institutes, foundations, and universities.

Karl E. Peters, PhD (Columbia University), is Professor Emeritus of Philosophy and Religion at Rollins College, Winter Park, Florida; coeditor of *Zygon: Journal of Religion and Science*; president of the Center for Advanced Study in Religion and Science; and author of *Dancing with the Sacred: Evolution, Ecology, and God* (2002). He is also the author of several scholarly articles on science and religion.

Rev. Michael L. Spezio, PhD, has a doctorate in biochemistry from Cornell University and a doctorate in cognitive/systems neuroscience from the University of Oregon. He is currently a postdoctoral scholar at the California Institute of Technology (Caltech) investigating neural networks of human social cognition, emotion, and complex judgment. He has an MDiv from the Pittsburgh Theological Seminary, is an ordained minister in the Presbyterian Church (USA), and works actively in the field of religion and science.

Edith L. B. Turner is on the faculty of the Department of Anthropology at the University of Virginia. She specializes in ritual, religion, healing, and aspects of consciousness including shamanism. Among her publications are *The Spirit and the Drum* (1987), *Experiencing Ritual: A New Interpretation of African Healing* (1992), and *The Hands Feel It: Healing and Spirit Presence among a Northern Alaskan People* (1996). She is the editor of the journal *Anthropology and Humanism.*

Fraser Watts is Starbridge Lecturer in Theology and Natural Science in the University of Cambridge, a fellow of Queens' College, University of Cambridge, and director of the Psychology and Religion Research Programme in the Centre for Advanced Religious and Theological Studies. He is a psychologist by training, and a former president of the British Psychological Society. He is a priest in the Church of England, a chaplain of St. Edward King and Martyr, Cambridge, and also an adviser in pastoral care and counseling for the Diocese of Ely. His recent books are *Theology and Psychology* (2002) and *Psychology for Christian Ministry* (with Rebecca Nye and Sara Savage; 2002). With Sara Savage, he has recently developed the Beta Course, a video-based course linking Christian faith, personal growth, and pastoral care.